Growing up V

Thomas J. Gorman

Growing up Working Class

Hidden Injuries and the Development of Angry White Men and Women

Thomas J. Gorman
Queens College, CUNY
Queens, New York, USA

ISBN 978-3-319-86504-1   ISBN 978-3-319-58898-8   (eBook)
DOI 10.1007/978-3-319-58898-8

Cover illustration: © Steinphoto / Getty Images
Cover design by Henry Petrides

Printed on acid-free paper

This Palgrave Macmillan imprint is published by Springer Nature
The registered company is Springer International Publishing AG
The registered company address is: Gewerbestrasse 11, 6330 Cham, Switzerland

I dedicate this book to all the current and former residents
of my old neighborhood.

ACKNOWLEDGMENTS

When I would read the acknowledgments page in a book, I used to wonder how authors could thank all the people who helped them write that text. Now, I find myself facing that very task. I am tempted just to say, "Thanks to all, you know who you are." But I have decided not to do that and to thank those who helped me in various ways to write this book. If I forget anyone, I apologize. To begin, I must thank all those who live and lived in my old neighborhood. They may not agree with everything I have written about that neighborhood, but this book is dedicated to them. A few notable new and old friends helped me clear up in my mind some issues related to the manuscript—Victor Gullotta, Linda Hasman, and my lifetime good friend, Thomas Crockett. Also, I want to thank Maggi Kolb Ostrowicki, who gave me permission to visit her mom's house back in the old neighborhood so I could take measurements of the typical apartment. That sketch is included in the Appendix to Chap. 1.

The Administrations of both Queens College and Queensborough Community College coordinated to create my current position at Queens College. Those at Queens College who were instrumental in that arrangement were Dr. Dana Weinberg and Dean Elizabeth Hendrey, along with the support of Professor Suzanne Strickland. At Queens College, I was able to secure a sabbatical, which gave me the time to write most of this book. A very special thanks goes to Dr. Andrew Beveridge (Chair of the Department of Sociology and President of Social Explorer) and Dr. Charles Smith (Professor Emeritus) at Queens College in all that they did in securing my position and providing me with a sabbatical; they both went above and beyond the call of duty.

At Queens College I was helped in negotiating the data tables presented in the Appendix to Chap. 1 by two people well versed in Social Explorer: Susan Weber-Stoger and Sydney Beveridge. In addition, Sydney Beveridge at Social Explorer went on to assist me in interpreting the census data, and later she edited about half the manuscript, which helped remind me what the written word should look like in the other half of the book. And to top it off, Sydney created (in Social Explorer) the map of my old neighborhood that appears in Chap. 1.

None of this would have been possible without the talented and hard-working individuals at Palgrave Macmillan, especially my editor Alexis Nelson and her assistant Kyra Saniewski. So, a big thank-you goes to Alexis Nelson for believing in the importance of this kind of work. Evanjalin Hephsiah and Soundarrajan Sudha were my production contacts and they both did a great job. The copy editor and cover designer also did outstanding work.

Of course, my family—of procreation—(Carolyn, Connor, Sean, and Erin) needs to be thanked for putting up with me writing this book to all hours of the night, looking like a zombie most days, and having all my books scattered around the house. It helped that my wife, Carolyn, whom I met while we were graduate students in sociology at SUNY Stony Brook, still understands academic culture and all of its idiosyncrasies. She is currently in the business world and she is an excellent sociologist.

And yes, thanks mom and dad (and my brother and sister). While some may see this book as an attempt to air a family's—of orientation—dirty laundry, I have written it with love and compassion for all of you. I think it is a story that needs to be told, including the good and the bad, to show the strength and resilience of our family and the working class. Hopefully, this kind of instruction can contribute to a more inclusive society.

CONTENTS

LIST OF PHOTOS

LIST OF MAPS

List of Tables

LIST OF BOXES

Introduction

An in-depth article in the *New York Times Magazine* (Tough 2014) explored one of the main reasons talented poor and working-class students drop out of college—their lack of self-confidence. In response to questions I asked working-class men and women (1998a, b) about their past experiences with schooling, current experiences at work, and future aspirations for their children's educational achievement and occupations, the common response concerned what they considered a key for their children's success—which they did not have, and still lack today—"self-assuredness." This segment of the working class had a tendency to lash out at middle- and upper-middle-class, college-educated, white-collar workers, calling them "just paper pushers" and accusing them of "looking down on them." A segment of the working class being frustrated, bitter, and angry is not a new phenomenon.

Anger finds other outlets, too. Consider this: in another recent article in the *New York Times Magazine*, Sharlet (2016) reported on the meteoric rise in popularity of Donald Trump for the 2016 Republican Party Presidential nomination. In the article, one man at a Trump rally explained the candidate's appeal: "He stands up there and says what we all think, we all want to punch somebody in the face, and he says it all for us." An electrician at the rally rose from his stool in a local bar near the rally and shouted: "I don't care if you're a racist! If you'll just bring back one [expletive] steel mill!" (Sharlet 2016). How did we get here? What can account for the white, working-class anger and lashing out at established

© The Author(s) 2017
T.J. Gorman, *Growing up Working Class*,
DOI 10.1007/978-3-319-58898-8_1

institutions in the United States that has just now come to the media's attention (see Faludi 1999; Dionne 2015), but has been studied to various degrees previously by sociologists such as Kimmel (2013), Rubin (1994), and Gorman (1998a, b).

These reports are all connected to what Sennett and Cobb (1972) referred to as the hidden injuries of class. I experienced many of these "injuries" while growing up in a working-class neighborhood and relate to these issues through both personal and scholarly lenses. The following auto-ethnography of my youth, along with some of my recent research, voices from social media, and demographic data from Social Explorer about a particular time and place—a neighborhood in New York City on the Brooklyn/Queens border in the 1960s—will provide a window into the development of such attitudes and behavior.

In 1972, Sennett and Cobb wrote:

> The position we take is that everyone in the society, rich and poor, plumber and professor is subject to a scheme of values that tells him he must validate the self in order to win others' respect and his own. For the plumber, the search for respect is thus thwarted, the.individual feels personally responsible for failures ... he will have a harder time at all because other people like himself think he doesn't have as much ability ... as the professor ... What we have to do is to illuminate a hidden scheme of values that sorts men into different classes .... (pp. 75–76)

However, there has not been enough attention given to the kinds of injuries experienced by working-class youth (see Morris 2011 for an exception). This book traces the various types of "injuries" from childhood into adulthood and their consequences for the working class (defined as blue-collar or lower-level white-collar workers—with a high school degree or less. Today, more and more researchers are using education as the key variable defining social class with the middle and upper middle class being defined as those with a 4-year degree or higher and the working class defined as those with a high school degree or less. Those individuals with a 2-year associate's degree could be defined as an intermediary group worth observing for various combinations of attitudes and behavior).

This manuscript is an auto-ethnography/ethnography embedded in sociological concepts (such as the hidden injuries of class) and theories (which other auto-ethnographies have not included). It helps add to the previous groundbreaking work on working-class culture by authors such as Howell (1973), Rubin (1976), Halle (1984), and Lareau (2003), as well as the work on social class reproduction theory by Macleod (1987), Willis

(1981), and Bowles and Gintis (1976). This manuscript looks at how social class (and other social institutions and social structures) shaped the manner in which my peers and I grew up in a working-class neighborhood on the Brooklyn/Queens border. This was a place and time where one's self-confidence was constantly being tested and battered. I have incorporated census data from Social Explorer, some of my previous research on class cultures, and commentary from social media to give my accounts context. This volume will break new ground by producing a rich ethnography.

DATA, THEORY, AND THE LITERATURE

The book uses a variety of data types—quantitative and qualitative. In Chap. 4 I use previously published data to show how the hidden injuries of class that begin in childhood and adolescence continue into adult lives. At the end of Chap. 2 I provide a number of (Census Bureau—Social Explorer) data tables to establish the demographic nature of the community and to give some background as to the changing face of the neighborhood of which many previous residents now disapprove. Those tables contain data such as income and education levels, crime rates, population density, Presidential voting patterns, and the (very important) racial and ethnic composition of the neighborhood, now and then. Chapter 5 contains interviews I conducted, from which the data and analysis have never been submitted for publication. I interviewed middle-class and working-class parents concerning their attitudes toward their children's participation in organized youth sports. The data suggests, again, that middle-class parents push their children to participate in organized youth sports to prepare them for middle-class occupations, as Lareau (2003) has asserted. Meanwhile, working-class parents tend to be more interested in youth sports to keep their children "off the streets" and for the pure enjoyment of the games—a more "hands off approach to parenting." Yet, I argue that this is not exactly what their children will need for upward social mobility in a hyper-capitalist economy. These data provide more evidence that the working class tend to "resist" middle-class ideologies of parenting designed to consciously shape their children's future lives. Then, Chap. 7 contains current comments (from social media) of past residents' frustration, anger, and bitterness. My auto ethnographic approach to the balance of the data is becoming a new and rich arena for scholarly work—(auto-)ethnographies that highlight the everyday indignities of growing up working class. I was, in essence, a participant observer, just like researchers who have written some of the richest sociological studies such as *Street Corner Society*

(Whyte, 1943). The only difference is that I was a participant observer of that particular neighborhood when I was younger.

My theoretical approach deals with the latest works on the white working class. This book can be viewed within the context of the current work on the "angry white working class," but with a few additional contributions to be outlined below. One of the more interesting aspects of the recent swath of books on the white working class is their similar conclusions, especially concerning the reasons for their perceived anger, bitterness, and resentment. The research spans a number of years and covers most of the United States. (In Chap. 4 I will present a reprint of an article I published in 1998 on white working-class anger and resentment. In addition, I will review the pertinent research dealing with social class cultures.) In fact, you could almost say that the research points to a somewhat unified understanding of the white working class in America.

There are some differences, however, to be found among the excellent research in the area. In *What's the Matter with Kansas*, Frank (2004) argues that the residents of Kansas have been duped by the Republican Party with a focus on Guns, God, and Gays, but that politicians do not do the citizens' economic bidding once in power. In *Strangers in Their Own Land*, however, Hochschild (2016) finds that when you listen closely to the working class (in Louisiana), they are well aware what is taking place in their communities. In their case, they are voting against the Democrats (and the Environmental Protection Agency) while siding with the chemical companies that are polluting their communities (but provide jobs for the locals). She finds that most residents in this "red" state have many of the same concerns as residents of "blue" states. They just don't like it when they think others are trying to get ahead of them in line unfairly for limited resources. Both books acknowledge a changing social, political, and economic landscape that has devastated many working-class communities.

And this is what the other new entries to this literature have uncovered. Gest (*The New Minority*, 2016) found that those who were disadvantaged politically, socially, and/or economically are more apt to vote for Donald Trump for President. They are weary of illegal immigrants and welfare recipients, even though some of them receive government assistance themselves. That is exactly what Jennifer Sherman (2009) found when she interviewed working-class residents in a rural California town. Her respondents blame liberals for the closing down of the logging industry on which many families in the town relied for jobs. Many of the residents, however, now rely on SSI and Disability Insurance to supplement their spotty employment. They seem to be able to compartmentalize the issue based on a notion that they are somehow morally superior to those (liberals) who live in urban areas and mooch off the government. They say that the value they place on "family" distinguishes them from others who don't—even though many of their families are "hard living" and splintered. (Also see Rubin 1986, who found white working-class residents on the "fault-line" blaming "other" ethnic and racial groups for the decline of the white working class.)

In 2013, Michael Kimmel was researching angry white men and set the stage for other work on this important sociological topic. The men he interviewed also blamed their current economic situation on liberals, immigrants, the government, and, especially, women and feminists. Kimmel found that the men had an "aggrieved entitlement" to power—to the way America had been after World War II (and to the politicians who are now promising to make America great again). Faludi (1999) also talked to men who felt they had been emasculated by similar social forces. And Katherine Cramer (2016) found, again, similar feelings in Wisconsin among the working-class residents to whom she spoke. They also resented the "liberal elite."

Hillbilly Elegy might be the most talked-about book in this genre. In it, J. D. Vance (2016) documents the decline of a rural working-class culture due to economic decline, but also because, the author argues, the culture has decayed. The author is at once sympathetic to his place of birth, and to the addiction that has harmed so many of his family and friends. Yet, he seems to think at the same time that the residents of the area, ultimately, have themselves to blame and need to take some personal responsibility for their plight. It's as if he is saying: "If I can do it so can you." Interestingly, prior to the 2016 Presidential election, a conservative commentator penned the following argument. He said:

> The truth is that these dysfunctional communities is that they deserve to die .... They are morally indefensible .... Immoral because it perpetuates a lie: that the white working-class that finds itself attracted to Trump has been victimized by outside forces. It hasn't .... They failed themselves. (Williamson 2016)

As the election approached, however, this kind of argument was lost among other conservative pundits, once it looked like Trump was going to blame the plight of the white working class on trade deals brokered by the Democrats and not on personal foibles. What makes this interest-ing is that the political party that had been for years telling poor and working-class whites, blacks, and Hispanic/Latinos to pull themselves up by their bootstraps now was offering a socio-economic structural analysis to explain white working-class economic displacement. Yes, I experienced some upward mobility, but it was a long, strange trip, with many personal turning points that—as I will describe in later chapters—could have easily had me ending up with a different path in life and active agents that sent me on a different direction. And there has been much personal collateral damage.

The two authors who take a—somewhat—similar methodological approach to my current work are Steedman (1986) and Walley (2013). However, the setting and theoretical approach of both are quite different from this book. Also, neither has the wide-ranging scope of this ethnography. And Barbara Jensen's *Reading Classes* (2012) is an excellent review of the literature on working-class culture, but it does not explore the variety of sites where the hidden injuries of class occur, nor provide the sheer volume of data contained in my text.

As I mentioned above, Morris (2011) explored the hidden injuries of class that rural youth experience. He found that the hidden injuries of class in the rural area he studied were caused mostly by parents who were either unemployed or underemployed, leading to families being unable to provide the necessities for growing teenagers, especially decent clothing. Interestingly, Morris uncovered the different means that boys and girls employ to offset the pain of those injuries. Boys for the most part tend to play up their masculinity by participating in sports such as boxing, working hard at part-time manual jobs, goofing around, fighting, and getting into trouble at school. All of this, of course, will just help keep the boys in their social class position. Girls, however, play up their femininity by being dependent and submissive to the boys. Yet, they also offset the hidden injuries they experience by trying to do well in school. This will give them a better chance for upward social mobility. Other studies, including my own, have found that women do not resist the ideology of upward social mobility through education as much as men.

With all this research in my theoretical tool box, I now argue, given my own past and current research, that the hidden injuries of class frustrate and anger the working class, including many working-class women (a fact that is often overlooked), leading them to lash out at middle- and upper-middle-class, white-collar workers (almost no one talks about that in the literature today), minorities, women, and—especially in my old neighborhood today—Muslims. This lashing out has in the past been shown to maintain the status quo or worsen the objective conditions of the working class. The anger has its roots in economic and ethnic/racial social changes. One key theoretical contribution I make (in addition to highlighting angry working-class women) is that working-class anger is not new; I documented it in 1994. It has just moved into the political arena. Another key theoretical contribution I make is to show that those in the middle class are really the "conformists," as opposed to Kohn's theoretical approach in *Class and Conformity* (1969), but that conformity is what helps members of the middle class succeed. Meanwhile, a large segment of the working class continues to "resist" dominant ideologies and institutions. Yet, another large segment of the working class is more like middle-class "conformists," and, I would argue, is more likely to be less bitter and more likely to experience upward social mobility. In the past, research has tended to argue that the working class either experienced hidden injuries of class (Rubin) or did not (Halle). I would hypothesize, based on my previous research and current data, that there are at least two segments of the working class (a continuum, really, from hard living to settled living), with one segment experiencing fewer hidden injuries of class than the other. Keeping these different segments of the working class theoretically distinct can help us understand the conflicting reports of whether the working class is bitter or not, and what we might expect to find in the future if current economic and technological conditions continue.

AUTO-ETHNOGRAPHY

My interest in undertaking this project—writing about my life from a sociological perspective—has been a goal of mine since my first course in sociology. That is when I discovered that there was a subject about my life: sociology. What I am going to do in this book is to put a human face on sociological analyses; you could call it a personal sociology. The qualitative, methodological approach—using interviews, social media commentary, and observations—has attempted to bring us closer to those being studied. Recently, sociology has taken a further step and tried to get even closer to the human and social experience by showing how sociologists are part of the field. In light of this trend of capturing the feelings and emotions of the researcher, auto-ethnographies have become popular in sociology. Auto-ethnographic accounts, beginning with the work of Carolyn Ellis (1995, 2004), have paved the way for more sociologists to put themselves in the research picture. These studies have ranged in focus from exploration of the experiences of sociologists in the field to the feelings of losing a loved one. However, there are a few problems with these studies. Some of the works lean too heavily on the "feelings" aspect of the subjects (auto-ethnographies), while other studies have emphasized the social context at the expense of the feelings of subjects (socio-biographies). My task in this book is to find the right balance between these two poles. We need to bring back the social context into auto-ethnographies. Would this book be categorized as an auto-ethnography or a socio-biography? From my perspective, that distinction is not all that important. I am following C. Wright Mills' call to connect history and biography. He taught us that this is where the sociological imagination will be found (Mills 1959). As an undergraduate and graduate student studying sociology, I often wrote about what it was like growing up in a working-class family in an urban setting. What better way for me to put all of my training in sociology and more than 20 years in the academy to work than by writing about my experiences growing up as a young boy and adolescent in an often-overlooked part of New York City during a particularly important period of time? Over the years my students have urged me to write such a sociological analysis of my old neighborhood. Indeed, in the classroom I use many examples from that time and place to clarify key concepts in sociology, and I have also asked my students to write about their own lives using those concepts. It is time for me to do the same. There is no better way for me to practice using my sociological imagination, and to connect the macro and micro elements of society.

One objection from critics will be that this report will be biased, in that the accounts will be just from my observations over time. Yet, we have always relied on the observations of sociologists, and this type of analysis is one of our discipline's main methods of collecting data. Some of the "classics" in the field of sociology are observation studies (such as *Street Corner Society* [Whyte 1943]). The only difference here is that I was the observer in a field I occupied in the past—I just have to recreate my field notes. Memories are tricky and can be exaggerated or distorted, and I have thought about this matter and read all I could on the topic. However, my training as a sociologist guided me through recreating those field notes as objectively as possible. When employing interview and questionnaire methodological techniques, we always have to worry that our respondents have accurate memories. My training as a sociologist, plus my vigilance in trying to recreate the setting accurately, will minimize the bias in these accounts. As a matter of fact, I would argue that having a sociologist describe past social worlds is a good way to minimize the bias that comes along with relying on research respondents (if a "sympathetic understanding"—Max Weber—is what we want) Also, as you will see in later chapters, I compare my memories of the neighborhood with those of others who lived in that same neighborhood at the same time (supplemented by census data and a recent literary work by an old friend of mine from that same time and place).

What does research say about relying on memories for data? Pursuing just that topic alone forces one to confront a vast literature. There seems to be a consensus that at my current age, I am primed to remember events for the time period covered in this book (for a summary of the research, see Rubin 1986). When I took a graduate school friend of mine from a rural southern town to my old neighborhood, she stood in front of my childhood home and exclaimed, "I studied places like this in a book I read for a course in urban sociology." "Well," I replied, "I lived it."

Is it, as some argue, narcissistic on the part of sociologists to put themselves at the center of a study. Actually, I think this accusation comes from academics who, from my experience in the field, can be very private people and reticent about putting themselves "out there" for others to see. There seems to be an unfortunate reluctance on the part of academics to talk about their personal lives. I find the few publications where sociologists have talked about their lives fascinating (Horowitz 1969; Riley 1988; Berger 1990). Yet, they have, for the most part, discussed the social contexts that drove them to pursue a life in the academy at the expense of their thoughts and feelings about such decisions. In those accounts of their lives, the authors rarely used their wonderful sociological imaginations to put their experiences into sociological terms.

Do I have any reservations about laying out my dirty laundry in front of my colleagues? Absolutely! However, it is necessary for sociology to fulfill Mills' (1959) mandate to connect personal troubles with public issues, history with biography, and the individual with society. These kinds of stories need to be told; this story needs to be told—the inside sociological story of what it is like to grow up in a working-class family in an urban working-class neighborhood, and both the immediate and possible long-term consequences of doing so.

Ethical and privacy concerns have to be at the forefront of any research project, and this one is no different. In keeping with standard research protocol, I have tried to keep the identities of those referred to in this book anonymous—I have not used anyone's name, and for those who could be identified by someone with detailed knowledge of that time and place (one or two at most), I have made sure not to discuss any incriminating events. It must be remembered that my main interest is not in the particular people from that time and place, but rather in providing an analysis of the experiences of what it is like to live and grow up in a working-class, urban environment, coupled with a discussion of the consequences.

What Is New Here?

Like any project in sociology, the discussion will revolve around the topics of social class, race, gender, religion, politics, generations, neighborhoods, education, and social psychology. It is these substantive areas of sociological inquiry that guided me and my analyses through that time and place. To get into the zone necessary for writing this kind of book, I immersed myself in that time and place. I listened to music from that era in the background, and I built an HO scale model of the main streets of the old neighborhood. In addition, I have reconnected with many of my old friends on social media, and I have visited my old neighborhood a number of times over the last few years (including a reunion of the members of City Line). As research has suggested, those memories have been strengthened—and kept fresh in my mind—by talking about them and using them in classroom discussions (Rubin 1986).

This book will be helpful to students, sociologists, and the general public in connecting with these issues and sociological concepts. My approach can deepen a student's understanding of sociology by showing how it is related to our everyday lives. The general reader will be introduced to the principles of sociology as applied to someone's life course and to the sociological perspective. My hope is that scholars will find my auto-ethnographic approach and the strong social, cultural, and economic context interesting and useful.

This volume will break new ground by producing a rich ethnography:

1) Including a detailed description of what it was like to grow up working class in an urban environment from a sociologist's perspective.
2) Providing a solid social context and theoretical explanation.
3) Supported by census tract data and comments from past residents of the community.
4) Highlighting a particular, important, but not previously explored geographic area in New York City, consisting of white working-class

residents, mostly Catholic Irish, Italians, and Germans, but now populated by many different peoples—including many Muslims, which has recently prompted a number of former residents to join the backlash bandwagon.

5) Describing the kinds of hidden injuries of class young people can experience, and showing that these injuries shape them from an early age.

6) Providing a sociological explanation for what has previously been described as "angry white men" (and the rise of some recent political figures such as Donald Trump).

7) Parsing how the tendency for angry white men (and women) to lash out at the wrong social forces usually works against their best interests.

8) Offering an account of the connections between working-class orientations toward schooling, sports, politics, and economics.

9) Sharing a preliminary look at some former residents of City Line who now occupy different rungs on the social class ladder, being a product of the interaction of structure and agency.

ORGANIZATION OF THE BOOK

The Introduction contains the central argument of the text, its contribution to the field, and the reasons why this kind of work and research is necessary. Also, the chapter briefly covers two important related areas: the role of memory and the importance of ethics. The reader is introduced to the geographic location of the particular Brooklyn-Queens neighborhood, its housing stock—railroad rooms in row houses—and their importance as settings for the hidden injuries of class. Finally, important demographic data about that time and place is analyzed using the award-winning program Social Explorer.

Chapter 2 turns its attention toward the local (micro) context of the hidden injuries of class (Sennett and Cobb 1972). What about the local area and the families who lived there sets the stage for some to live in "worlds of pain"? During this chapter I examine the micro aspects of class-related injuries of youth: an alcoholic father and other family problems that are unseen; ethnic identity; rampant sexism and racism, the moms' and dads' jobs (and their ability—at that unique time period—to provide blue-collar workers without a college degree with a decent lifestyle); and the stoops, blocks, main avenues, bars, and overall urban village environment.

In Chap. 3, I start to delve deeply into the hidden injuries of class. Sennett and Cobb argue that members of the working class experience hidden injuries of class—frustration, anger, and bitterness—during their search for dignity in a capitalist society, because in such an economic system the members of the working class are denied their fair share of self-worth (badges of ability based on educational credentials and occupational prestige). We will explore my experiences with the educational system and its effects on my developing self-confidence (with self-confidence being a central indicator of the overall effects of the injuries that research suggests can cause anger). We will also see how my parents' and peers' attitudes toward education—their "cultural capital"—are crucial for understanding how working-class kids get working-class jobs (Willis 1981). My early years attending a Catholic elementary school, and then a vocationally oriented high school, will be explored for their benefits and drawbacks. Finally, two important concepts will be brought into the discussion: "tracking" and the "hidden curriculum." Clearly, I was on track to reproduce my parents' social class position until a major turning point in my life: the divorce from my first wife (the "I" being important for this kind of research; see Ellis 1995, 2004). My divorce was a major "turning point" in my life, and sent me onto a new career path.

In Chap. 4, I show how the hidden injuries of class continue into adulthood and curdle. In my previous research on social class (reprinted in that chapter), I found that a large segment of the white working class are angry: they lash out at middle- and upper-middle-class, college-educated, white-collar workers. Their frustration with their current economic situation pushes them to lash out at the "other." The lack of self-confidence, again, rears its head as an important issue for understanding their feelings, even as adults. The working-class parents used words such as "maybe" and "hopefully" when discussing their children's chances of going to college. Interestingly, working-class women were found to be somewhat less angry and bitter. Some possible explanations for this finding are offered. Meanwhile, middle-class parents "assumed" their children will attend college and go on to successful "careers." This chapter will also introduce the idea behind "hard-" vs. "settled-living" working-class families.[1]

Educational Reality: A Comparison

Educational credentials are one of the main badges of ability (Sennett and Cobb 1972) that are awarded in a capitalist system. In comparing my educational career and my family's cultural capital with the findings from my previous research (in the second part of Chap. 4), we will see that the story is not one-dimensional (structure). The active participation of important figures (agency) can help some working-class kids to not get working-class jobs (Willis 1981). Even though I attended a vocationally oriented high school and community college, active agents in my life interceded and helped mitigate the hidden injuries of class. Still, my lack of self-confidence rose and fell like a roller coaster throughout my acquisition of BA, MA, and PhD degrees (and even into my professional career).

While Sennett and Cobb concentrated on educational credentials and occupational prestige as the focus for the hidden injuries of class, Chap. 5 explores other important fields where the injuries escalate. These include friends and peers, girlfriends and boyfriends, and leisure activities such as one's prowess at various sporting activities. Here, I will also discuss the debilitating effects of "rank-outs" (sometimes called "verbal sparring" or "the dozens"). Our version was nasty, vicious (aimed at the weaknesses of working-class families), and taken to heart (as recent research suggests) by working-class youth. The research on sports and leisure, including my own, is also important for understanding working-class and middle-class identities. Finally, this chapter will look at another important area for the self-confidence of working-class youth (again, because they tend to take it to heart): love interests who are "out of one's league." Finally, I will look at the norms and values found in the examined neighborhood, for better or worse.

The larger macro-social context of the hidden injuries of class cannot be ignored and will be highlighted in Chap. 6. While the world was watching events unfold in 1968 (Democratic Convention, Robert Kennedy and Martin Luther King assassinated, and the TET Offensive in Vietnam), I was worried—because of a lack of self-confidence—about making an error and losing the Catholic Youth Organization Championship baseball game. We eventually won that game on a key play in which I was involved, which temporarily helped my self-confidence. Despite being in a major "world capital," our little neighborhood seemed to be living in a bubble, impervious to the political and cultural changes of the 1960s, until the Vietnam War and the cultural spread of sex, drugs, and rock and roll came to our small corner of the world. Many of those who fight wars come from neighborhoods like City Line. In fact, I found myself, at times, feeling guilty for not having served in the military at that time (that value being a product of my social class). Also, during this time working-class wages peaked, but some people today seem to have forgotten that fact, and tend to blame others (blacks, Hispanics, and Muslims) for their own social and economic struggles.

In Chap. 7, the reader gets to hear other voices who are from that time and place by using comments from social media, without using any names or other identifying information, and where all comments have been somewhat altered, combined, and summarized to guarantee anonymity. Some former City Line residents from my era seem to be currently angry (usually about the economy and those "others" who now occupy the streets where *they* grew up). Others, however, do not seem angry at the changes to their old neighborhood. Some seem to have positive memories of that time and place (another recent book of 12 stories by Crockett [2015] highlights some of the injuries I talk about, though in a humorous way) and some do not. Some of the women are angry, because that time and place did not allow them to become who they could have become professionally. Meanwhile, some former residents say that they long for a time when the legendary John Gotti and other organized crime members lived in the area and kept the neighborhood "safe." Explanations for these attitudes will be offered in the conclusion.

In Chap. 8, I will present a summary and conclusion. Sennett and Cobb (1972, p. 186) said that "no matter how much he [the working-class individual] knows 'the system is rotten,' he has to fight a doubt about himself first to be able unreservedly to fight the world." Some individuals from my old neighborhood have experienced upward social mobility, while others have not. Some have lived "hard" lives, others have lived "settled lives." Indeed, some former residents talk about how moving away from the area helped them in their pursuit of the middle-class American Dream. Several of the factors that can account for my own career path from a low-level production assistant in a printing factory to a tenured associate professor at Queens College (CUNY) will be discussed. As noted above, in my previous research on social class I found a tendency for some members of the working class to respond to an assault on their dignity by lashing out at middle- and upper-middle-class, white-collar, college-educated workers. Their anger was misdirected; that anger did not improve their station. Today, I argue, those feelings seem to have spread into another arena—the political. We have been hearing much lately about angry, white, working-class males (and I would add that there also are a significant number of angry white women from the working class) spewing venom at the changing demographics and the lack of well-paying jobs in America, and turning toward certain political candidates such as Donald Trump. Their anger is still misdirected.

Overall, the first two chapters describe the area and the neighborhood, followed by a discussion of education, sports, and friends, since they were so influential in my youth, and the kind of hidden injuries of class that I experienced in those settings. The hidden injuries of class really start to hurt with my interactions with the educational system and continue into adolescence in Chaps. 3 and 4. I will then review previous research I conducted on social class in which a sample of 40 working-class parents (and a different sample of 20 working-class parents) spoke of their various life experiences. Their testaments show how the hidden injuries of class are experienced by both children and adults in a variety of settings. Those experiences help shape those parents' attitudes toward education, especially their children's education, and toward their children's participation in sports (and, I would argue, their attitudes toward other institutions such as politics). Following that review, I will put my youthful experiences into the context of the politics, economics, and other social institutions (such as the family and religion) of that time and place. Social media comments from former residents will show conflicting perspectives on the old neighborhood and provide the necessary information for a possible explanation for "angry (and not so angry) white men and women." Finally, I will summarize and draw some conclusions pertinent to working-class culture today.

The Site and the Community: City Line, Brooklyn, USA

This book focuses on the geographic area where I spent the first (almost) 30 years of my life, which is located on the Brooklyn/Queens border in New York City—known as City Line on the Brooklyn side of the border and Ozone Park on the Queens side. While walking down any of the main avenues that run from Ozone Park into City Line, you would never know you had just crossed from one borough of New York City into another (there are five such boroughs: Brooklyn, Queens, Manhattan, the Bronx, and Staten Island) because the streetscape would feel so similar.

Looking at the maps (Maps 1.1 and 1.2 in the Appendix to this chapter), you will see that City Line and Ozone Park are adjacent to the southern section of Long Island and are wholly within two of New York City's five boroughs: Brooklyn and Queens. The neighboring two counties are Nassau and Suffolk, but these two counties, while part of New York State, are not part of New York City (they make up Long Island). Brooklyn and Queens may be part of New York City, but residents from all the boroughs refer to visiting Manhattan as "going to the city," positioning themselves as outsiders. City Line received its name from the era when Brooklyn was the far end boundary of New York City: the actual city line. Ozone Park, as legend has it, received its name because of the cool, refreshing breezes that would cross the area from Jamaica Bay. The word "Ozone" had a positive connotation—as representing the fresh breezes from the ocean—when the area was first settled in the nineteenth century. It never occurred to me that the name of my hometown sounded strange to others, until one day when someone asked me, "What kind of a park is an 'OZONE' park?"

Much of the area was built around the turn of the twentieth century. It was a working-class town with a number of factories dotting the landscape. The book *The Story of Woodhaven and Ozone Park* (Seyfried 1986) is about the place and an adjacent neighborhood, and does a very nice job of outlining the area's development. In the early 1900s, working-class men and women moved out to the Brooklyn/Queens border and built their lives working in factories and businesses that produced candles, baked goods, furniture, cookware, beer, underwear, and dairy products. As late as the 1970s, the remnants of those heady manufacturing days along 101st Avenue came into view. During hot summer nights, one could peer through the open doors of buildings and see women working at their sewing machines. These women worked for clothing manufacturers (some would call these establishments sweat shops) as part of the city's larger fashion industry. One other factory still stands from those early manufacturing days, and anyone from the area would recognize the Lance and Grosjean Factory Co. Clock Tower on Atlantic Avenue, built in 1900. It has been used to manufacture various products over the years.

City Line and Ozone Park remain far removed geographically and, even more so, economically and culturally from the hustle and bustle of Manhattan, the place that most of the rest of the country associates with New York City (Empire State Building, Times Square, etc.). Out there was a place where the people who helped build New York City lived. The Independent Subway (El) Line runs right through the middle of the community and was instrumental in connecting working-class Queens and Brooklyn to "the city" and developing the area's neighborhoods (see Photo 1.1).

The border separating Brooklyn (City Line) from Queens (Ozone Park) meanders through a number of streets, dividing friends who lived on opposite sides of the same street into two different phone books

Photo 1.1   Independent Subway Line, A Train, El—it runs through Ozone Park on Liberty Avenue and goes underground at Drew Street

(*NY Daily News*, Liff 1999). One of my friends, who lived on 75th Street—which is technically Queens by about 150 feet—would later tell his high school students that he lived in Brooklyn because it made for a better story and gave him street credibility. To confuse matters even more, the houses on Drew Street (the borderline) have two addresses: one for Brooklyn and one for Queens. If you ask locals to draw the boundaries of City Line, arguments over blocks and street corners will ensue.

The boundaries of my social world were very clear and confined. I lived on 76th Street (between 97th and 101st Avenues—see Map 1.2 in the Appendix to this chapter and Photo 1.2), two blocks from the border that separated City Line from Ozone Park, and nearly all my life activities were defined by our local church, the St. Sylvester Parish.

Those borders included City Line, Brooklyn, and extended three blocks into Ozone Park, Queens. Neighborhood borders, while debated endlessly in the sociological literature on urban life, can be defined by "natural" effects, "invasion," the political economy, or "social construction," in that they became "real" only after members of the community have negotiated the boundaries (see Sampson 2012 for a nice review of the literature). The boundaries defining the St. Sylvester Parish—which

Photo 1.2   Home, 2nd Floor, 97-23 76th Street—the author lived there from 3½ years old till he was 16

the Catholic Brooklyn Diocese decreed (or socially constructed) included parts of Brooklyn and Queens, and included most of City Line and the first few blocks of Ozone Park—provided a map for my day-to-day life. Other parts of Ozone Park might be seen as neighborhoods "defended" against the incursion of African-Americans from other nearby neighborhoods, such as Jamaica.[2,3]

However the St. Sylvester Parish was created, it defined my social world: I spent almost all my time and energy in that universe, walking to school and church, playing basketball (P.S. 214) and baseball, hanging out and playing sports with friends, and shopping and eating (on Liberty Avenue). My family's apartment was on 76th Street, and anyone who lived beyond 77th Street had to attend a different Catholic elementary school: St. Elizabeth's on Atlantic Avenue and 86th Street (quite a distance from 76th Street by foot). While I could have walked the other way, past 77th

Street (further into Ozone Park, Queens), to hang out with kids at the park at P.S. 64 playground, I "chose" not to do so (a few people from 75th and 76th Streets did hang out at "64 park" further into Queens). The boundaries of St. Sylvester School (SSS) were socially constructed, but they would dictate my everyday life for many years.

My maternal grandparents moved to 87th Street and Atlantic Avenue after we all moved from Elderts Lane in Brooklyn, which was down the block from St. Sylvester Church (more on that later). Living on Elderts Lane established my credentials with those who think that true City Liners can only be from Brooklyn. Technically, City Line, Brooklyn is bounded by Ozone Park to the East, Conduit Highway to the South, Atlantic Avenue to the North, and Euclid Avenue to the West. Neighborhood boundaries are also socially constructed, however. Here is all you really need to know for this volume: my social world encompassed the geographic region beginning on 77th Street in Ozone Park, Queens (which included Angelo's Candy Store, Severolli's Bakery, and Aldo's Pizzeria) and extended up 101st Avenue in Queens, where it turns into Liberty Avenue—City Line, Brooklyn—up to and including the Earl Movie Theatre (and maybe a block or two further), and then north to SSS on the corner of McKinley Avenue and Grant Avenue. This was (and is) my definition of City Line, and I will refer to that area in this book either by name or as "the neighborhood." Photo 1.3 shows where Liberty Avenue meets 101st Avenue at Drew Street—two blocks from where I lived on 76th Street—separating City Line, Brooklyn from Ozone Park, Queens. These are the storefronts that lined "The Avenue."

Other maps outlining the boundaries of City Line show a slightly larger geographic region (including the area south of the Conduit Highway), although that is not how I would define City Line. Indeed, most neighborhood boundaries will be debated endlessly by local residents, but those differences will not be a problem for the current research as the core areas and details are consistent. Anytime I am referring to Ozone Park specifically, I will be sure to be clear that I am not talking about City Line or about both neighborhoods.

As you can see from the recent photographs of the area, the physical structures have held up well over the years. Much of the housing consists of brick, two- to three-story, row housing with railroad-style apartments, similar to many working-class areas of other big cities in the United States (for

Photo 1.3   Liberty Avenue—"The Avenue" looking west from Drew Street, the Brooklyn/Queens border

an interesting history of row housing in the country in general and specifically in Baltimore, see Belfoure 2001). For those not familiar with row housing, you can see (Photo 2.2) that my block was filled with two-story houses, connected together in a row. Railroad apartments follow a specific interconnected layout. For example, from my parents' bedroom (see Map 1.3 in the Appendix to this chapter) in the front of the apartment, one could see straight through my bedroom (no door), through the living room, and into the dining room. The dimensions for each room are indicated on the diagram and add up to approximately 740 square feet, quite a difference from the average home today, which clocks in at about 2500 square feet.

As one moves further east and deeper into Ozone Park, Queens, the housing changes from row housing to somewhat larger, semi-attached and unattached houses (see Photo 1.4 for the apartment my family rented on 106th Street in Ozone Park in 1969, where I was so proud that there was a little space between the houses).

City Line is closer to the lower-income areas of East New York, but Ozone Park and City Line blend together in my mind. The only difference I noticed over the years was that we had some space between our house and the neighbor's house when we lived in Ozone Park. The demographic

Photo 1.4   106th Street, Ozone Park, Queens, 1973—author looking proud of the newfound space between our apartment and others

differences between City Line and Ozone Park are discussed at the end of this chapter. Overall, residents in Ozone Park had a slightly higher educational level, median family income, and lower levels of poverty. Even though I technically lived in Ozone Park after I moved from City Line, I had many more friends from City Line and still "hung out" there. Thus, one could argue that I understood more about City Line culture than I did about Ozone Park culture.

The area just described—City Line—includes a type of shopping district that may not be familiar to many people, especially if you grew up in a rural or suburban environment and are used to strip malls, larger shopping malls, or big box stores. As you can see (Photo 1.3), each block contains (and contained) a number of different small stores, stretching from 101st Avenue all the way up Liberty Avenue, such as shoe stores, bakeries, small grocery stores, clothing stores, a funeral home, candy stores, banks, drug stores, hardware stores, barbers, and so on. There was a store on the "Avenue" (as locals called it) for just about any need one had. To go food shopping, my mother would take her small shopping cart up the Avenue each day to the small grocery store she loved: Crystals. She would buy one or two bags of groceries for that day and return home with them in her cart. The next day she would follow the same routine, because the idea of driving to an isolated large grocery store and packing a car with a dozen bags of groceries for the week would have seemed like something out of a science fiction movie to her. After all, who could have afforded to shop for two week's worth of groceries?

When we lived on 76th Street, each night it was my job to go around the corner to the candy store to get my father the *Daily News* and *Daily Mirror* (each five cents) and two packs of King Size Chesterfield Cigarettes (there were few stores then that asked for proof of age when buying cigarettes—alcohol was a different story). While waiting for the newspapers to arrive, I would bide my time drinking an egg cream (a seltzer, chocolate syrup, and milk concoction with no actual egg or cream), Cherry Coke (the cherry syrup and Coke coming from the soda fountain), or a Lime Rickey. If my mother had given me an extra quarter, I might have waited two doors down at Aldo's, two stores away, eating some of the best pizza ever made (where we would get the best pizza pie every Friday, given it was a heavily Catholic neighborhood; patrons of Flora's Pizzeria further up Liberty Avenue might disagree with me). During the holiday season in this solidly Catholic area we knew it was the Christmas season: festive lights hung across Liberty Avenue, adorning most of City Line and creating a magical feeling for a young lad. Everyone in the neighborhood walked or biked to their destinations on the Avenue.

Each block could be described as its own neighborhood. For example, there was rivalry between my block—76th Street—and the next block—75th Street. Yet, most of the children in the area went to only one of two elementary schools, St. Sylvester (Catholic) or P.S. 64, although the overwhelming majority of my friends went to St. Sylvester on Grant Avenue (see Map 1.2).

While I was growing up in City Line, it was almost impossible to find someone whose ancestry was not white and Catholic, whether Italian, Irish, or German. In particular, the area had a strong Italian flavor to it. The tables at the end of the chapter give a breakdown of the neighborhood census tracts by ethnicity (via Social Explorer) and a full rundown and analysis of the demographic profile of both Ozone Park and City Line. However, today the neighborhood is heavily populated by immigrants from Bangladesh, Guyana, and the Caribbean, and has become significantly more Hispanic and African-American. The change in neighborhood demographics has produced much consternation among many former and longtime residents of my generation who used to populate those same streets.

Longtime residents of the neighborhood complain that the current residents are disruptive, with loud music coming from homes, especially from traditional Guyanese and Indian weddings that some residents say go on for days, the types and smells of food, men standing on corners harassing women passing by, graffiti and crime in the area, the presence of mosques, and just about anything that is different from the City Line of their past. Interestingly, some of our own norms would be seen today as crass to others. For example, when I was a kid it was very common to see clotheslines dominating the view out of any back window. I raise this point because when I lived in a different—upper-middle-class—neighborhood in Queens many years later, some residents complained vehemently that someone had strung up a clothesline that made the neighborhood—in their words—look like a "third world country." There are, in fact, upper-middle-class neighborhoods where clotheslines are not allowed by regulation—a case of a social norm reflecting the values of the community to the degree that it is written into law. The custom of sitting on our stoop all hours of the day and night back then was normal to us, but would seem somewhat odd to those who live in quiet, upper-middle-class neighborhoods. So, I think my friends would be somewhat surprised to learn that from a middle/upper-middle-class perspective, some of our norms from the old working-class neighborhood would now be seen to be as strange and unwelcome as they find some of the new residents' normative behavior.

There is very little written about this neighborhood in the numerous books about New York City, even in those that survey the many neighborhoods that define each borough. It is an ignored neighborhood on the western tip of Brooklyn and the eastern tip of Queens. There have been a few sociological and historical studies of other Brooklyn neighborhoods, such as Canarsie, Brownsville, and East New York, and some books on New York City reference areas that are nearby, such as Jamaica or Forest Hills, Queens, or East New York, Brooklyn (of which City Line is technically part), but there is little about Ozone Park and almost nothing about City Line. Much can be learned from an examination of this neighborhood on the borders of Brooklyn and Queens in the 1960s and 1970s.

DEMOGRAPHIC TABLES

The overall population (Table 1.1 in the Appendix to this chapter, where all the raw data can be found) of the old neighborhood has increased over time along with growth across the city, with the Brooklyn side becoming more densely populated than the Queens side (except for Census Tract 02, which is closer to Conduit Boulevard; see Map 1.2 for the location of each census tract). To understand the differences in population density between Ozone Park and City Line, one must keep in mind that Ozone Park has fewer blocks with row housing, instead favoring semi-detached and detached homes. As one moves more toward Tudor Village (near Conduit Boulevard), one starts to come across single-family homes.

The data shows that during the time I was growing up in City Line, population density ranged from 40,000 to 50,000 residents per square mile (U. S. Census Bureau, Population Density, 1950–2000). To give you some perspective on how crowded that was, consider that New York City is the most densely populated city in the United States today, at approximately 27,000 people per square mile. Queens County's population density comes in at approximately 20,000 and Brooklyn at about 35,000. Only Manhattan, one of the most crowded areas in the world, exceeds City Line at approximately 69,000 residents per square mile (much of which can be accounted for, largely, by the area's many high-rise apartments). City Line achieved this density despite not having many apartment buildings. When Crockett (2015) talks about hearing his next-door neighbor going through his daily activities of all kinds, he is not kidding. We lived literally on top of each other.

The racial and ethnic demographics tell a story of change (Table 1.4). The neighborhood was fairly homogenous up until 1970, with just a few Hispanic residents in a sea of white. By the 1980s we see the beginning of "white flight" from many parts of the city including City Line (usually to Long Island, Staten Island, or even Howard Beach, to stay close to the old neighborhood). Meanwhile, Ozone Park, for the most part, remained overwhelmingly white (Irish, Italian, and German). By the 1990s, white flight took off in City Line, with the white population dropping to the middle of the 30 percent range. The percentage of whites in Ozone Park at that time stayed in the 70 percent range. In Ozone Park, white flight lagged by approximately ten years. The movement of new people to the area seemed to begin on the western edge of the neighborhood and move east. To be sure, some residents of Ozone Park will credit organized crime figures there with keeping their streets mostly white (and relatively crime free). Indeed, when one old resident of Ozone Park recently heard that an African-American man may have committed a crime in the area, he said that John Gotti would have never let *them* into the neighborhood (*NY Daily* News, Salinger 2014). Recently, the number of white residents in both City Line and Ozone Park appears to have reverted to levels seen in the 1960s. Looking at the data closely reveals that most of them are "Hispanic whites." My lesson on the "social construction of race" (that there is only one "race"), I believe, would not be well received, and I am almost sure that these white residents would not have been considered "white" in my old neighborhood. City Line today is heavily populated by Bangladeshis (Table 1.10), and Ozone Park has a large and growing Guyanese population (most of whom are Catholic). When many residents talk about how the neighborhood has "changed" (changed for the worse), these group shifts are the changes they have in mind. I have been back to that area a number of times recently and I can verify that its physical structure looks relatively unchanged from what I remember. So, to what other "changes" could the former residents be referring?

Despite the perception that the new Muslim population has overrun the neighborhood, past residents of City Line and Ozone Park might be surprised to find out that Muslims remain pretty much in the minority in East New York and Ozone Park. PUMA data for 2010 indicated that for East New York, Protestants comprise approximately 46 percent of the total population, while Catholics make up another 25 percent. In Ozone Park, Protestants constitute about 30 percent of the population, while Catholics make up another 64 percent (much of the large Guyanese population is Catholic). In Woodhaven and Richmond Hill, there are approximately 22 percent of the population who are Protestant and 56 percent Catholic.

When looking directly at the mostly Muslim Bangladeshi population in City Line, we can see that they have become a significant group, but are not the majority. In the Census Tracts—1188, 042, and 044—with the highest percentage of Bengalis, they comprise approximately 35 percent, 30 percent, and 39 percent respectively (Asian American Federation Census 2013). When we look at the data from a different document (The Newest New Yorkers 2013), we can see that about 44 percent of Cypress Hills/City Line residents are foreign born. The three largest groups that make up the foreign-born population come from the Dominican Republic (34 percent), followed by Guyana at 14.7 percent (both groups are mostly Catholic), and Bangladesh (mostly Muslim) at 10.4 percent. The foreign-born groups are summarized in Boxes 1.1, 1.2, and 1.3.

Box 1.1   Origins of foreign-born residents of City Line

Country of origin	%
Dominican Republic	34
Guyana	14.7
Bangladesh	10.4
Ecuador	6.9
Mexico	4.3
China	3.9
Trinidad and Tobago	3.6
Columbia	3.3
Honduras	2.5
Guatemala	1.7
Others	14.8

Box 1.2   Origins of foreign-born residents of Woodhaven

Country of origin	%
Dominican Republic	18.5
Ecuador	12.6
Guyana	9.7
China	8.9
Bangladesh	8.2
Columbia	5.4
Philippines	4.0
Mexico	3.6
Poland	3.4
India	3.1
Others	22.6

The proportion of foreign-born residents (Table 1.9) hovers around the 50 percent level in most local census tracts today in both neighborhoods. It is interesting that the foreign-born rate was also relatively high back in the 1950s and 1960s (around 20 percent). I can remember a number of "old-timers" speaking Italian in the shops and on the streets, but that kind of diversity seems to be remembered fondly by many ex-residents today (although the same does not apply to the current foreign-born residents).

When looking at the highest level of education completed (Table 1.4), the percentage of adults who never graduated high school continues to

Box 1.3 Origins of foreign-born residents of South Ozone Park

Country of origin	%
Guyana	46.5
Trinidad and Tobago	14.4
India	5.4
Dominican Republic	3.7
Ecuador	3.6
Jamaica	3.0
Mexico	2.6
El Salvador	2.1
Columbia	1.8
China	1.7
Other	15.2

Box 1.4 Residents with some college education or a college degree

Census Tract	%
1184	6.0
1186	8.0
1188	3.5
1202	8.0
06	7.0
034	8.0
036	6.0
042	7.0
044	7.0

decrease over time. It is true that one did not need a high school degree back in the 1950s to find a well-paying job (as my father did), but it is still an interesting finding. Also, the fact that the number of persons with "some college" or a "BA degree" continues to increase is a very important trend for the new residents of the area in their pursuit of the American Dream. The demographics illustrate how City Line exhibited more working-class characteristics than many other areas of its day. For instance, the percentage of those from my old neighborhood who had "some college" or more in 1950 and 1970 is far lower compared to those from other areas of Queens such as Forest Hills and Bayside, and lower than areas on the North Shore of Long Island.

In 1970, the percentages of both the City Line and Ozone Park adult population that had attended some college and/or had a college degree is indicated in Box 1.4.

Some of the other Queens County neighborhoods and parts of the city had a better-educated and more professional adult population. The percentages for other nearby areas, such as Bayside, Forest Hills, and Flushing, Queens, who had some college or more came in at between 35 and 40 percent of the population, with professionals and managers making up about 45–47 percent of the population. Parts of the Upper East Side of Manhattan had approximately 55 percent of their population as professional and managers, and 59–62 percent with some college or more as their educational level. On the North Shore of Long Island, there were areas where about 56–61 percent were professionals and managers and about 60–65 percent with had some college or more as their educational level.

In 1980, when my peers would have already graduated college, the percentage of adults from the census tracts in my old neighborhood who had some college or more as their educational attainment is shown in Box 1.5.

While those numbers indicate a slight increase from 1970 in the percentage of residents in City Line and Ozone Park who had attended some college or more, the increase in college attendance exploded in several other parts of New York City, such as Bayside (47–52%), Kew Gardens and Flushing (72–77%), the Upper East Side of Manhattan (73–82%), and parts of the North Shore of Long Island.

There is no doubt that City Line and Ozone Park were (and are today) working-class neighborhoods, no matter whether you use occupation and/ or educational level to determine this. The incomes of blue-collar workers were higher than today, but occupation and educational level provide a better indicator of the residents' relation to the means of production. The data show that "craft, operatives, and laborers" constitute a very large part of the adult working population (Table 1.5). In 1950 and 1970, the

Box 1.5 Residents with some college education or a college degree

Census tract	%
1184	8
1186	12
1188	14
1202	10
06	19
034	8
036	13
042	12
044	15

percentage of "professional and technical, and managers" in the area adds up to only about 10 percent of the population (compare that to the professional and managers category in other areas of New York City, which, as discussed above, is much larger). The "clerical" category in the neighborhood is fairly large, but contains some occupations that would be considered working class, while others would be considered middle class. The percentage of women participating in the labor force across the area's Census Tracts in the 1950s, '60s, and '70s was in the 30% range; in the 1980s, '90s, and 2000s it was in the 40–50% range; and in 2010 and 2014 in the 40–60% range. These numbers were surprisingly high to me, but they should not have been. Working-class women have been in the work force longer than middle-class women. The percentage of working women in the area today is somewhat lower than the national average, but that may possibly be because of the cultural beliefs of the current residents.

The neighborhood was a stable, working-class place with a low unemployment rate (Table 1.8) until the 1980s and 1990s, when it went through a period of high crime rates and rampant drug use. Today, the civilian unemployment rate has decreased, but remains high in both City Line and Ozone Park (2013). You find the same trend when looking at the percentage of families below the poverty line. The unemployment rate is not that high given the percentage of families below the poverty line, an indication that there are many "working poor" residents. This is where the low minimum wage and the lack of well-paid jobs for the working class today (as compared to when my friends and I lived in the area) come into play. (The most recent Census data for 2015 indicates a trend of lower civilian unemployment rates across City Line and Ozone Park. Census Tract 1184-5.25%, 1186-9.37%, 1188-7.6%, 1202-3.07%, Census Tract 6-13.9%, 34-14.5%, 36-5.73%, 42-14.6%, 44-8.69%).

It is interesting to note that the median household income (Table 1.2) across all the local census tracts is below the nationwide median in 1950, possibly reflecting the early years of the population's careers after World War II. It then rises in 1960, and by 1970 the average family income (a different but related measure) is above the average for New York State and the country as a whole (except for Census Tract 1188, which is slightly below New York State). Yes, well-paying, blue-collar, working-class jobs *were* still available at that time. This also shows that families in some neighborhoods were doing somewhat better than others across the region. By 1980 that trend starts to change, as median household income stagnates (except for most of Ozone Park) or decreases, while the civilian unemployment rate and the percentage of families below the poverty line increase (except for Census Tract 06). Median household income is remarkably high today, higher than for the area in the 1950s and the 1960s (where it is slightly below that for the city and country). This social fact may reflect a pattern, whereby there may be more than one family within each household, especially given the large percentage of families living below the poverty line. (The number of residents per household does increase over time for many areas.) Poor immigrant families may pool their resources to survive in a new country. (When investigating my own grandparents, I found that my paternal grandfather, grandmother, and their two children lived in the same household with my paternal great-grandfather and great-grandmother—and my grandmother's father). Census Tract 1202 has a much smaller population than the other census tracts and, therefore, the data varies quite a lot over the decades. The census tracts in Ozone Park had a consistently higher median household income than the nearby Brooklyn census tracts.

An analysis of voting patterns (Table 1.6) reveals the movement of the residents of City Line and Ozone Park to the right on the political spectrum over time. In City Line the vote was strong for Kennedy in 1960 and for Johnson in 1964, but the vote was split in 1968 between Humphrey, on the one hand, and Nixon and Wallace, on the other—running on "law and order" platforms, at the time code for getting tough with African-Americans. The vote was strong for Nixon in 1972, and then split (for the Democrats and Republicans) again in 1976 and 1980 (after Watergate). Ozone Park looks to be split between an area that historically votes Democrat and an area that has voted historically Republican.

The change in New York City crime rates over time is quite remarkable (Table 1.7). As has been discussed and debated endlessly, the overall crime rate for the city, as well as that the local police precincts in the area (75th, 102nd, and 106th), has decreased drastically since the 1990s. There are as many explanations for this phenomenon as there are criminologists. Can it be attributed to tougher policing, demographic changes in the age cohort most likely to commit crimes, the decline of the popularity of certain drugs such as crack cocaine, the rise in abortions (a very controversial explanation), or a combination of these? Yet, while the numbers make the crime rate decline plain, many people still believe that crime rates have gotten worse over time in New York City (Weill 2015). Could it be that people got so used to social problems increasing in the city in the 1970s and 1980s that it just seems impossible for them to have improved? Maybe people don't read or listen to the local news in newspapers and on television. It is also likely that it simply upsets most past residents' image of the current state of the neighborhood as crime ridden. Studies have found that people tend to continue to believe many falsehoods, even after they have been disproven. Nevertheless, the streets of East New York—a neighborhood in New York City with historically high rates of crime—are as safe, or safer, than when I grew up. Incidentally, studies also show that crime rates are lower for immigrants than for the population at large. "When a lot of immigrants come to communities, crime tends to drop," says Phillip Kasinitz, who teaches sociology at the CUNY Graduate Center (cited in Rose 2013). This drop in crime rates over time is one of the biggest changes to happen to New York City and the Brooklyn/Queens neighborhoods under study here, and the shift continues to shape the lives of people who live in the working-class neighborhoods of City Line and Ozone Park. That area, however, was the scene for my experience of the hidden injuries of class, which Chap. 2 will explore.

APPENDIX

Map 1.1 Large-view map of New York City

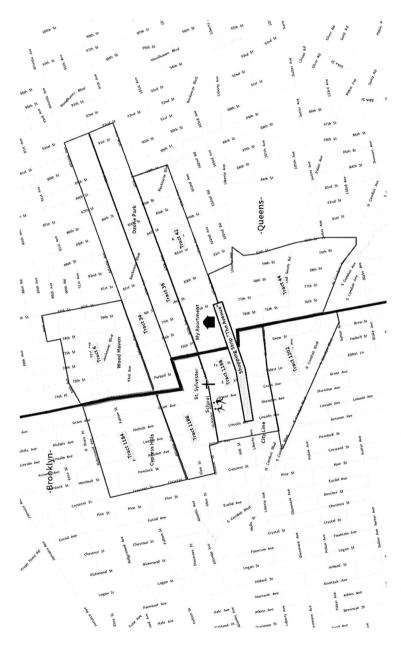

Map 1.2 Close-up map of my old neighborhood

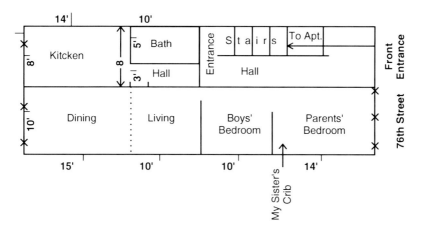

Map 1.3   Apartment schematic

DATA TABLES (BY CENSUS TRACT AND YEAR)

Table 1.1   Total population

	Brooklyn				Queens				
	Cypress Hills	City Line	-----------	-----------	Woodhaven	Ozone Park	-----------	-----------	-----------
	1184	1186	1188	1202	6	34	36	42	44
1950	3903	2307	3995	1257	2994	1865	2831	3598	1813
1960	3656	2109	3415	1095	2841	1721	2646	3221	2517
1970	3404	2221	3272	948	2749	1608	2782	2962	2766
1980	3550	2085	2921	1032	2687	1805	2411	2668	2532
1990	4087	2452	4037	1279	2762	1570	2408	2750	2414
2000	5106	3133	4560	1916	3717	2332	3099	3740	3139
2010	5316	3466	4165	1488	3137	2214	3210	4073	3364
2013	5229	2982	4263	2109	3796	2147	3536	4872	3765

Source: U. S. Census Bureau. Total Population. 1950–2013. Accessed via Social Explorer.

Table 1.2   Median household income

	Brooklyn Cypress Hills	City Line			Queens Woodhaven	Ozone Park		US—— NY State——			Median Household Income 2012 Dollars
	1184	1186	1188	1202	6	34	36	---------- 51915 / 57096	42	44	Average Family Income 2012=60000
1950	33629	41964	33182	NA	39243	34449	36899	----------	31796	32558	
1960	A	B	A	B	B	B	A	----------	B	B	1960 Median A=38783—to— B=46540 to 54296 46539
1970	61215	77343	56504	61371	73433	81490	70868	63048	63048	78087	Average Family Income for 1970
1980	39648	44512	31068	39531	58123	55216	57639	44081	44081	64444	
1990	51773	42756	43501	53448	65332	71459	51392	58332	58332	67058	
2000	45628	44043	29882	49255	62325	52878	59863	45478	45478	48708	
2010	44749	51838	24729	66306	51611	61091	55442	54333	54333	53106	
2013	42315	48916	30090	33642	58148	74865	65317	57000	57000	47986	

Source: U. S. Census Bureau. Median Household Income, 1950–2013. Accessed via Social Explorer.

Table 1.3 Highest level of education

Highest Level of Education—Percent

Year	CYPRESS HILLS (1184)					CITY (1186)					LINE (1188)					1202					WOODHAVEN (0006)					OZONE (0034)					PARK (0036)					0042					0044				
	LH	H	SC	BA	M+	LH	H	SC	BA	M+	LH	H	SC	BA	M+	LH	H	SC	BA	M+	LH	H	SC	BA	M+	LH	H	SC	BA	M+	LH	H	SC	BA	M+	LH	H	SC	BA	M+	LH	H	SC	BA	M+
1950	73	20	3	3	—	69	20	4	4		74	15	2	1		—	—	—	—	—	73	17	3	2		65	21	4	7		72	14	3	2		75	13	2	2		70	14	3	3	
1960	51			6		54			6		48			3		87	12	0	1		56			7		55			7		53			4		50			4		59			6	
1970	63	28	5	1	0.4	45	28	5	1	2	46	25	2	1	0.3	44			4		45	32	6	1	0.2	45	32	4	2	2	45	32	4	1	1	45	25	5	2	1	44	28	4	1	2
1980	56	36	7	2		60	28	10	2		59	27	10	4		42	30	5	1	2	46	36	11	8		59	33	7	2		45	42	8	6		49	38	7	5		49	36	10	6	
1990	45	32	16	7	1	48	31	17	3	1	51	26	16	5	2	57	29	7	3		40	32	15	11	1	37	32	22	7	3	36	37	15	9	3	39	36	17	5	3	33	40	17	7	3
2000	47	24	20	*	2	42	30	21	5	2	56	23	14	6	1	45	29	16	6	5	40	35	14	9	2	35	32	24	5	5	40	34	20	3	4	38	35	17	8	2	36	34	21	7	2
2010	28	72	25	1	1	20	80	27	10	2	31	69	24	9	3	27	73	39	20	10	25	75	37	16	6	19	82	40	15	6	12	88	43	19	6	24	76	39	17	3	22	78	39	20	5
2013	33	67	25	8	2	25	75	24	8	2	35	65	25	9	2	24	76	31	12	4	31	69	35	16	5	18	81	44	14	7	14	86	59	37	14	24	76	39	15	2	32	68	36	18	5

LH=Less than High School, H=High School, SC=Some College, BA=4 year College, M+=Masters and Above.

Source: U. S. Census Bureau. Highest Level of Education Completed, 1950–2013. Accessed via Social Explorer.

Table 1.4 Race/ethnicity

RACE/ETHNICITY (percent)

Values in each cell are given in the order **W B A O H**.

Year	CYPRESS HILLS 1184	CITY 1186	LINE 1188	1202	WOODHAVEN 0006	OZONE 0034	PARK 0036	0042	0044
1950	99	99	99	99	99	99	99	99	99
1960	99	99	99	99	99	99	99	99	99
1970	99 1 1 1	98 2	99 3	96 1 4 6	99 1	99 1	99 1	99 3	99 1
1980	75 5 2 18 39	72 5 1 23 39	72 2 3 24 34	77 2 2 19 25	97 0 1 2 7	96 0 2 2 10	98 0 0 2 8	95 0 1 4 12	98 1 0 2 6
1990	31 18 14 37 64	38 19 14 28 57	33 18 12 35 55	13 14 29 45 35	73 5 13 9 27	77 2 12 8 25	79 2 6 12 30	72 3 10 14 28	82 3 9 6 21
2000	28 19 11 35 64	26 17 11 38 60	18 18 19 32 35	17 33 37 10 20	41 9 13 40 50	42 10 12 35 52	47 7 11 40 47	38 8 15 38 46	36 5 23 36 32
2010	42 12 11 32 69	49 27 4 20 63	24 17 33 22 42	38 27 18 15 44	37 13 21 29 58	22 9 18 41 63	21 10 26 34 52	29 18 29 18 37	19 8 51 18 28
2013	52 20 14 10 58	53 26 7 10 59	28 50 11 10 35	38 27 18 15 44	34 10 22 31 58	30 10 20 29 55	23 8 44 16 38	29 7 41 16 42	22 8 52 12 26

W-White, B-Black, A-Asian, O-Other, H-Hispanic

Source: U. S. Census Bureau. Race/Ethnicity, 1950–2013. Accessed via Social Explorer.

Table 1.5 Occupational categories

	Brooklyn Cypress Hills	City Line	----------	----------	Occupational Categories--1950 / 1970 (percent) Queens Woodhaven	Ozone Park	----------	----------	----------
	1184	1186	1188	1202	6	34	36	42	44
Professional	6.3	8.5	5.1	4.7	6.6	8.2	5	4	4
Technical	8.2	13.5	3.5	7.3	7.6	8.5	4.8	7.1	7.9
Managers	6	5.9	6	8	9.1	6.2	3.9	6.6	8.6
	7.5	4.8	8	11.3	6.1	5.4	4.3	5.4	4.7
Clerical	31.8	28.7	23.2	20.5	28.8	24.6	22.8	22.1	14.4
	33.3	32	31.1	34	32.4	32.5	37.8	31.6	31.2
Sales	6.4	6.8	6.1	5	6.4	7.1	5.4	6.3	3
	3.9	9.2	3.8	3.7	4.2	5.5	3.6	4.8	6.8
Craft/	17.3	18.1	19.7	19.5	20.7	20.1	20.7	18.1	17.9
Foreman	12.7	12.6	17.5	17.5	14.5	15.2	14.1	15.9	17.9
Operatives	19.7	21.1	25.4	32.6	15.1	19.8	28.2	27.7	38.8
	19.9	15.1	22.5	16.1	18.8	17.7	16.9	16.2	20
Private	0.7	0.4	0.4	0	0.4	0.4	0.9	0.3	0.1
Household	0.3	0.4	0	0	0	0	1.5	0	0
Service	7.3	7.8	8.6	5.2	7.4	6.3	6.8	7	5.6
	9.7	5.7	13.3	3.7	10.1	10.7	9.3	10.9	7.5
Laborers	3.3	2.4	4.4	3.5	2.3	5	5.5	5.8	6.9
	4	6.3	6.7	5.1	5.7	3.7	6.9	7.6	3.6

Source: U. S. Census Bureau. Occupational Categories, 1950–1970. Accessed via Social Explorer.

Table 1.6 Presidential voting results

PRESIDENTIAL VOTING RESULTS

	BROOKLYN AD 22			QUEENS AD 13			Queens AD 12		
	DEM	REP	INDEP	DEM	REP	INDEP	DEM	REP	INDEP
1960	19801	14314		16649	30350		48639	32196	
1964	17759	10509		18687	24201		61076	26686	
	Brooklyn AD 38			Queens AD 28			Queens AD 29		
1968	12103	10913	2027	22404	16051	2191	20352	21699	3245
	Brooklyn AD 38			Queens AD 31			Queens AD 32		
1972	4653	10890		13240	33938		23468	16018	
1976	5924	5096		17355	20276		25135	8505	
1980	4321	3250	1142	12985	18415	1885	21088	9456	1077

Source: New York Times, Times Machine, November 9, 1960; November 5, 1964; November 8, 1968; November 9, 1972, November 4, 1976; November 6, 1980.

Table 1.7   Crimes for selected precincts

CRIMES FOR SELECTED PRECINCTS IN NYC

	BROOKLYN 75th East New York Including City Line				QUEENS 102nd Woodhaven/Richmond Hill				Queens 106th Ozone Park				New York City Total			
	Murder	Rape	Robbery	Burglary	Murder	Rape	Robbery	Burglary	Murder	Rape	Robbery	Burglary	Murder	Rape	Robbery	Burglary
1968	24	50	1168	5115	2	6	106	905	6	10	296	1416	1185 (1965–836)	2527	59857	250918
1973	51	115	1916	3137	3	17	360	929	11	31	585	1586	2040	4852	80795	246246
1976	(13633 Total Felonies)				(4098 Total Felonies)				(7080 Total Felonies)				1969	4663	95718	318919
1990	109	133	3452	2433	6	29	1067	1847	15	31	832	1348	2605	5368	112380	208813
1993	126				12				21				2420			
													2013			
2001	35	89	1146	568	2	21	459	622	4	19	344	272	960	3546	36555	80400
2014	21	70	817	530	3	15	235	293	2	25	272	251	648	2577	27241	56442

Source: Police Department, City of New York, CompStat, New York Times, December 2, 1974, April 10, 1977.

Table 1.8   Civilian unemployment rate

					Civilian Unemployment Rate (percent)				
	Brooklyn				Queens				
	Cypress Hills	City Line	----------	------------	Woodhaven	Ozone Park	-----------	-----------	-----------
	1184	1186	1188	1202	6	34	36	42	44
1950	5.1	5.8	9.3	1.7	3	6.6	4.4	7	10.5
1960	4.79	3.25	5.92	6.86	4.68	3.4	5.08	5.1	2.44
1970	3.8	6.3	3.9	3.7	4.1	6	1.9	4.2	4.6
1980	9.3	8.6	7.6	5.8	3.8	12.3	6.5	7.1	6.1
1990	11.8	5.8	8	13.05	8.2	2.5	10.9	7.2	4.4
2000	13.9	17.7	15.8	12.9	8.1	6	9.8	6.9	10.9
2010	5.2	7.45	15.4	1.33	12.72	8.69	13.89	12.62	7.96
2013	7.38	11	12.74	5.03	15.01	17.45	7.73	14.72	11.39

Source: U. S. Census Bureau, Civilian Unemployment Rate, 1950–2013.

Table 1.9   Place of birth: foreign born

					Foreign Born	(percent)			
	Brooklyn				Queens				
	Cypress Hills	City Line	-----------	------------	Woodhaven	Ozone Park	-----------	-----------	-----------
	1184	1186	1188	1202	6	34	36	42	44
1950	13.9	14.9	14.7	19.1	10.8	14.7	18	16.1	21.6
1960 NA									
1970	15.8	15.1	9.2	22.7	16.5	17.1	10.3	11.4	10.3
1980	18.7	17	24.1	16.6	14.8	12.7	10.8	13.2	19.3
1990	35.6	35.4	37.7	51.65	26.2	23.9	18.9	25.8	21.6
2000	45.9	48.5	53	54	45.6	34.7	45.7	47.2	46.5
2010	46.46	49.02	52.48	62.1	59.23	51.99	45.76	41.79	54.31
2013	58.42	43.49	53.25	42.06	46.42	40.52	55.71	54.31	55.7

Source: U. S. Census Bureau, Foreign Born, 1950–2013.

Table 1.10   Selected ethnicity

	Brooklyn				Selected Ethnicity--1970 Queens		Native and Foreign Born (percent)		
	Cypress Hills	City Line	----------	----------	Woodhaven	Ozone Park	----------	----------	----------
	1184	1186	1188	1202	6	34	36	42	44
Italian	41.25	58	63.6	73.7	40.6	39.8	48.5	63.4	74.3
Irish	11.4	5.5	5.6	3.3	11	14.6	4.2	7.1	3.3
German	12.7	8.5	6	8.3	16	18.3	10.9	4.4	5.3

	Brooklyn				Selected Ethnicity--2013 Queens				
	Cypress Hills	City Line	----------	----------	Woodhaven	Ozone Park	----------	----------	----------
	1184	1186	1188	1202	6	34	36	42	44
Italian	1.4	1.94	0.55	6.12	1.02	5.96	3.69	7.1	7.44
Irish	0.57	0.44	0	0.4	3.15	3.96	2.75	1.34	1.18
German	0.57	0	0.2	0	1.3	3.5	0	0.4	1.92
Guyanese	5.87	11.45	7.51	8.92	12.84	7.7	6.87	11.13	5.58
Other	83.84	78.9	77.8	77.72	72.56	66.45	79.04	73.62	77.1

Source: U. S. Census Bureau, Selected Ethnicity, 1970, 2013.

NOTES

1. "Hard-living" families, according to Howell (1973), tend to be composed of seven elements: heavy drinking, marital instability, toughness (profanity and violence), political alienation, rootlessness, present-time orientation, and a strong sense of individualism. As one moves away from "hard living" to the "settled living" end of the continuum, one finds less of these seven elements.
2. Interestingly, there is a part of Jamaica, Queens, that borders Long Island and whose business owners are trying to have the main avenue running though it changed from Jamaica Avenue to Jericho Turnpike, because (as everyone in that area knows, but does not admit publicly) Jamaica Avenue is closely associated with a mostly black population. Renaming advocates hope that more suburban residents from Long Island might shop on that stretch of Jamaica Avenue if it were instead called Jericho Turnpike (which it turns into once you cross the Queens/Nassau border).
3. With the recent closing of St. Sylvester School (but not the church yet), there have been accusations that its closing and merging with other local Catholic schools, creating the Salve Regina Academy a mile deeper into Brooklyn, were related more to the power that some Catholic parishes in the area have over other parishes.

CHAPTER 2

Where Does the Concrete End? The Local Context of the Hidden Injuries of Class

It is now time to turn to the local (micro) context of the hidden injuries of class. What is it about the neighborhood and the families living there that sets the stage for some to live in "worlds of pain"? In this chapter I will explore the neighborhood and the importance of the stoop, the avenue, summer evenings, apartment layouts, neighborhood density, gangs, the jobs the residents held and how these factors shaped their worlds, and more about the demographic characteristics of the area. Finally, I will give an account of the alcoholism that invaded families' lives, especially my own family.

BEGINNINGS: RESIDENCES, COMMUNITY, AND STOOPS

I came into this world on July 15, 1953, in Canarsie, Brooklyn. We lived in an attached, brick, two-family rental, and then moved to Elderts Lane on the Brooklyn side of City Line, which was on the Brooklyn/Queens border. My memories of that house are of just one or two "snapshots," because we moved when I was 3 years old to the other side of that border, to 76th Street in Ozone Park, Queens. The house on Elderts Lane (see Photo 2.1) was on the same block as the church that I would later attend—St. Sylvester.

It is funny to call that dwelling a "house," since my wife, who comes from a suburb, thought I meant a "little blue cottage," not an attached home on a crowded block. I told her she would not find any little blue cottages around there. It turned out that this was the closest my family would come to owning a home. The house belonged to my maternal grandparents and we shared the two-family residence. That arrangement fell apart

© The Author(s) 2017
T.J. Gorman, *Growing up Working Class*,
DOI 10.1007/978-3-319-58898-8_2

Photo 2.1   Elderts Lane House—with the red stoop, City Line, Brooklyn

after a year because my grandparents could not, and would not, put up with my father's drinking. In fact, they told my mother to leave my father and she followed their advice—for a year. She was a strong and compassionate woman; leaving your husband took courage in that era when there were few work opportunities for women outside the home.

So, my family packed up and headed four blocks east over the Brooklyn border into Queens, to 97-23 76th Street, Ozone Park, NY. (My maternal grandparents moved nearby to 87th Street in Woodhaven, Queens.) That address is inscribed in my mind along with our phone number: VI(rginia) 8-2643. I lived there until I was 16 years old, and this is where most of the working-class life that I describe in this book took place and shaped me forever. My memories of that place (Photo 1.2) are filled with laughter, pain, sorrow, hope, and futility.

To begin to understand the neighborhood and my relationship to it, one has to understand the importance of the stoop. The stoop was *the* place where many of one's daily activities occurred: playing stoopball; reading the *Long Island Press* or the *Daily News*, mostly for the sports section, comics, and movies (many of the girls read "Dear Abby"); listening to the ballgame; arguing with friends about sports; or just watching the world go by. As we got older, the discussions turned toward music, concerts, girls, and, yes, drugs. It was shocking to move to the suburbs years later as a graduate student to find the stoops and streets virtually empty; it was July 4, 1984, and not a soul could be found on my street in Stony Brook, NY. At that point in time, I could only imagine what was happening on the streets of my old neighborhood that same day: the sound of firecrackers, the sight of children running up and down the street—and on their stoops—with sparklers, and the smell of all those fireworks that lasted into the next day. That date highlighted the carnival-like atmosphere that permeated the day-to-day events taking place on many blocks in the neighborhood. The legendary John Gotti held an annual mega-party each July 4 about a mile away, right in the middle of the streets of Ozone Park, until Mayor Giuliani shut it down in 1996.

Our apartment was a rental, and with renting comes restrictions, so the stoop did not belong to my family. I understood this, and began to understand something about social class and the hidden injuries of class—ownership defines privilege. For instance, when my ball hit the stoop and bounced up to strike the awning, making a terrible banging noise, my mother would tell me to stop, because the landlord might complain (and raise the rent). We also were not allowed to use the backyard or the basement, and pets were prohibited. Social class differences show up in many ways.

Each night on my block in good weather, a party atmosphere reigned: people standing and talking to each other across their "gates" (the area inside the fenced-off areas in front of the houses), kids playing in those gates and in front of homes, teenagers on other stoops flirting with each other, and a Mr. Softee ice-cream truck coming down the block with its tuneful delights lighting up the street, literally and figuratively. That tune is playing in my mind right now: "The creamiest soft ice cream comes from Mr. Softee...." I would stand in the middle of 76th Street throwing a ball (a Pensy Pinky or a Spalding) up in the air to see if I could get it to disappear above the street light and then catch it, maybe with one hand, at the last second. That kind of scene of kids and bustle after dark on a suburban street in a middle-class neighborhood is hard to imagine. If someone witnessed those activities on a block in a middle-class suburb, they would probably call the police.

Beyond the summer heat, the party-like atmosphere also came from the fact that there were many families crowded together in a small space and from the tendency of the working class not to worry how it looked to others. One upper-middle-class man once said to me, during an interview for my research for a different project, that he wished he could sit on his stoop in his well-to-do neighborhood and drink a beer. But, he said, "I can't" (it's just not done). You will not find men sitting on stoops drinking beer in their T-shirts in middle-class and upper-middle-class neighborhoods. It is difficult to find people out anywhere—except in their backyards—in those types of neighborhoods. This kind of hanging out was one way the working class coped with its limited material conditions. It is the middle class, as I have argued elsewhere (Gorman 1998a, b), who are more likely, overall, to conform to societal norms. The working class tend to think that middle-class people are "snooty," and may resist some middle-class ideologies. By being outside on a hot summer night, the working class can converse, cajole, and laugh together about what they lack. The grown-ups loved it too. My mom had quite a reputation for standing in the gate and talking with her neighbors about the kids, the local schools, and their husbands. Sometimes, on a terribly hot night, you would find whole families on their stoops, watching their TV! One time a family did that on 75th Street and allowed others to watch Tom Seaver almost throw a no-hitter for the Mets.

The night always appealed to me more than the day. When I say always, I really mean I learned that way of life. My wife is a day person; I am a night person. She also grew up in a working-class family, but in a suburb. The nights, of course, were cooler than the days. The second-floor apartments were very hot (and had no side windows in row houses) and almost nobody had air conditioning. It was a time for working-class people to get together after a long day's work. Why socialize in someone's crowded, hot apartment? And the night had the effect of cooling off the hot concrete, the hot stoop, and cloaking the entire neighborhood (and my family) in a shadow, hiding all its imperfections. The tendency has been noted in studies of working-class families for them to have different leisure activities, and not to socialize with—to host—other families in the neighborhood, as is found among middle-class families (Komarovsky 1962; Gans 1967; Rubin 1976; Halle 1984). That kind of socializing is very difficult in hot, cramped apartments, as opposed to more open, cooler, single-family homes. What these early studies missed, naturally, was the socializing that took place on the stoops and in the gates of working-class city blocks and communities. City Line, in many ways, was an "urban village": people knew each other, especially on the block, had shared values, walked almost everywhere, attended a common school and church (SSS), and, coincidently, were overwhelmingly Italian-American. Most adults had to leave the area each day to go to work in Manhattan, but many young people worked locally (see Gans 1962).

It was "cool" to be out at night, literally and figuratively. Even when I was young I could stay out later than my friends. A few of those friends would then use that fact to put down my family and me; they would laugh and say, "Doesn't she [my mom] ever go in her own house?" Even when we did go back in the apartment, I would stay up late, even later than my mom wanted. The local CBS station ran a series of movies almost till dawn: *The Late Show*, *The Late, Late Show*, and (I kid you not) *The Late, Late Show Part II*. The theme music for the show was the music from *Gone with the Wind*. (The first time I watched *Gone with the Wind* I wanted to know why they used the music from *The Late Show*.) To stay awake through the night (when school was not in session) I would sometimes put my head partially in the freezer section of the refrigerator to cool off—it gave me a strange sense of the good life. Again, I felt as if that time was my own: it was quiet and no one else was around. It also was a way to escape the frenzied atmosphere of the outside world.

NEIGHBORHOOD DENSITY AND APARTMENT LAYOUTS

It is important to understand the density of each block in the area to fully appreciate the environment. The block—between 101st and 97th Avenues (Map 1.2)—had approximately 25 two-family homes (some blocks had three-family homes) on each side of the street (see Photo 2.2).

That adds up to a total of about *100* families living on just *one block* of many! This is the same amount of space that might hold only five or so homes and families in many suburban communities (see the discussion on density in the Appendix to Chapter 1). I was not aware of just how crowded those streets were until I moved to a suburb in Stony Brook, Long Island, as a graduate student at the age of 31. When I would go back to visit the old neighborhood, I started to see for the first time the density of that part of Queens. It was shocking when compared to what I have now become used to in the suburbs. By the way, families at that time owned at least one car, and, lacking garages, parked their cars on the street. People from outside New York City sometimes think that everyone in the city takes mass transportation to get around. That may be true for many trying to get to work,

Photo 2.2 Author's block, 76th Street, Ozone Park—between 97th and 101st Avenues

but not in the "outer boroughs" of Brooklyn, Queens, the Bronx, and Staten Island. Yet, what did we know—we were kids. This fact that our memories of that time and place are memories from childhood will come up again in a later section, when it seems that some of my friends have forgotten that fact when discussing their current perceptions of the area. Most of those friends do not live there any longer. I have asked them if they would move back there now if it were just like it was then. From their large homes in suburban areas, some said "yes," while others said emphatically "*no*."

Research on the effects of urban density (Hunter 1974) suggests that there are differences in perceptions of and reactions to density among residents of a particular neighborhood. People tend to perceive their neighborhoods based on how happy they are with the rest of their life. That is, if someone is unhappy or unsatisfied with their life, high density will just magnify the problems (Freedman 1975; Grove and Hughes 1983). Other research reminds us that one cannot easily pull apart density effects and social structure (Gove and Hughes 1983). This reminds me of when I told my mentor at SUNY Stony Brook, Dr. Kenneth A. Feldman, that I wanted to isolate the variable responsible for why working-class kids get working-class jobs. He answered that the factors are everywhere: in the air, in the water, and all around.[1] Jacobs (1961) has noted that people can perceive city blocks differently based on a number of factors. My own feelings of claustrophobia growing up in Brooklyn and Queens must have been shaped by doing so in a "hard-living" family. Yet, to varying degrees, those are the kinds of conditions that a number of families experienced. Later, I will report on how other people who grew up on the same blocks now feel about their old neighborhood. There were, without a doubt, "settled-living" working-class families in the neighborhood: families with fewer financial worries and fewer problems associated with drugs, alcohol, and abusive relationships, who took vacations and now have many photos of those happy times. And indeed, row housing has never been associated with only the working class. In fact, early row housing designs in Baltimore included spacious quarters for middle- and upper-middle class families (Belfoure 2001).

Areas of high density also have their benefits, however, especially during the baby boom years. Playmates and friends were plentiful. There was never a problem getting enough people together for a game of stickball, football, or wiffle ball. Many years later, I asked some children on a nearby block in Ozone Park if they wanted me to be the official catcher for their wiffle ball game, because they looked a little short on players. I told them, "When I was a kid we used to have a wiffle ball league with 4–5 teams and 4–5 players on each team." One of the kids said to me, "We don't have enough kids around here to do that." I had forgotten my sociology for a moment. Age and sex segregation were everyday realities for us baby boomers in City Line/Ozone Park. Even so, for some reason that I am still trying to understand, a few of my friends were three years older than me. It was not necessary. Maybe I was trying to be seen as one of the older guys, but I paid for it dearly. Nevertheless, our friendship group consisted of myself, a group of about five kids a year or two younger than me, and my older friends. We called the younger ones the "little kids." Today many parents would probably intervene to try to rectify the disparity in the power and influence that the older group had over the younger kids. This would definitely happen in middle- and upper-middle-class communities. In my neighborhood at that time, parents, for the most part, stayed out of their children's affairs. The idea of overly involved, "helicopter parenting" would have been ridiculed. All in all, even friendship patterns were shaped by neighborhood density. There will be much more about friendship groups in later chapters.

Each two-family house included two apartments. The bottom floor was usually occupied by the landlord because it was cooler, and had easier access to the front door, basement, and backyard. I never played in our backyard and we had to ask permission to use the basement. The backyards were small (postage-stamp size, as one of my current in-laws from the suburbs likes to say), but could accommodate a small swimming pool, like the one the next-door neighbors had purchased. As previously noted, the top floor was hot and the apartment was not wired for air conditioning; nor could we afford it anyway. The small fan we kept in the window helped cool the apartment, but it was weak, and turned into another target for my "friends" during rank-out sessions—they called the fan a "pinwheel." Really, I should start putting the word "friends" in quotations for some of these guys. I will say more about this later, but I will give one example of the behavior of one of those "friends": He had the nerve to raise the temperature on the thermostat in our hallway to 90 degrees one day, setting off a flurry of complaints and arguments with the landlord that night.

As noted earlier, the apartment had railroad-car rooms. Railroad apartments offer absolutely no privacy. Someone could stand on one side of the apartment (my parents' bedroom) and look through my bedroom and the living room (which my parents called the "parlor") and into the dining room (which was just an extension of the living room). My brother and I slept in a room right next to my parents' bedroom, making for close quarters (see Map 1.3). The two bedrooms were really one room with a large opening between the two beds, and a small wall separating them. Maybe someone thought that the layout, and its lack of privacy, was a way for the working class to practice birth control.

Feeling so cramped in our living arrangements, in both the house and the neighborhood, I asked my father one day, "Where does the concrete end?" In thinking back, I now realize that was a profound question. My brother and I shared a bed in one bedroom, and my sister slept in a crib, and then was a very small bed in my parents' bedroom (just on the other side of a small wall). This living arrangement only added to my feeling of claustrophobia and my search for an end to the concrete. For the most part, I think it was more than the actual concrete that felt so oppressive, and I will talk about those factors as we go along: lack of role models, lack of privacy, lack of green space, lack of vacations, lack of cool air. Jane Jacobs (1961) and the "New Urbanists" who followed her understand this about cities: they can be what we make them. I am quite sure that the "hipsters" currently gentrifying different parts of Brooklyn, not too far from where I grew up, find their environments to be exciting, creative, and maybe even liberating. It is true that research has found that high urban density tends to intensify already positive or negative feelings toward a neighborhood (see Freedman 1975; Gove and Hughes 1983; Ekstam 2015). Therefore, my feelings of claustrophobia were influenced by more than just physical density.

It is noteworthy, though, that when a few of my old friends visit the old neighborhood they find the area to be drab and gray, with one person saying it was basically a "slum." And when some former residents see photos of the old neighborhood, they want to know when the photo was taken, as if they cannot remember it being so dull and crowded. A few have even said, "I don't remember the neighborhood looking like that." I always remember thinking that the area was kind of dreary looking, though. Indeed, it takes a strong commitment to get the picture right when trying to paint a portrait of a certain time and place. My training in sociology will help me get as close to an accurate picture as possible. Later in the book, I will explore the various opinions that others have about growing up in City Line and Ozone Park.

To have so little privacy for two teenage boys and a married couple must have added to the stress of daily life. Remember, you would have had to walk through my bedroom to get to my parents' bedroom. By the time we moved to another part of Ozone Park in 1969, I was 16 and my brother was 23; I am sure that we could have used our own individual rooms. One's social-sexual development could be compromised under such conditions. Our parents would not have had to tell us to keep our doors open if a member of the opposite sex would have visited. The idea of having one's own room was only a dream to us—but to tell you the truth, I cannot remember pining for it, since we had as much or as little as everyone around us had. Like many of the families in the neighborhood, we had plastic covers on the furniture in the living room for a while. To some people this is an indication of faulty design taste, but it is really an indication that the owners were finally able to afford something they were proud of and wanted to protect. A small kitchen lacking a dishwasher or a dryer, along with a very small bathroom (for five people), rounded out the rest of the apartment. This layout could be found in most of the apartments on the block, adding to the sameness of everyday life.

The physical layout had an impact on our homework. It was quite impossible to go to your room to do your homework, especially in the sense of being able to close the door to get a little privacy. I would do my homework at the kitchen table, at the dining-room table, or on the couch, which were all within a few feet of each other. The television playing and my father banging on the table with his fist demanding supper (after coming home from the bar) left little room for an environment conducive to academic achievement. The image of suburban, middle-class teenagers doing their homework on their beds in their own rooms (while maybe talking to their friends on the phone) was a fantasy for me. All of the sights (vomit and snot), sounds (music and/or television to help cover the other noises), and smells (booze, smoke, and supper cooking) intermingled in this tiny apartment (see Photos 2.3 and 2.4 for the kitchen and living room/dining room during a birthday party for me as a child).

Photo 2.3 Kitchen, 76th Street apartment—author's mom is behind him and his dad is behind his mom

Photo 2.4   Living room/dining room, 76th Street apartment

Those two rooms comprise the entire apartment—except for the two small bedrooms. I never smoked, but I must have inhaled enough King Size Chesterfields to be counted among the heavy smokers of the world. Later in life, an ear, nose, and throat specialist told me to stop smoking after looking in my mouth, and was astonished to hear that I had never smoked a day in my life.

Nevertheless, as you can see from some of the photos, we still managed to have some good times in that apartment, thanks to the strength and determination of my mother. She kept the house clean, cooked dinners, and washed the clothes, while still tending to my dad. Sometimes we had a

Swanson frozen dinner on a bad night, and, of course, my friends made fun of that, too. My dad was a great guy when he was sober, a man with a good heart and one of the hardest workers I ever knew—until alcohol turned him into a different person. The extended family Christmas party was held in our apartment until my maternal grandparents died and we moved on.

I liked to stay up late to watch movies, but I also enjoyed the local independent stations, especially Channel 11 (WPIX) for baby boomer favorites *The Three Stooges, Superman,* and *Popeye.* Staying in the house and playing by myself never bothered me, especially since I had those nasty older friends. I had a vivid imagination: I played made-up games of horseracing using dice, wrestling matches with dinosaurs, and baseball games using a pencil for the bat and a rolled-up piece of paper for the ball. *Home Run Derby* (an actual television show) was another game I loved to play in the house. Using an old tennis racket (I have no idea how we got it) and my sister's little broom, I would fashion a pair of socks or a piece of aluminum foil (hiding it because it was expensive) into a ball and hit it from my parents' bedroom into my room, and all the way through the apartment if I hit it just right—which was only possible with railroad-arranged rooms. All of this practice hitting a ball and bouncing it off the ceiling at various speeds only made me a better hitter in stickball, wiffle ball, and baseball.

Families without the means to travel rarely left the concrete habitat. My family did not go on vacations or venture much outside the city limits. We went to see my brother graduate from the Marines in Paris Island, South Carolina in 1966, and we went to Jones Beach once and Lake Ronkonkoma in nearby Long Island once, too. In addition to the money issue, my mother was always worried about my father's drinking problem. He drank on the train to South Carolina, and was shocked when he found out that the county we were visiting was "dry." My aunt, who had moved up the career ladder from secretary to office manager in a large corporation, tried her best to give us three kids what my parents could not provide. She took it upon herself to take us on a few vacations to Cape Cod, MA, Atlantic City, NJ, and upstate New York. We always knew she would get us the best gifts for Christmas as well. Yet, even without directly experiencing other environments that would later confirm my suspicion that everyone did not live the way we and others in my neighborhood did, my feelings of claustrophobia sprouted early in my life; I just did not know what to call them or how to express them or whom to confide in. The shows on television like *My Three Sons, Dennis the Menace, Leave It to Beaver,* and *Father Knows Best* portrayed a world and a lifestyle that were far beyond anything within my family's purview, or that of almost any family from the neighborhood. Single-family, detached homes with plenty of space and a bedroom for each child, big backyards, professional fathers, and mothers who cleaned the house in a party dress and pearls and reasoned with their children were out of reach. The farm life on *Lassie* seemed to be even farther away.

You would think I would have run out of the house every chance I had, given some of what I have just portrayed, but I didn't. My mother always said I handled my father's drinking the best among the three kids. Still, it was no picnic. It was my family and I remember clearly wondering where the concrete ended—where the smoke, noise, smells, crowded living arrangements, friends' ridicule, and stress finished—and where Lassie's farm began.

THE "AVENUE": ITS EFFECTS
ON A WORKING-CLASS COMMUNITY

As mentioned previously, Liberty Avenue runs through Queens into Brooklyn. The stretch of Liberty Avenue that meanders into Brooklyn is called City Line. This row of mom and pop storefronts was incorporated into New York City in 1898. The stores on the avenue allowed residents of the neighborhood to shop for anything and everything. There were very few large grocery stores at the time, save for a medium-sized Safeway on our corner that gave away Green Stamps to its customers to redeem household items. My mother licked the backs of countless blocks of green stamps, filling many books in the hope of getting a new toaster or coffee pot. (There were times after we moved from 76th Street that we experienced short bouts of poverty—because my dad was out of work—and I and other family members were forced to sell personal property to get by: vinyl records, a stamp collection, used textbooks, and old jewelry.)

All of the stores along Liberty Avenue were lined up one after another: dry cleaner, pizza store, candy shop, clothes store, shoe store, real estate offices, and, of course, a number of bar and grills. The most popular stores at that time were a Woolworths, a bar/restaurant called Nathans, a deli called Kucks, a clothes store called Johns Bargain Store, and a movie theatre called The Earle. I especially liked the barber shop, because the owner saved half-priced coupons for the Earle Theatre for me. What made the avenue a perfect place for all of us kids—and adults—was its proximity to where we lived. While not exactly what the New Urbanists might have drawn on their boards, it was a place made for walking. We walked to school; we walked to the store; we walked to the movie theatre; we walked to our friends' houses;

and we walked around the corner to get the newspaper and cigarettes for dad, and a new Spalding ball. And with most families having just one car— for financial and density reasons—the mothers (who were mostly home-makers in those days, though a surprising number did go to work; see the demographic tables at the end of Chap. 1) would walk up and down Liberty Avenue with a push cart in hand for *that day's* shopping. The push cart could not hold more than a day's groceries. All of this walking is one of the reasons that living in the city is seen as a healthy lifestyle today. Nevertheless, it meant that us kids could also get to any store necessary to satisfy our sweet teeth, at any time: a late-night bottle of soda or a slice of pizza was always just a block or two away. When my mom, later in life, had to move to an area of Ozone Park not within reach of an avenue for shopping, she complained about how quiet and boring she found the neighborhood—a feeling that would seem strange to many middle-class suburbanites who might seek such a setting.

As we got older, we walked to get mass transportation—subway and buses—to get to school. At just 13 and 14 years of age, we took the sub-ways and buses by ourselves. This means of getting to school would surely shock many middle-class suburbanites, but we just took it as "normal." The "El" that carried the A-Train (the subject of the famous song "Take the A Train," Strayhorn, 1939) from southern Queens through Brooklyn and into Manhattan was just two blocks away, with the sounds of rum-bling and screeching subway cars always reminding us of their pres-ence (along with the low-flying planes from nearby JFK International Airport). Some families living directly under the El enjoyed convenience while enduring the noise. It added one more ingredient to the mix of sights, sounds, and concrete of our little "urban village" (see Photo 1.1).

On the way to the stores, one would bump into friends (and enemies) on the "Avenue" (see Crockett 2015 for a relevant amusing story). These interactions helped refine our interpersonal abilities and how to/how not to deal with bullies. These encounters were lessons in socialization. Even though it was not a crime-infested area, growing up in City Line gave us all a thick skin; and working-class individuals need a thick skin to survive. Yet, the Avenue also added to the feeling of a never-ending sea of con-crete. There was block after block of store after store. Where could people go to find some space—at least some space between the houses and the stores where they do their daily shopping? See how proud I look to have a *little* space between our house and the neighbor's after we moved to another part of Ozone Park (Photo 1.4).

Another element that helped define the neighborhood was the (over-representative) number of bars (or gin mills, as my dad called them). Up and down the main avenues of the neighborhood were the favorite watering holes: Nathans, Buldocks, Mr. G's, 77 Street Club, Colonial House, Neir's, The Main Bar, Ralphies, and countless more. This points to another distinction between middle-class and working-class communities: having a "cocktail" or two for the working class is a much more public pastime. Indeed, there were no private cocktail parties or two-martini business lunches in the lives of most residents of City Line and Ozone Park. In fact, I imagine some of my friends would laugh at the very mention of words such as "cocktails" and "two-martini lunches" to describe the type of drinking environments in which alcohol was consumed in the old neighborhood. To the men and women who frequented drinking establishments in working-class communities, the norm was to show up at the local bar (if you had not been barred from it for past indiscretions), meet your friends, and stand or sit on a stool in front of the bartender, who would keep filling your glass and continue taking the money you had originally placed on the counter. Then, at the end of a (long) night, you would leave a nice tip for the bartender (who might then buy one for you "on the house"). Inevitably, someone would have too much to drink and for reasons one can only imagine—sports, girl- or boyfriends, politics—throw a punch at someone else who had had too much to drink, and the fights would begin (usually finishing somewhere outside the bar). There were many bars because there was lots of business. As you might guess, my dad was barred from a number of the establishments dotting the avenues. He would come home every so often with a black eye, but he was always adamant about the ill fate of the other fellow.

One particular drinking and "dining" establishment remains an icon for those who can remember such places: Nathans. Don't be misled, this "Nathans" had nothing to do with the Nathans franchise that is famous for its hotdogs, which started in Coney Island, Brooklyn. This Nathans originally had one side for those wishing to drink, and another side for those wishing to fill their stomachs with such delicacies such as (greasy) cheeseburgers on club rolls, hotdogs, knishes, French fries, and pastrami sandwiches. (I still miss those cheeseburgers on club, even though you had to soak up the grease with a napkin.) Nathans was a central watering hole for the working-class men and women of the neighborhood. It was one of the stores long remembered by former residents of City Line, along with Kucks Delicatessen, Mom's Candy Store, Jerry's Record Shop,

Woolworth's 5 and 10 Cents Store, Aldo's Pizza, Angelo's Candy Store, Max's Candy Store, Castelli's Bakery, Serivolli's Bakery, and the Earl Theatre. The bars were the places where the hard-working men and women of City Line tried to find some entertainment and leisure, and to forget about their everyday problems.

One other bar in the local area—Andy's Topless Bar—was a place where a number of young men (including me) got their first look at the anatomy of the opposite sex. One night, a good friend and I (at the age of about 15 or 16), each claiming later to have had six beers (when all we had really had was one six-pack), pushed open the doors and walked to the back of the bar, pretending we weren't interested in the women dancing on the stage, then turned around and walked out. That was a good move on our part, because I am sure we would have been thrown out by one of the bouncers. Tutti's was another local tavern with a particular story. It was known for its décor, especially all the different artifacts that were hanging from the ceiling. Anything you could possibly think of—including the kitchen sink—was probably hanging from Tutti's ceiling (there was also, supposedly, a microphone in the women's bathroom). Neir's had its own old-fashioned bowling alley, and Nathans had its famous shuffleboard bowling game. There were many good times to be had in these and the other bars in the neighborhood, and they were the places we could be found after hanging out on street corners and stoops became passé (keep in mind that the drinking age at that time in New York State was 18). What I find most telling is that while we were hanging out in these places at ages 17 and 18, we were not studying for the SAT (SAT scores and social class background are highly correlated).

Some of the neighborhood's other claims to fame include the filming of many of the scenes from *Goodfellas* in Neir's (one of the oldest bars in the city), and when Jack Kerouak sat in a local tavern planning to go on the road. Bernadette Peters and Cyndi Lauper, two women from the world of entertainment, are from the general area, and their connection to the neighborhood is a point of pride for many residents.

GANGS

Gang activity was present in our neighborhood, in both City Line and Ozone Park. Gangs can give the powerless a feeling of power. My group of friends was located in a demilitarized zone between two well-known gangs: Ozone Park (OZ) in Queens and Fountain and Pitkin (F&P) in Brooklyn, respectively. A few recent books speak to the issue of gang violence in Brooklyn and Queens, especially on the tough streets of East New York, Brooklyn (Trigoboff 2013; Quarantello 2013). The impact of organized gang activity will be discussed later in the book.

A few of the teenagers on my block and one or two surrounding blocks belonged to OZ and F&P. Therefore, we were geographically and socio-logically situated in a gap of turf between two gangs. For the most part the gangs left us alone—we were, to some degree, seen as athletes. It did help, however, to have a friend or two in the gangs. For instance, one night I was on my way around the block to get the newspaper and a pack of ciga-rettes for my dad. A voice I recognized as belonging to an OZ gang mem-ber said to me, "Hey, where are you going?" I thought, "Oh crap." Was he "calling me out," challenging me to a fight? To my surprise, a voice from another OZ member said, "Leave him alone, he's my friend." The gang member who came to my defense was a young guy I had befriended one night in the slot-car racing store next to Angelo's Candy Store: when he ran out of money, I had let him use my control to play with my car. Thus, I was free to live another day.

My group of friends mostly stayed away from illegal activities. We did get into the drug scene heavily in the late 1960s and early 1970s, but we continued to play sports and do well enough in school (I usually drank beer and smoked some pot). In fact, I feel very strongly that our participa-tion in sports is one of the main factors that saved many of us from the vagaries of the city streets (more on sports later). The "bad guys," as the Beach Boys song says, "left us alone." I think they saw us as non-threatening and our activities as superfluous. Illegal gang activity in the immediate area was minimal, except for a reported murder in a local public schoolyard. Others have told me that there was much more illegal gang activity a little further into Brooklyn from City Line.

The importance that "turf" played in the neighborhood should not be downplayed; it was a fact of life that made sense given the congested nature of the environment. The little space between my residence and the one next door provided me with the feeling of my own little piece of turf—I played in that space many times (see Photo 1.2). There was a strong feeling that one's patch of brick and concrete was one's own piece of property, even if it was a rental. To ensure one's turf rights, a practice developed whereby residents would try to save the parking spaces for their car in front of their homes by placing garbage cans in the parking spot they vacated. You would pull out of the space just a little bit, get out of your car, put your garbage can in that space, then get back in your car and drive away. You can imagine how that practice sat with my father coming home from his night shift in the milk factory (with a few alcoholic refreshments embellishing his perspective). He rebelled against this cultural norm, born of crowded conditions, by backing right over the (at that time) metal can, and then throwing the crushed can back into that person's yard. I must admit, I loved it. Still, culture clashes could occur. One day a friend of mine (not from the neighborhood) drove down my block in Ozone Park and, not aware of the "garbage can" norm, got out of her car and proceeded to move a can to free up a space. When she got back into the car, I warned her that her actions were probably going to start a fight with the neighbor. She said, "That's ridiculous." I replied, "OK, you'll see." Even before she had finished parallel parking her car into the spot, the neighbor was out on his stoop yelling at us with a bat in his hand. Only my newly developed diplomatic manner prevented a physical altercation that would have probably seen me on the losing side—he was a big guy.

The area is also famous for being one of the locales for the legendary John Gotti and other organized crime members, especially farther into Ozone Park (where many houses proudly display a statue of the Blessed Virgin Mary in their small front gardens). When my mom came home one day from grocery shopping with her little pushcart (along 101st Avenue and Woodhaven Boulevard), she was shaking and said, "John Gotti looked right at me on the Avenue." "Ma," I said, "I don't think John Gotti is out to get you and your little cart of groceries." There were rumors that a few members of Gotti's gang lived in City Line, but no one really wanted to know. Moreover, there were rumors that one person from the neighborhood who had wronged Gotti had suddenly disappeared, adding to the atmosphere of most people not wanting to know anything. There is some debate among past residents as to whether having John Gotti and his friends hanging out in the area was a good thing or not (see Tobias 2014).

The neighborhood and its two local police precincts also became known for racial tensions and police crime. On one occasion that made the headlines, some officers from the 106th Precinct became involved in the "stun gun incident," where black youths were tortured with a hand-held stun gun after arrests for selling marijuana. In addition, the vast corruption (selling drugs and protection) uncovered at 75th Precinct was recently documented in the movie *The Seven-Five* (the 75th Precinct was known as the most dangerous in the city and possibly the country). In the 1980s in Howard Beach, about a half-mile further down Crossbay Boulevard from Ozone Park, a group of young white males chased a group of young black males out of a pizza store. One of the young black men trying to escape the attackers was struck by a car and killed. Some of the area residents wondered why blacks were in *their* neighborhood.

Some of the most contentious rivalries were between neighboring blocks, however. My block, 76th Street (between 97th and 101st Avenues), would play 75th Street—between the same avenues—in many sporting events, snowball fights, and water-balloon battles. As you can see from Map 1.2, I am talking about just one section of 76th Street. In fact, there was a rivalry between our block and 76th Street between 95th Avenue and Atlantic Avenue. This might be difficult for anyone who has not lived in such an environment to appreciate. For example, my wife (who is from an upstate New York suburb) once said to me: "What kind of a name is 76th Street for a block?" For her it was a non-descript address. That totally misses the social fact that, for those who lived on that block in that environment, "76th Street" was very important for their identity. For my wife, a family should live on "Maple Lane" or some such "homey" address. When one of my very first friends moved from 76th Street to 75th Street (literally around the corner), it was as if he had moved to another country.

The Neighborhood and Race/Ethnicity

Along with a tight community came anxiety about outsiders and newcomers. The families on my block and in the immediate area were mostly second- and third-generation immigrants from Italy, Ireland, and Germany. The residents were all white and almost all Catholic back then. The racial and ethnic make-up today is very different: African-American, Latino, and South Asian (see the demographic tables in Chap. 1 for a complete breakdown). The neighborhood has transformed into a diverse community. I can remember when the first (possibly) non-white resident enrolled in SSS, and the anxious whispering that followed. Going farther into Brooklyn (East New York) would bring us into contact with more non-whites, and the local community mostly stayed put.

When I was growing up, it was common to hear some people in my neighborhood talk about "niggers and spicks" with an ease that might make you think they were talking about the weather. Even when "choosing sides" for any kind of children's game, you might hear a distorted rhyme: "Eaney Meaney Miney Moe, Catch a 'Nigger' by the Toe, and If He Hollers Let Him Go, Eaney Meaney Miney Moe." The word used should be "tiger" and not "nigger," but this kind of thinking was ingrained in our heads. So oblivious was I to the racist ideology (and other ideologies) we were exposed to that one day in freshman year of high school, when a friend joked to another classmate "suck cock," I riffed, "a big black one." I was trying to play along and be cool, but felt only embarrassment. My shame was met with just a stare from one of the few African-American students, a guy I would later befriend. Some people took pride in their bigotry. One friend from our group was said to have ridden the subways so he could pick fist fights with black kids. Family members, friends, and neighbors pounded the usual racial and ethnic stereotypes into us. Actually, it was common knowledge that many residents liked having the mafia in the area because they "kept out the criminal element" (coded language for African-Americans). Even today, I have heard a number of people from the old neighborhood repeat hateful words about others.

It was quite a shock, but necessary for our social development, to experience other races, ethnic groups, and religions in high school. We did not experience many members of other religious groups either. Only a few non-Catholics lived in the neighborhood, and I had just one non-Catholic friend. When we were in SSS, we saw filmstrips about other religious groups such as Protestants (the term always said in a whisper, as if they were lost souls).

All of these attitudes about "others" distorted our thinking about different groups and cultures, and led to misdirected anger for a large segment of the working-class population. When you combine these early learned attitudes about "others" with early hidden injuries of class that foster insecurities, plus "worlds of pain" (Rubin 1976) later on in life because of limited educational, occupational, and income opportunities, it can create people who are angry, bitter, and ready to lash out at those they think are responsible for their situation. This connection is very important for understanding the balance of this book.

What makes this study different from other ethnographies of New York (such as *Canarsie* by Jonathan Rieder, 1985) is that the neighborhood was heavily Italian-American, supplemented by German and Irish-Americans. There were few Jews (though there was a synagogue on 75th Street), few non-Catholics, and almost no people of color. Other ethnographies, such as Pritchett's (2002) historical study of Brownsville, just a little down the road from City Line, have pointed out that by the mid-1960s, almost all white residents had left—this was not the case in City Line. Tales of what had happened in neighborhoods such as Brownsville were used by the locals of the area in which I lived as evidence of what would happen to our neighborhood if black people "moved in."

Even with some Irish and German families in the area, the neighborhood took on a distinctly Italian flavor. Italian delicatessens, restaurants, and pizzerias dotted the landscape. A few older Italian women who had lost their husbands could be seen walking the streets dressed in black mourning clothes—an Italian tradition. The food you could purchase in the neighborhood was delicious, whether you visited Aldo's or Flora's for pizza, or even a cheeseburger on club and French fries at Nathans. One of the delights in visiting a friend's house was you knew that his or her mother probably had something good cooking on the stove. In my own family, my father was 100% Irish and my mom was half Irish, but the half Italian side of her dominated the smells of our kitchen. My mom would put a "pot of sauce" on the stove on Sundays, maybe topped off with fresh ravioli from Severolli's bakery around the corner, and her meatballs were delectable. (Unfortunately, each member of the family would quite often eat at different times, due to the "distractions" my father provided.) When I went to graduate school, I mentioned in class that my mom used to make a great dish of pasta and peas, whereupon another graduate student from an upper-middle-class neighborhood said "Yuck." When I mentioned this incident to someone versed in health and nutrition, she told me, "Your friend didn't understand because that's 'poor people's food.'"

Ethnic pride was palpable in the neighborhood. In a number of homes, Italian was still spoken by grandparents and some parents (see the census tables in Chap. 1 for the number of foreign-born residents then and now). When I visited my wife's family in Western, NY—a suburban community—for the first time, I naturally asked them about their ethnic background. To my shock, one of my wife's brothers had to ask his father, because he did not know. In my neighborhood we all knew everyone's background and our own down to the fraction, and some used this information to hurt others during "rank-out" sessions.

THE FAMILIES: THE WORKING CLASS WORKING HARD

It was not unusual at that time for a family to have three, four, or more children. In the overwhelming majority of families in City Line/Ozone Park, the husband went to work while the wife stayed home and did just about everything else that needed to be done. Feminism had not (fully) visited our neighborhood, yet. One woman, whose husband died meaning she *had to* go to work, would elicit whispers of sympathy from other women talking to each other in their gates.

The fathers worked in many different blue-collar/working-class occupations, such as tool and die/metal worker, factory help, foreman, longshoreman, taxi driver, postal worker, transit worker, or doorman. My father worked for Bordens (milk and dairy products) for 25 years and worked his way up to foreman in one of the local plants. Previously, he had worked in the shipyards. My maternal grandfather also worked for Bordens and had helped my dad acquire his job. My grandfather worked in the factory on Atlantic Avenue in Woodhaven, and my father worked at the plant in Long Island City, Queens. These types of occupations gave blue-collar workers, with only a high school degree or less, a fairly comfortable living and a chance at joining the middle class. Some made it, some did not, but a number of their children experienced upward social mobility and reached the middle class by going to college (usually a city college). My maternal grandfather, with only a sixth-grade education according to census information, worked his way up at Bordens from laborer to foreman to lower-level manager, and gave my mother a taste of middle-class life, at least as far as he could with his income. The men worked hard (as their wives did at home), usually with their hands and backs. Before he worked for Bordens, my father had worked for Bethlehem Steel, delivered coal and ice, and had driven a lumber truck on various shifts, day and night; his father and grandfather also drove coal trucks. After Bordens my father drove a cab for over 25 years, right up till the day he died at 79 years old. That was a tough way to make a living.

I always have to laugh to myself when I hear my middle- to upper-middle-class relatives say they are "broke." What they mean is that they are "tight" for money that month. When my mom used to say we were "broke" we really were broke—no stocks, no bonds, no insurance, no checking account, and very little in the savings account. I used to make sure I brought home a few White Castle Burgers if I had the chance—and the money—to pick them up after hanging out with the guys, because I knew some people at home may not have had supper that night.

My father would have been happy to see me find a job like those he had, but the economy was changing from a manufacturing base to a service-oriented, white-collar workplace. Those kinds of jobs allowed the children of the working class to change from a blue-collar to a white-collar uniform, but did not guarantee any more income, prestige, or power. Cyndi Lauper has said that she used to watch the men coming and going to work in those factories in Ozone Park (Gustafson 2014), and that it was a picture of the struggle of laborers trying to make it better for the next generation. A few former residents, on reading her comments, said they did not understand what she meant.

While the neighborhood was distinctly working class, there was a range in income. A few of my friends had parents who owned a local store and had more money than my family. The working-class families in City Line could be categorized along a continuum of hard living to settled living— from dysfunctional, poor families to other families on the cusp of being middle class (or at least lower middle class). Although some families had a little more money than others, most families embraced working-class cultural capital (the attitudes and dispositions that social class position offers; see Bourdieu and Passerson 1977). One family may have had a slightly better car or living room or bedroom set, but almost all the men on the block (and in the neighborhood) were part of the larger proletariat. These were the men and women who went through the Great Depression and fought in World War II.

Also, some of my friends' parents were homeowners, making them (settled living) working class with just a little more money than other working-class families in the area. Keep in mind that it took a lot less money to purchase a house in those days, about half of what it requires today (as a percentage of family income). A longshoreman, mailperson, transit worker, or tool and die craftsman could own a home on just a single salary. That income differential among families would come up during our "rank-out" sessions (more on that later).

Ethnic and racial pride sometimes substitutes for class consciousness (Kimmel 2013). Back then in City Line, if someone was white and/or Italian-American, that person was considered middle class, but anyone of color, no matter what occupation they held, would be seen as lower on the socio-economic scale—except of course for entertainers, sports figures, and politicians. Only fame could overcome such marginalization.

THE LATER YEARS AND ALCOHOLISM

My family felt the effects of the larger changes in the economy when Bordens moved its plants out of New York City in the late 1960s. The company offered my father a position in Watertown, NY, but he turned it down when he found out that due to the 200 inches of snow a year, he would need a flag on his car antenna to find it. My family would have been more at home on Mars than there. (I now live in upstate New York.) Sometimes I wonder what my life would have been like if we had moved to Watertown when I was 16 years old. Like many New York City natives, I do not drive a car and never got a license. That would not have been possible in Watertown, NY. By the way, I sincerely believe my lack of confidence early on contributed to my never having learned to drive, but I would have had to contend with that in Watertown.

Driving became my father's next career after working at Bordens. After a few short stints in jobs such as driving a diaper service truck, he spent the next 25 years driving a taxi in Queens. Interestingly, his father also drove for a living—a coal truck—as did his grandfather. He was smart not to drink while driving his taxi, but as he got older it became more and more difficult to drive a taxi, spend the night at the bar, and then get up the next day to go to work. Alcoholism (and later in the 1960s, drug abuse) was a problem for a number of families in the neighborhood. Alcoholism cuts across social classes, but again, working-class families do not have the connections, resources, and educational background necessary to get help for an alcoholic relative or other family members. For example, not only is therapy expensive, it is also difficult to take time off work. In addition, the machismo that my dad (and many other men in the area) subscribed to prevents some from declaring that they need help for an addiction (or to have the kind of connections and information necessary to treat addictions). My father's common refrain (especially when drunk) was "Fuck 'em, save six for pallbearers" (a refrain from World War II). He would shout this from the top of his lungs while at the same time banging the table with his big fists. The sound of the table vibrating and the dishes hitting the floor would send electric-like shocks through my body. Keep in mind, I was just a few feet away in the living room. Did Robert Young do that on television in *Father Knows Best*; or crassly say he was going to "shit, shower, and shave" before going to work?

When my father was sober, he used to joke about the other alcoholics in the neighborhood. Even my mother had to laugh at those remarks, but then she would scream back at him, "And what are you?" His pat answer was, "I'm Jim Gorman and I'm a fucking Irishman." There was a lot of cursing in my apartment, back and forth between my parents. Most of those curse words would make you blush: "Mother-fucker," "cock sucker," and "cunt" were tossed around like a red rubber ball. My father would be cursing most often (usually calling others those curse words when drunk), but my mother would verbally retaliate with something such as "And what good are the Irish if they are going to get soused all the time?" Whereupon he would say something on the order of "Well, at least I am not a fucking guinea [an ethnic slur for someone of Italian descent], the only good guinea is a dead guinea." Any racial/ethnic group could be the target of his attack. It is strong language for modern ears, but common in my household.

It is remarkable that my father, who used to frequent many of the bars in our Italian-American neighborhood, was not in more fights than he was. He used to tell stories of belonging to Irish gangs that fought Italian gangs when he was a teenager in Brooklyn (see Moses 2015 for a recent exploration of the love–hate relationship between the Irish and Italians of New York City). My parents told us the story that my paternal grandfather would not allow my mother in his house because she was half Italian (and half Irish). Earlier family lore tells the story that my great-great-grandparents dropped the "O" from the family name O'Gorman because the nineteenth century was not a good time to be Irish in New York, since the Irish were ostracized by other groups. Indeed, I have tried to relay that story to my students, and some of my friends from the old neighborhood who have made derogatory remarks about certain racial/ethnic groups that today are the target of the same kinds of comments. The targets may change, but the language remains coarse and offensive.

Meanwhile, I would be trying to do homework while all of this fighting was going on a few feet away—the banging, sneezing, farting, vomiting, arguing, and smoking. The yelling would go on for a while until my mother could get my father to bed, and we all could breathe a sigh of relief—for that night. Before going to bed he would have a sneezing and coughing fit (20–25 sneezes, at least). The liquid that came out of his nose and mouth would pool on the kitchen floor. When he finally agreed to go to bed, he would stagger into the bedroom, asking my mother, "Marge, did I eat?" If he had not eaten at that point, my mother, exhausted, would then make him a dinner that he probably would not remember in the morning. When he woke up the next morning, he would go to work, and the cycle would start all over again. If, as in later years, he was not able to make it to work, he would say, "Hey Marge, give me $20" for another round of drinking. They would argue and my mother would yell at him for an hour or two, or until she finally gave him the money. Sometimes, he would leave without the money and say, "I'll just borrow it." Quite often, I would be thinking, "Just give him the money so we can have some peace and quiet for a while." The research that suggests a sense of lethargy sometimes overtakes low-income people (in dysfunctional familial situations) resonated with my experience. I felt it from time to time, and it is difficult to fight.

Each family's story of addiction is unique. My father never hit any of us (he was a loud alcoholic)—and when he was sober he was a different man. He was an addict. I usually felt bad for him, and, of course, for my mother. He (like many other men of his time, place, and social class) worked hard, and drank hard. For him, a six-pack of beer (or two) represented just the "chasers" for the whiskey—"a beer and a ball," in his terms. He and many of his peers were socialized into a type of masculinity in which one was tough, a hard worker, street smart, not able to show any signs of emotion, racist and sexist. This is the kind of world some working-class men and women long for today, and they are looking for a politician to help bring back those days. That is the kind of behavior my father saw in others in his family and neighborhood while growing up working class, and that is what he emulated. As mentioned earlier, alcoholism, and later drug abuse, were quite prevalent in our little part of New York City. Nevertheless, Jim Gorman could show what was underneath that tough exterior. On Sunday morning, he started the day smiling and would bring home the newspapers and bags of rolls and bakery goods, which he knew we all liked. He would also tell my mother to make sure I had some money in my pocket.

My father would have been very happy if I had stayed in the blue-collar printing industry; we would have talked about shop politics, unions, and "manly" topics. When I went back to (graduate) school he was perplexed, but he came around to being very proud of my accomplishments; before he died he bragged, "My son's a professor." If he had not been an alcoholic, our lives would have been somewhat different—especially financially—but we still would have been working class, just a more "settled-living working-class" existence (Howell 1973). I would have accepted that lifestyle happily; I saw a few examples of settled-living families on my block. My father would do anything to help someone he liked, but you did not want to get on his bad side. Drinking was, for many men of his time, place, and social class, a way of dealing with alienated labor (Thio and Taylor 2012)—albeit decently paid alienated labor (without a college degree), as compared to the kind of salary one would make today for his type of job and his level of education.

Some research suggests that the consumption of alcohol is shaped by social class. While many studies demonstrate that alcohol consumption rises along with income, heavy consumption of alcohol at any one time is more associated with working-class drinkers (Thio and Taylor 2012). These studies, however, miss the impact, especially financial, that drinking has on the working class. Drinking robs the working class of a greater percentage of their earned and potential income than those of greater means. On payday, my mother would wait about an hour or two after he arrived at the "gin mill." Then she would go around the corner to tell the bartender to stop serving him. She knew my father hated it when she showed up at the bar; it was not very manly to have your wife turn up and pull you out by the ear. He would visit a number of different bars to throw off her routine.

Middle-class drinkers have other resources in which to draw from to get help for them and their families. Besides financial resources, middle-class addicts have friends and contacts who are more in tune with the latest information on the causes, symptoms, and treatment for alcohol and drug abuse. When my father was in one of the local hospitals for liver and lung problems, the hospital staff sent in a priest to talk to him about his addictions. That was not the best way to reach a secular man like my father, and he threw the priest out of the room. He continued, with the help of some "friends," to smoke while hooked up to an oxygen machine. People chalked it up to the fact he was a "character," the classic example being the time he underwent a hernia surgery: when the wound opened up while he was in hospital, he walked into the nurse's station with his intestines in his hands and asked, "Is this supposed to be this way?" A former coworker laughed uncontrollably when I told him this story, as he had grown up in a similar family environment. My father's antics would force us to have a "good laugh" as a way of coping. We also had a "good laugh" when my dad stole a Siamese fighting fish in a small bowl from a pet store, after I had told him how expensive it was. And we would all squirm when my dad pulled out his teeth at the kitchen table with the other end of a piece of string tied to the kitchen door handle.

There were no 12-step programs for my father, no social workers, no expensive rehabilitation facilities, no big house to separate him from the rest of the family. This was a man who would be sick to his stomach every night. He once vomited up pasta shells into the kitchen sink, with the sauce, cheese, and meat intact. It was all stuck together in a clump—a gruesome block of red muck at the bottom of a white kitchen sink. That image still keeps me from eating pasta shells to this day; just thinking about it turns my stomach. Wetting and defecating in his pants at the kitchen table happened too, and my mother would just clean up after him. To paraphrase a recent book title, I don't know how she did it. Recently, an old friend told her parents that she had reconnected with Tom Gorman, and the first words out of my friend's mom's mouth were "That poor woman" (meaning my mom). Jim Gorman died, believe it or not, from smoking, not drinking. There was nothing left of his lungs. My brother used to like to say that my father broke all the Metropolitan Life mortality tables. To keep his sanity when my father was drunk, my brother would make believe he was in a prisoner-of-war camp. A very close relative did not attend my father's wake or funeral (which I think he now regrets).

One day, a colleague of mine in the Psychology Department (informally) diagnosed my lack of trust in institutions and bureacracies as a result of my father's drinking habit. But, I had told my colleague relevant stories: that on those rare occasions when we were going somewhere as a family, my father would leave the apartment to "go get the car," only to stop off at the bar and forget to come back to pick us up. That usually put an end to our anticipated outing. And another story I told my colleague was the time my father walked into our apartment and fell to the floor dead drunk in the middle of a gaggle of adolescents at my sister's "sweet 16" party. The holidays were always filled with these kinds of surprises; the pity is that my mother loved the Christmas season. Again, I can remember waking up one Thanksgiving morning to my father telling my mother he had "wrapped the car around a pole on Atlantic Avenue." There were so many times he wound up drunk at a special occasion and ruined it for us. At my first wedding, he passed out and had to be taken home early; for my second wedding, my mother told me that the rest of the family wanted him to stay home. My uncle walked her to her seat in the church. Even though I approved of that decision, it still haunts me to this day, and I wish I could apologize to him. With the utmost respect to my psychology colleagues, maybe my lack of trust was warranted—a rational reaction to untrustworthy people and situations like an alcoholic father, a few older "friends" who betrayed me time after time, and a failed first marriage.

Did my father's drinking shape my memories and experiences of growing up in City Line? Of course it did, but that is the point—that is part of the experience of growing up for a number of working-class kids. It might be a little different for others: maybe neglect, maybe abuse, or maybe drug use. A few of my old friends have described such family lives to me on social media. One of my old friends, who once described the neighborhood as a slum, recently called it a "cancer." I would not go that far, but there were good times and bad times. Let me say this before moving on to a new chapter: my father loved our family. He would do anything for us if he could.

Why didn't he stop drinking? That is the vile nature of alcoholism. The middle class have more of a stake in stopping their drinking—white-collar job, nice house, and social standing in the neighborhood. There is not as much for working-class drinkers to lose.

When my dad was in the Navy during World War II as a Seabee stationed in Rhode Island, he wrote to my mother almost every day. We used to tease my dad about the letters after we found a pile of them in a dresser drawer, but when I came across them again, it was an invitation to see him in a whole new light. Here is one of those letters in full:

1-10-43

Dearest Margie:

It sure is a blue day for me here. There is no mail for me and no sun out. All in all this a blue day. You are writing every day aren't you. They, meaning the mail clerks, are very slow about things here anyway. I suppose that is the cause of the delay.

Well, we went to church then ate breakfast and the noon chow was good but we had to stay in doors today on account of the rain. It gets very mushy here when it rains. You know the warm snow melts into the dirt making mud.

I must have read all the papers in this barrack all I did was read all day long. We will be able to get books later on then we will have something to do when we are not writing. I feel pretty good. I still have a little cold but it don't mean much. The doctor gave me some awful tasting liquid but it is good for a cold.

Right now we have Jack Benny on the Radio. I remember your brother used to listen to it so maybe you are in the parlor now sitting the favorited couch resting and waiting for me. Maybe you are looking at my pictures—I hope so because I am thinking about you baby. I always sit and dream about you and get a kick out of it. I often see you in that favorite pink woolen dress, the one with the hem or that stuff going all around the skirt. I used to love to see it on you with the pink pearls and your black shining hair against the pink dress. Oh, how I wish I could see you in that little dress now and the other dresses that I like. I like the new one your work the last night but I hope you fixed the neckline. It was a little too low.

Did my sister write or call or let you know about the date she wants you to come to her house? I hope so. Some new fellows moved into the next unit the other day. I pity them for the next 21 days. They will be sorry—what a beating some of them fellows are going to take. Most of the fellows can't take the cold weather so they get sick then the rest of the fellows have to do all the work for the rest of the platoon.

I didn't have any mail at all—most of the fellows realize that the mail condition is bad so they want more mail clerks but the men in charge told us that we would be out of the boot period and all our worries would be over. That is the toughest period of training. I hope so.

Give my regards to the family and everyone. And baby you take my love just for you and store it in your heart for a time till I take it out and hug you in my arms and never let you go. Baby at church I said a few prayers for you and to get our wish to be together. I told God that we were never meant to be separated. I hope he answers it.

Forever and ever Baby,

Jimmy

NOTES

1. I owe a lifetime of thanks to Professor Feldman for my social and intellectual development, but the analyses in this book are solely my responsibility.

CHAPTER 3

Education: The Hidden Injuries
of Class Begin in Earnest

Sennett and Cobb (1972) argue that members of the working class experience hidden injuries of class (frustration, anger, and bitterness) during their search for dignity in a capitalist society, because in such an economic system, working-class people are denied their fair share of self-worth: educational credentials and occupational prestige (badges of ability). I have argued (1998a, b) that understanding the effects of the hidden injuries of class can explain the attitudes of parents toward education as stemming from their class-specific experiences in their own family, at school, and at the workplace. The "lashing out" I described by white, working-class Americans can help explain what has recently been referred to as the rise of "angry white men." I found that working-class people have a tendency to respond to the assault on their dignity by lashing out at college-educated, white-collar workers (who have been referred to recently by some members of the working class as being part of the "elite"), but this ultimately leads to those in the working class reproducing their social class position for themselves and their children.

After all the dust settles, what we have left are working-class men and women with damaged selves and little confidence in their ability to help them navigate professional social worlds—such as challenging their children's teachers and other professionals and authorities, and "leaning in" at their workplaces. The "hidden injuries of class," as a concept, is now part of accepted wisdom in the social sciences, and has been utilized by sociologists ranging from Lillian Rubin's (1976), portrayal of the working-class family, to

© The Author(s) 2017
T.J. Gorman, *Growing up Working Class*,
DOI 10.1007/978-3-319-58898-8_3

journalists such as E. J. Dionne (2015), trying to explain the recent spike in drug abuse and suicide among white, working-class Americans.

Educational credentials constitute one of the main badges of ability awarded to the middle class. How did the hidden injuries of growing up working class come into play in my own educational career? We will see that the story is not one-dimensional—active agents helped this working-class kid (eventually) get a non-working-class job.

My career began as a textbook model of how "working-class kids get working-class jobs" (Willis 1981). Yet, a long, strange trip from a typical working-class educational track to a new world of graduate school, academic scholarly conferences, and papers turned me into a full-time, tenured Associate Professor of Sociology at Queens College in New York City. When I look back at my educational career through the eyes of a sociologist, I see that it diverged from the predictable path after my early 20s back in the 1960s and 1970s. Part of the answer to how this change took place also shows the complexity of our lives, challenging sociology to constantly struggle with the agency–structure continuum. Are we free agents able to make and remake the world, or are we just products of our society?

My father only had a tenth-grade education, whereas my mother finished high school; she did fairly well in school, but social norms at the time for women and her family's lack of cultural capital (Bourdieu 1977) worked against her attending college. No one else in her family had been to college, and she was not expected to change that trend. Instead, she had considered becoming a Catholic nun at a time when joining the clergy was viewed as a notable career move for "smart" working-class men and women. Many of us who attended Catholic grammar school at least thought about that option at one time or another. That career option was an "achievable" means of social mobility in working-class families.

My mother's religious upbringing was probably the reason she chose to send me to the neighborhood Catholic school: St. Sylvester (SSS). As for my father, he used to say that public school students just cut out and paste pictures all day (even though he and my brother went to public schools). I never found out his source for that statement. My sister, from whom my parents never expected much in the way of academic ability, also went to SSS for the first three years, but then transferred to public schools for the rest of her education when money got tight. My parents would also joke about my sister when she struggled in high school. In saying "she barely knew the alphabet" they weren't being mean spirited, but were rather upholding the lowered expectations for females at the time.

In a neighborhood where social status markers are few and far between, it was a feather in one's hat to be able to say that one's son or daughter attends a Catholic school (especially when tuition was instituted). In addition, this was a time in New York City's history when "white flight" was starting to take its toll on the city's resources (for public schools). The white parents who remained became suspicious of public schools and the non-white populations who attended.[1]

ELEMENTARY SCHOOL

Attending kindergarten was not a requirement (or even a social norm) in New York City in the 1950s when I was young. Most mothers stayed at home and took care of the kids. Therefore, my first contact with formal schooling came when I entered the first grade at SSS in Brooklyn (even though we lived two blocks into Queens). I can remember marching up the stairs to "The Stars and Stripes" for the first time; I would march up those same stairs to that song twice a day for the next eight years. We went home for lunch each day because the school lacked lunchroom facilities for all students. A few kids were crying on the first day: I was choked up, but kept a stiff upper lip. I was in a class labeled as 1-2. There were three classes for each grade: 1-1, 1-2, and 1-3. We found out soon enough that those classes were our academic rankings. For most of the next eight years I was a "2." There will be more on tracking later in the chapter.

Let me say this right from the start: I survived my first eight years of schooling by being a conformist (which turns out, I argue later, to be the best way for the working class to break out of the reproduction of social class relations). I learned early to stand in line quietly, fold my hands at my desk, and keep quiet. My biggest fear was that a teacher or nun might humiliate me in front of my friends by yelling at me or hitting me. The "lay" teachers could be as harsh as some of the nuns. Overall, I was very lucky with the crop of nuns and lay teachers I had at SSS over those eight years. My feelings about my time there are mixed; my classmates are also split. Some of my friends have very fond memories of those years. Others have memories that can only be described as nightmarish: nuns humiliating them, hitting them, and making their lives a living hell. It is important to remember that many of these friends with nightmarish memories went to "better" high schools than I did. Why is that important? Well, compared to the minimal academic challenges of my high school, SSS provided me with a solid academic background. Was I petrified of the nuns? Yes, every single moment I was in that school. Was it the best academic environment I could have had? Absolutely not. Still, I did learn the three Rs—reading, writing, and arithmetic.

My wife, who is 9 years my junior, attended Catholic schools for 16 years, and tells me that the "fire and brimstone" approach is no longer found there (probably with the continuing changes that Vatican II instituted in the early 1960s). Although she reports being humiliated in class by the nuns, she faced very little physical intimidation. It appears that fewer of my female friends experienced physical abuse and intimidation at SSS also, and among my old friends it is the girls who seem to have the more positive memories.

When I walk through my children's schools in the middle-class suburbs of upstate New York, I am struck by the laughter, openness, bright colors, and variety of dress of the students and teachers. That is definitely not what I experienced during the first eight years of my strictly regimented schooling. It made me a nervous wreck. From marching up the stairs in the morning in unison, each class led by a nun, to the desks that were bolted to the floor in rows—like a shop floor (Kohn 1969)—to the mandatory attendance at 9 o'clock Sunday Mass (not the 10 or 11 o'clock mass), our days were run in a very controlled way. A couple of my friends who attended public schools would sometimes wait outside on a day off to make fun of our rigid school culture.

It was an intimidating environment. I was regularly so scared that one day I urinated in my pants on a line in church rather than ask the nun if I could go to the bathroom. The nun saw what had happened, but turned away in a manner that I understood to mean she was not going to turn me in to the principal.[2] So some of the nuns were nice. And I did receive a solid, very basic, very old-school education. If it were not for SSS, I would not have ever made it to college.

When I think about my formal education, the following words come to mind: conformity (see Kohn 1969), worry, stress, and a lack of confidence. These feelings were exacerbated by the atmosphere of the Catholic grammar school. The best way for me to alleviate the stress I felt, and my worries about my parents' reactions if I received a bad report card, was to conform to the wishes of the nuns and lay faculty. There were a few students who rebelled against the intimidating behavior of many of the nuns by acting up in class, not doing homework, or even physically fighting back: I witnessed one classmate put one of my lay teachers in a headlock, and I heard about another fellow who punched a nun in the face. Of course, he was expelled that very day. Yet, not me: I sat in classes for eight years with my hands folded, like they showed us on the first day of school. Even with that, I got whacked with a large ruler (turned over for maximum effect) in the third grade for whispering to my neighbor behind me. After the lay teacher hit me, she knew she had hit me too hard and rubbed my hand (I was a skinny kid, with skinny little hands) while she continued talking to the class. I was beyond crying, I was in shock. The rest of the class let out a gasp. (She also told my mom I was a "Chatty Kathy"—one of the first dolls to talk—for whispering to my neighbor.) That incident plus a few minor sideburn-pulling events (mine were seen as too long) are the only times I felt the nuns' wrath, although others will tell you worse stories. To be fair, a number of my friends are going to be upset at my assessment of SSS. They would relate tales of pain and humiliation at the hands of the nuns. One or two of the friends I have reconnected with on social media have said they hope that certain nuns burn in hell.

When I tell my current college students about being hit by the teacher with a ruler, they ask if I sued the school. They are very surprised when I say that if I had told my mother I would also have been in trouble with my parents, because nuns and lay teachers were assumed to be in the right. It was a very different time. Furthermore, working-class parents have been shown as likely to leave school decisions to the teachers and administrators. Middle-class parents, however, have more of a tendency to challenge the decisions of teachers and administrators (Lareau 1989, 2003). Diagramming sentences, practicing cursive writing, and memorizing the multiplication tables were everyday experiences. The "back-to-basics" approach may or may not be the best way to learn, but it helped me overcome my mediocre high school education. It is incredible how many of us did learn under these conditions, but somehow we did. Now, would I recommend a return to those teaching practices? No! Yet, for some combination of reasons (they are difficult to pull apart), it worked for me (and for many others from the old neighborhood, so they tell me).

The classrooms at SSS were overflowing with students, approximately 60 students in each class. Imagine having that many kids in a classroom. The classes were so crowded that each classroom was equipped with an air filter. Today, middle-class parents in the suburbs are worried if the number of children in a class reaches 20. At my daughter's elementary and middle schools, there were approximately 17 in each class. Research has consistently suggested that class size is a key component of why some kids learn and others do not (for a review, see NCTE 2014). By the time I graduated

SSS in 1967, we still had over 50 students in my class, one of three classes to graduate that year. With that many kids continually together, we probably developed immunities to a number of illnesses. To be blunt, in a class of 60, the odds of someone vomiting or urinating on the floor (afraid to raise their hand) on any given day was quite high.

A mixture of religious beliefs and social class structures came to a head at the school. As in most Catholic schools of that era, everyone had to wear a school uniform—boys a white shirt, blue pants, tie, and black shoes; girls a plaid jumper, white blouse, blue tie, and, of course, black patent leather shoes. The uniform was available at one particular store on Liberty Avenue. It did have the beneficial effect of helping to level out any differences in the narrow range of income between the families in the parish (the church and school boundaries), and thus was aimed at avoiding any stigma—though I remember you could tell that some of the kids had more than one uniform, and had fancier jackets and coats.

There were separate entrances for boys and girls at SSS (and at many Catholic schools at that time). That separation of the sexes just worsened my awkwardness around girls and confused feelings about sex. There was one girl in particular on whom I had a major crush, but I thought those feelings were "sinful" (though all I ever thought about doing—being still fairly young—was holding her hand, or maybe, just maybe, putting my arm around her shoulders). One nun even lined the boys up at the back of the classroom because one of them had been seen on Atlantic Avenue with his arm around a girl; this was probably not good for our social-sexual development. The girls were also put under the microscope—with the boys waiting in the hall—when a lay teacher went around the room and smelled each girl because she thought she smelled "feminine odor." What makes these stories relevant is the fact that, as working-class kids, we did not have anyone who could help us understand the birds and the bees. These kinds of conversations are rare in working-class families, and we certainly did not get sex education in a Catholic school (see Miller et al. 1999; Kohn 1969; Lareau 1989; Rubin 1976). Reading about the condemned movies in the Catholic newspaper *The Tablet* made me want to see them even more.

The ease with which some of the boys could interact with girls escaped me. To say I was awkward around girls in elementary school would be an understatement (see Photo 5.2). Privacy was at a premium even if one did have a girlfriend. We were a little too young for cars, and the apartments were wide open for parental inspection. In fact, when I kissed my first girlfriend approximately 25 feet from a group of people out in front of their house, I could hear one person in that group say "That's not real love." It might or might not have been true, but it certainly did not help my confidence interacting with girls. Being nervous and lacking confidence were everyday feelings for me at SSS (and for the working class in general). Remember, I had a very nervous mother and an alcoholic father. I am trying to keep the important variables separate for discussion purposes, but in reality they all interact: social class, family, religion, school, friends, gender, sports, race, generational factors, neighborhood, and social-psychological variables such as self-confidence.

In the 1960s, even at rigid SSS, revolution began to bubble. Each week, as I said earlier, the entire student body was expected to be at 9 o'clock Mass. The nuns took attendance, and if you were not present you had some explaining to do on Monday morning. One of the first revolutionary acts I ever witnessed happened in Mass one Sunday. Someone played a transistor radio loudly, and the song reverberating from the boys' side of the church was "These Boots Were Made for Walkin'" by Nancy Sinatra. The nuns proceeded to run up and down the aisles to try to catch the culprit. They never found him; I am really surprised they did not pat us down after Mass. This was definitely an act of resistance. What I find interesting, looking back, is that while this event seemed so radical to me at the time (as did my friend punching a nun), the world outside was starting to be rocked by even more radical events. Did the sixties pass us by in City Line? Later in the book, I will address the generation in which we grew up: the micro world of City Line interacting with the macro events of the 1960s (civil rights, feminism, the Vietnam War, the Cold War, and the assassinations of King, Kennedy, and Malcolm X).

As mentioned earlier, there was an obvious system of "tracking" at SSS. From the first grade though the eighth grade, each student was assigned to one of three classes, either 1-1, 1-2, or 1-3. The 1s were thought to be the smartest kids, the 2s to be average students, and the 3s to be the troublemakers. It was assumed that we were assigned our track through standardized testing. It is not that we were taught different subjects, which is another form of tracking usually not found until high school level. In thinking back, however, it seems clear that academic achievement levels were different for each class, and it gave the school a way to keep the "troublemakers" from interfering with the "smart" kids. Much research has shown the problems with "tracking," and the difficulty in changing tracks once assigned a label (see Rosenbaum 1976;

Oakes 1982 for a good overview). It is definitely a label: I can remember thinking that I was a mediocre student: not so good, but not so bad. No one wanted to be a "3." Comedian George Carlin would joke that there were "4s" in his school—they got their school pictures taken front and side view. When it came time to go to high school, it seemed that many of the children from 8-1 went to Catholic—college prep—high schools (seen as among the better high schools in the city), along with a few of the kids from 8-2. Meanwhile, many of those from 8-2, mostly boys, went to public high schools, especially the vocationally oriented ones. It would make for an interesting study to plot the educational levels and careers of members of the three eighth-grade classes.

Sociological research (Rosenbaum 1976; Oakes 1982 and 2005 for an update) has shown that, once tracked, a student has a difficult time moving up a level. In fact, movement down the tracks is more likely than movement up. One year I did move: from 5-2 to 6-3. I never moved from a "2" to a "1." These labels stick to children and can become self-fulfilling prophesies, where the expectations of a student's abilities become a reality. Thinking back, I truly felt that the 1s *were* smarter than anyone else. Interestingly, there were probably a number of children labeled 2s who could probably have been 1s if there had been enough room in the class. Sometimes, tracking is a matter of just keeping the school running smoothly rather than serving students (Rosenbaum 1976). Could it be there were exactly 60 1s, 60 2s, and 60 3s for eight years? The statistical chances of that are small. One of the pernicious effects of tracking is that I never interacted with the 1s or the 3s. Even though some of the 2s attended college prep high schools, I was not among them.

My own horror stories from St. Sylvester School and Church are quite sad. I am not going to whitewash those memories. For example, I can remember wanting to die immediately after receiving my First Holy Communion, which would guarantee my passage into heaven. Can you think of a more horrible thought for a 7-year-old to have? Yet, the education I received, even with the negatives I have outlined, gave me habits and a focus that helped me, after a vocationally oriented high school, to do well in college and beyond. It might be that the nuns instilled in me a sense of guilt and shame—and fear—when I had not done well in school. Much of the work was rote learning, but we did master how to parse a sentence, and memorize multiplication tables, and learned geographic and historical information such as capital cities and important dates in history (I loved making product maps of countries, where I used little capsules

I purchased at Johns Pharmacy around the corner to hold the different signature products for each country). We even read quite a lot, much of it from our Baltimore Catechism, but we read, nonetheless: each of us, one by one, up and down the rows, taking turns reading passages aloud. We also read from the St. Joseph Sunday Missal, which was used for Sunday Catholic Mass, and that week's songs and gospel. And, of course, we read the SRA (Spirituality and Resilience Assessment) color-coded packets that were popular at that time in many schools. Students moved up in color as they progressed. It was not all rote learning at SSS, either: I can remember reading *The Bridges at Toko Ri* in the eighth grade, and having to act out the plot in front of the class with two of my good friends. One of them will always be Admiral Tarrant to me.

I was recognized as a "good student" by the seventh grade and was rewarded by being chosen as a safety guard, but I dropped out of being an altar boy—because I thought I couldn't handle learning Latin. I needed someone to tell me I was made of the right stuff. I did, however, "star" in two school plays in the first and second grades, with one nun in particular asking for me to be in the second-grade play after she deemed my performance the previous year to be excellent. That was a boost to my self-confidence.

St. Sylvester closed its doors in August 2011, consolidating with two other local Catholic grammar schools. When I visited SSS two weeks after it closed, I sat on the entry steps for the boys' side and tried to remember all the days I had walked up those stairs. It is true that my positive assessment of my years there came only after receiving a less challenging high school curriculum than many of my friends.

Did such a teaching environment leave a negative residue? For some people, it did, and they have told me this time and again. While some students did rebel, that could be seen as just a natural response to being mistreated in an attempt to impose conformity (Humphries 1981). Could 60 children in a classroom have learned the same material in another, less intimidating way? I don't know. There is an entire industry devoted to studying the differences between Catholic school and public school. Overall, the research suggests that there does not seem to be any difference in learning outcomes when you control for a number of variables (start with Coleman 1987; then see Elder 2013; Braun 2006). Some studies have suggested that Catholic schools do a better job (even controlling for other variables), while others claim that public schools educate children more effectively. The Catholic school environment may have been "hellish," but in my era the students still learned the three Rs.

It is important to put my early educational experiences into the larger social context. At that time, the outer boroughs of New York City were starting to experience the effects of white flight. Large numbers of white, Irish, Italians, Germans, and others were packing up their homes and apartments to move to Long Island and Staten Island (see the demographic tables in Chap. 1). This left the inner cities with a dwindling tax base to help fund public schools, and the Catholic schools with plummeting enrollment. Nevertheless, for many working class whites who remained in the city, Catholic schools seemed to be the only way left to guarantee their children a decent education.

In my first four years at SSS, the tuition was free. The church assumed that families were supporting both church and school with their Sunday offerings. Envelopes were mailed to each family every week in time for Mass (with the family's name pre-printed on the front of the envelope, laying on a little more guilt). Then at Mass, a basket was passed down all the rows and one either put in cash, a check, or coins (a comic strip once showed Dennis the Menace taking change from his donation—I never thought of that). Only in later years did SSS begin to charge. At first, the school required the children to sell chance books (with the chance of winning a prize of some sort), as a precursor to an actual tuition bill. My mother would buy the whole book instead of me having to go around the neighborhood selling them. The neighbors, most likely, had their own chance books. Indeed, my mom tried to put on the best face for our family; my father's drinking embarrassed her. She used to say endlessly, "Being poor sucks." In later years we had to bring five or ten dollars to school each month in a brown envelope. Now, the Catholic schools in the area face the problem that they are serving a mostly poor, non-white population that cannot afford the tuition.

And to be perfectly honest, when someone said that the public schools were not as good as they used to be, they most likely meant there were more and more blacks and Puerto Ricans flooding the schools (Puerto Rican stood for anyone with Hispanic/Latino ancestry or heritage). Racism ran deep in the neighborhood, and the language that many people used was probably not much different from what you might have heard in the past from some in the deep South or from Archie Bunker. Of course, not everyone was racist—racist language used to upset my mom, for instance. I can remember her coming home one day looking very flustered. She said that Mr. X had just told her he'd been elected block captain and his job was to keep "niggers" from buying houses in the area. My mom also once told me that a group of neighbors got together on our block in Ozone Park and told our landlord to take down a "FOR SALE" sign from the front of the house—it was understood that the real estate agents controlled the sale of homes in the area, and thus the racial composition of the block. (I apologize for some of the words I have used, but to leave them out would be to whitewash the hateful language I grew up hearing quite often in my old neighborhood. It is part of the data.)

Ironically, one of the first "dark-skinned" residents to move into City Line/Ozone Park was Asian-Indian. It seemed to confuse the people on the block and in the local area: should they like the new people or not? They were dark skinned, actually darker skinned than many African-Americans, but they weren't "black." While this event was not a precursor to the residents promoting cultural relativism or the social construction of race, it did make the people on that particular block (and in the local area) stop and think about their attitudes toward others (at least for a moment). So after all that social struggle, it is sad that public schools are as segregated today as they were then—but this time it's for economic reasons.[3] The Supreme Court decision on racial segregation in schools (Brown *v.* Board of Education, 1954) said nothing about economic segregation, or disparate funding and educational resources.

High School

When it came time to decide which high school each student wanted to attend after eighth grade—we didn't have a middle or junior high school— there were basically only three choices: going to one of the local public high schools (John Adams or Franklin K. Lane for our location), taking the "co-ops" for admission to a Catholic high school, or applying to one of the vocational, technical, or specialty high schools scattered around New York City.

Family history was my only guidance when I made this decision. My older brother and my three older friends had attended John Adams. My mother was not overly impressed with the Catholic Church, and was thus reluctant to keep me in parochial school (and she told me we could not afford Catholic high school). She used to tell us that a priest once said she should continue to have children even if it endangered her health; she said she told him to go to hell. She was a bit of a radical for her time and place. My parents were not equipped with the kind of information necessary to make an informed choice, because they lacked the cultural capital (Bourdieu 1977)—certain attitudes and dispositions that are class specific—that could have helped them decide which high school I should attend. I do not ever remember thinking about college until I was a senior in high school, and neither did my parents. Can you imagine such a lack of attention to higher education happening in a middle- to upper-middle-class family today? While college attendance was becoming more the norm in many middle-class families in the late 1960s and early 1970s, it was not for the working class.[4] I took the "co-ops," thinking they were necessary for all the high schools in New York City, although the exam scores were used to determine which Catholic high school one could attend. I was accepted at one Catholic high school and put on a waiting list at another, Bishop Laughlin. Some friends who were behind me on the waiting list eventually were accepted, but my mother had already told me we couldn't afford it.

One fateful day in the eighth grade, at our kitchen table, I asked my mom what I should do when I grew up. Before I tell you her answer to my question, let me make a few points to keep in mind. My dad was not involved in most decisions regarding our schooling—he only wanted to see the results on our report cards. He would also say, "I better not hear anything bad about you from my friends in the bar." I used to wonder who on earth in the bar would know me, but it kept me on my toes. (It is a little absurd, though, to think I would have been in trouble if one guy hanging out in a bar—and not home with his family—told another guy hanging out in the same bar—and not home with his family—something I should not have been involved in.) My mother persevered in the face of limited financial resources and an alcoholic husband, but she knew almost nothing about colleges and careers. There is no one person to blame for this reality. It is just some of the "pain" found in working-class families.[5]

There were few, if any, professional role models in the neighborhood. My parents did not have any friends who were professionals, so the concept of inviting professionals over to the apartment for cocktails was absurd. It would have not done any good either if there had been a "take my child to work" movement back then, not for the kids in the working-class families on the block who wanted to move up the social class ladder.

A little reflection would have revealed that my interests revolved around the sciences. I had plastic dinosaurs, a tropical fish tank, a chemistry set, a microscope, a spaceship called Astro Base, and a telescope (see Photo 3.1). My aunt, who had experienced some upward social mobility in her job as an office manager for a large real estate developer, bought me these items. In addition, most of the movies I watched were about science and science fiction, and I loved television shows such as *Lost in Space*, *The Time Tunnel*, *Voyage to the Bottom of the Sea*, *Star Trek*, and *The Twilight Zone*. Yet,

Photo 3.1 New microscope, Christmas gift—and the author continues his love of science and looks on while a relative tests a new telescope

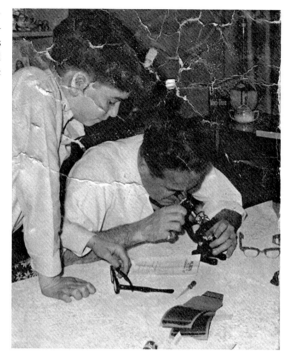

when it came time to answer my question about career choices, my mom answered, "Why not be a printer like your uncle?" "What does a printer do?" I asked, imagining someone sitting at a desk printing letters all day. She followed with, "They work the machines that make the books, magazines, and newspapers." Wow, I thought, I have a career path. To my mom (and eventually, my dad) this was a solid working(-class) occupation to which to aspire (which also had a strong union at that time and place).

Printing in New York City was then one of the largest manufacturing categories. Little did we know, however, that the printing industry had already peaked, and was just starting to go through technological transformations. This, combined with the movement of printing plants to the south and west (seeking fewer unionized environments), would leave the industry unrecognizable and put many people out of work. Still, in hindsight my mom's advice to me to enter the printing trades seems a rational choice at the time and set the stage for the next 20 years of my life. To her, any job that could give someone enough income, like my uncle had as a linotype operator, to support a family of seven, is a good one. On his one income, he and his wife were able to buy two homes: one in Brooklyn and an additional summer home in the Poconos. When I tell my students that such a lifestyle was possible for a blue-collar worker then, they look at me as if I'm lying. Then we continue the lesson and introduce the concept of "deindustrialization" (Bluestone and Harrison 1982), the process whereby the US economy changed from manufacturing to a service orientation.

In the printing industry's heyday, my uncle set type on a "linotype" machine. This machine had a typewriter-like keyboard that dropped pieces of metal with letters on top. At the end of the line, the operator would hit a "return" key, and the "line of type" would be molded together. Technological changes shaped that occupation, first by a method by which computer tapes ran a number of linotype machines at one time, and second by inventing a method of printing—offset—by which (hot type) lines of type produced by the linotype machine were no longer needed. Hard copies could be printed out from computers to be photographed for making flat printing plates.

One should not, however, perceive my mother's advice to me as an indicator of the stereotype that working-class parents do not value education. My own research (1998) illustrates the strong commitment (and value) of working-class parents toward providing their children with a quality education—a good high school education. They are just not sure of the need for a college education. A number of research articles still reflect that position (Longman 2017). Other researchers have documented that working-class parents are sometimes simply afraid of losing their children to an alien way of life at a university (see Rubin 1976; Lareau 1989). Of course, this resistance to the dominant ideology of using higher education as a means of ensuring upward mobility helps reproduce social class relations. Although I understand Rosenbaum's (2004) position that other countries—Germany and Japan—seem to be able to provide gainful employment to those who do not have a college degree, the position that college is not for everyone sometimes appears to be promulgated by those who want *their* children to go to college.

Counter to the norm, a couple of older neighborhood kids, including one of my brother's friends, had gone to private colleges. My mother would say—with emphasis—that he went to *Catholic* college, as if that somehow meant it was a better college. Even though she knew we couldn't afford Catholic high school, my mom (like many others in the neighborhood) was still impressed with those who had the means to continue to give their children a Catholic education (Similarly, she used to talk about *Jewish* doctors, as if that meant they were better at their job). These are the stereotypes she heard growing up in Flatbush, Brooklyn. What such a person studied, or how he gained admission to a college, or how his family was able to afford college, must have been a mystery to my mom. While a few of my friends did attend Catholic high school, I think it was not always so much a matter of a higher family income (though most did not have a family member who drank away half of their income). I would argue that the reason some families chose to send their children to a Catholic high school had more to do with the low opinion many in the neighborhood had of public schools, and the variety of children that would be attending public schools with their children—that is, blacks and Puerto Ricans. For example, one woman my mom knew from the neighborhood was horrified that my mom was allowing her child to attend a vocationally oriented public high school instead of a Catholic high school. She told my mom, "I would never let my daughter go to a public high school." My mom hated the thought that someone was "looking down" on her. She did seem to understand that there were two segments of the working class—there were some families who lived a more "settled" life, who could sometimes flaunt their perceived higher status. By the way, that woman's daughter became pregnant in Catholic high school, which prompted my mother to laugh and say "Good!"

After talking to my uncle about his field, I searched for a high school that prepared someone for the printing industry. Sure, my mom could have suggested I be a doctor, a lawyer, a scientist (especially with my interest in science), or a politician, but these careers were not part of her cultural (capital) repertoire. A middle- or upper-middle-class parent today would have been reading about and searching for all there is to know to get their child a spot in the Bronx High School of Science—one of the top high schools in the country. This is not to blame my mom. She loved her children very much, but she was from the working class. Many of my friends from SSS who were not going to a Catholic high school were heading to one particular public high school—and it offered, among many vocational subjects, printing. So, off I went to Thomas A. Edison Vocational and Technical High School in Jamaica, NY.

Tracked education would structure my high school experience just as it had shaped my time in grammar school. There were two tracks at Edison: the vocational and the technical. Here again, a certain amount of cultural capital is necessary to understand the differences. In essence, the technical track prepared students for college and the vocational track prepared students for the work world. In the technical track, students took college prep classes such as algebra, geometry, trigonometry, biology, chemistry, and physics. In the vocational track, students took one or two basic courses in math and science, geared toward working in a particular shop environment. A student could major in electronics, chemistry, and computer technology in the technical track, or in woodworking, plumbing, printing, auto mechanics, mechanical drawing, and electrical installation in the vocational track. As a 14-year-old boy who had just graduated from a very strict Catholic elementary school, I was looking for the easiest route through high school.

As I was preparing for my traditional, working-class trajectory, my above-average academic performance threw a wrench in the usual progression. I scored high on the entrance exam that each student took on entering Edison, so the school counselor put me in the college prep math sequence, even though I was in the vocational track. He said I might need it one day, and he was right; though I later opted out of 11th-grade trigonometry, against his wishes, and had to retake it later at Queens College. Meanwhile, the rest of my friends in the vocational track were taking basic math, where they learned how to work with fractions. This event is an illustration of how social class trajectories (and social structure in general) can be modified and shaped by individual decisions (the structure/agency debate). The decision to track a student into a certain reading group, or into a non-college curriculum in high school, or even into a community college as opposed to a four-year liberal arts college, puts that student onto a particular educational/career path that may prove difficult to change. As with most systems of tracking, Edison's was fairly rigid—I cannot remember many students transferring from the vocational to the technical track. A vocational track student was already too far behind the technical students academically by the time he entered his sophomore year. On the other hand, a few technical track students did slip "down" to the vocational track.

So, while my friends were adding and subtracting fractions in basic math, I was trying to understand algebraic expressions and geometric proofs. Admittedly, I was jealous of those who were taking the easier type of math needed for shop class. The vocational track students would take six weeks of each career track and then choose a major to study for the next three years. Electrical installation was fairly interesting, but my mother used to tease me after I came home one day and told her,

"My thing wouldn't light up." Auto mechanics seemed to be something from another planet—I have never driven a car to this day—and I was all thumbs in woodworking and mechanical drawing (almost no thumbs in woodworking, actually). Yes, my family was working class, but it did not represent the handyman kind of working-class family so often portrayed on television (as in *Roseanne*). Rather, my friends and I followed more of the sports-oriented working-class stereotype. Remember, there was little space in those apartments for tools, and almost no one had a garage. Given that printing was seen as a noble working-class profession (and I think still is), I decided in the ninth grade—after taking six weeks of each vocational shop—to major in printing. (I love to drop off exams to the print shop at the college in which I now work: I can smell the ink, see the paper, and hear the printing presses.)

A vocational track student would spend four to five of the eight periods in a school day in shop. That meant I only had three to four periods for academic subjects, plus gym. The academic courses were moderately rigorous: science, English, and social studies. The advanced math courses outside the vocational track were the most difficult subjects I had to take. My shop-oriented schedule at Edison is the reason I give so much credit to SSS for the habits of mind I acquired during my first 12 years of schooling. The vocational track at Edison ultimately reinforced the idea that work means getting one's hands dirty (very dirty in printing). It would be a mistake to think that students disliked the vocational track, however; most loved it, including me. Thus, the memories I have of my time at Edison include some of the happiest moments of my life. Undoubtedly, strong bonds are developed when you are with the same group of classmates for 4–5 hours a day over three years. Being happy in school and learning a good trade almost certainly made my parents happy, too.

What about the structure of Thomas Edison High School? At that time it was a single-sex educational institution—only boys attended. An ex-Marine drill instructor ran the lunchroom with a (literally) strong hand. As with most systems of tracking, the students in the vocational track rarely interacted with the students in the technical track. Yet, it was sometimes possible to have friends from other cliques: I was able to hang out with the "jocks" as well as the "nerds."[6] Most of my time during my four years in Edison, though, was spent with students who were in the vocational track. This system kept the vocational students in the dark about academic issues and college-oriented matters. This quote is from my Edison Senior Yearbook (1971):

> Unlike an academic high school, Edison prepares its students to enter the adult world directly. It offers the job training, the means whereby they can immediately earn a living. Thus, we turned our attention and energies to that end.

What is not spoken of is the fact that the technical track student would have had the additional option of attending college. Looking through the yearbook reveals that most of the honor students were from the technical track.

Socializing with friends of like mind reinforced a job-oriented outlook for the vocational track and a college-oriented outlook for the technical track (following socialization theory). A student in the vocational track could, if he so chose, go to school for only half the day in his senior year, with the other half-day spent at a shop-related job. This was just another way in which the vocational student was put at a disadvantage if he wanted to attend college after graduation: he would not have the high school coursework necessary for most colleges. Finally, when school was finished for the day, I observed most of the technical track students take the bus toward Whitestone, College Point, and Bayside (middle-class and upper-middle-class parts of Queens), while the vocational students tended to take the bus the other way toward Jamaica, Woodhaven, and Ozone Park/City Line (working-class parts of Queens). Separation by class permeated home, school, and our journeys between the two.

Much has been written about the "hidden curriculum" of schooling, referring to its unstated goals in a capitalist society. Bowles and Gintis (1976) argue that the hidden curriculum found in working-class high schools consistently penalizes three personality traits: creativity, aggressiveness, and independence. In contrast, the personality traits that are rewarded include punctuality, predictability, and identification with the school. In short, these authors maintain that middle-class students are given more room for creativity and spontaneity than working-class students, due to the needs of a capitalist system continuing to transform from a manufacturing- to a service-oriented/information age. Another quote from Edison's (1971) yearbook indicates that such a "hidden curriculum" was an ever-present part of the school's mission: "Victories over the physical, emotional, and social problems facing Edison students helped make Edison unique and its students *industrious, upright, and dependable* (my emphasis)." It is possible that these three values helped bolster the self-concept of the vocational students (and possibly some of the technical students), but their basic function was to make vocational students compliant workers for industry.

However, the hidden curriculum is not an all-encompassing and deterministic concept. My counselor at Edison became somewhat of an active agent by placing me in a few technical track liberal arts courses that later helped me acquire a bachelor's degree. Rosenbaum (1976) found that language classes "chosen" at an early age send students along very different and unequal tracks. Instead of "cooling me out" (Clark 1960), my counselor intervened and disrupted the social class/educational assembly line that spits students out into their respective positions in society based on their social class background.

Many of my fellow vocational track friends did not stand a chance of acquiring the necessary requirements to attend college. At a 20-year high school reunion of my printing shop class at Howard Beach, Queens, one of our teachers admitted that he knew we'd been using outdated machinery and that he'd been giving us busywork in shop class. One of my classmates was very upset after the event. He said to me that his daughter had just applied to college, and he wished he had been given that opportunity. The printing program he was in at Edison just did not prepare him for that option. His anger was real and palpable. I felt nothing but sadness for him and others he represented. The teacher who was at that reunion dinner was very surprised to find out I already had a master's degree in sociology. This was a telling reaction. For some reason I never mentioned that I was also pursuing a doctoral degree—maybe I did not want to be seen as lost to an "alien way of life" (Rubin 1976).

There was a second person in my high school who intervened and asked me to consider applying to college (even though I was in the vocational track): believe it or not, it was my printing shop teacher, Mr. F. Never have I seen a teacher treat students with so much respect. He taught us more than just the basics of running a printing press—he talked to us about many unrelated subjects, such as history, sex, current events (telling us in 1971 the important role China would have in the world in the future), and life in general. And he always kept a keen sense of humor. One day, for instance, he was showing us a film about World War II, and just as the chair of the Graphics Department entered the classroom, there was a scene in the film of a wooden building exploding, sending all the wood down a river. Mr. F. shut off the filmstrip and told the chair that the film was about paper making. I have never laughed so much as when the chair left the classroom, visibly happy. At that moment, Mr. F. gained the respect of every member of the class, and he became someone you could go to with your school-related and personal problems. A far cry from the stereotype of a shop teacher, this man helped me immeasurably with my future plans.

Mr. F. had a closet full of books he invited us to borrow. One day, while waiting for class to end, I started to read through a psychology book, and continued to read it throughout the year. It fascinated me. In fact, I copied a large portion of this psychology textbook into a notebook (which I still have). I started to do more and more of this kind of work during shop-class time, but Mr. F. never told me to stop. Then he said he wanted to talk to me about my future.

The only other time I had ever thought about my future was when a friend of mine from 76th Street asked me (around the same year) what I wanted to do after high school—I told him I would probably "work in an office somewhere just like my brother," who was an inventory clerk for a book publisher. You would be safe to think that this comment was naïve, to say the least. It still makes me smile (and makes me sad) that I failed to consider that people who work in offices have certain skills and knowledge. I am a firm supporter of the "take your daughter to work" movement. However, I wish someone, especially an upper-class professional (the kind we didn't know), had taken me to work, too. Then I could have seen that there are a number of career opportunities, if one acquires the proper credentials. Again, in our household there was little talk about the world of work or the wide variety of careers available for young people. Today, at my children's (middle-class) schools, there are a number of career days and other times when people from different walks of life come to speak to students about the range of jobs available and the level of education necessary for each. At our school, the nuns and priests seemed always to be pushing a "vocation," and I took that to mean being a priest or nun like them. Meanwhile, my father came home every day and "cursed out" his S.O.B. foreman. I lacked those kinds of workplace role models, but my shop teacher helped close the gap.

Mr. F. asked me what I was planning to do after high school. Never having thought about it much, I replied I would probably look for a job running one of the printing presses we had learned about that year in class. "Tom," he said, "those kinds of jobs are becoming harder to find, especially with the technological changes that are remaking the printing industry." He was correct, because with the advent of computers, four-color quality copy machines, printing companies moving south, west, and overseas to escape union shops, and the rise of quick print shops such as Kinkos, the industry was rapidly changing (and quickly making any skills we learned at Edison almost obsolete). Mr. F. told me about a fairly new program at a two-community college in Brooklyn that prepared its students for (lower-level) white-collar jobs as estimators, planners, and assistant production managers in printing, advertising, and publishing. Somewhat in shock, I replied with one question: "College? How do you do that?" The word "do" was filled with many other questions. Yet, after I investigated the program further, I went home to tell my parents (really, my mom) that I wanted to apply to college. It was a community college, but a college, nonetheless.

A few of my classmates, with the prodding of Mr. F., also applied to New York City Community College (NYCCC) of the City University of New York (CUNY). This is another example of someone who stepped in to interrupt the insidious effects of social class (social capital). Thank you, Mr. F. Just as he was buoying up my prospects, the administration of Thomas A. Edison tried to stop me (and a few others) from graduating because of the length of our hair—which was well past my shoulders at that time (my aunt used to call me John the Baptist). My mother, like many parents in that time and place, usually did not get involved in school-related matters, but this time she leapt into action. She knew I had good grades, so she went to the guidance counselor's office and gave him an earful. Thanks to her advocacy, I graduated with my class, long hair and all. I was also rewarded with the Printing Industries Award, which I believe another student had anticipated winning. How is that for a working-class parent "valuing" education?[7]

COLLEGE AND BEYOND

When I told my mother I wanted to go to college, she asked (as most working-class parents would) how much it was going to cost. CUNY did not charge tuition until 1975, therefore it would be free, except for a fee of approximately $25 (and the cost of books). On hearing this rather very reasonable tuition bill (the equivalent of approximately $150 today), she uttered, with a strained face, "Oh, I don't know how we will swing that." It was a lot of money for my family at that time, but it is alarming that I almost did not go to college for $25. Tuition at Harvard University in 1971 was $2600 (Goldhaber 1971). How many working-class students still never have the chance to go to college because of financial difficulties or the fear of getting into additional debt? (Of course, student debt has become a very big social and political topic.) What a shame. What a waste of talent. There is a reason that CCNY (City College of New York, another CUNY campus) was known as the "poor man's Harvard," attracting smart students with lesser means. Many of the kids from City Line and Ozone Park would not have attended college without access to CUNY.

My Graphic Arts and Advertising Technology program at NYCCC was just a glorified, updated version of my high school curriculum. It was filled with mostly "white-collar" shop classes where I spent many hours learning about color theory, ink technology, black-and-white and color photography, layout design, art and mechanical production, paper making, typography, and printing management principles (see Box 3.1).

Box 3.1 Courses comprising the Graphic Arts Program at NYCCC
Semester 1

Foundations of Graphic Arts
Photo Processes—Black and White
Principles of Typography
Copy Preparation—Black and White
Typing I
English
Elective

Semester 2

Fundamentals of Estimating
Copy Preparation—Color
Format Analysis—Layouts
Photo Processes—Line and Halftone
Platemaking and Proving
Statistics
Social Science Elective

Semester 3

Color Reproduction Theory
Color Reproduction Technology
Intermediate Estimating
Photo Processes—Color
Organization of Advertising
English
Elective

(continued)

Box 3.1   (continued)
Semester 4

Production Management
Advanced Estimating
Quality Control Methods
Traffic Management
Principles of Science I
Elective

The class lab assignments had us running sophisticated cameras; marking up artwork; pricing paper, ink, and printing plates; and testing ink and paper for various properties, such as "pick" propensity. Most of my courses at NYCCC were related to graphic arts technology, but on rare occasions a liberal arts course was required to fill out the program. Over the two years I had a chance to take one course in statistics, two courses in English, two courses in the social sciences (I dropped sociology because I thought it was boring), and one course in science. This narrow curriculum, as I had experienced in high school, made it very difficult to be prepared to move on to the next level: a four-year liberal arts college.[8]

In keeping with my working-class background and my lack of confidence, I was happy with the program. It would be interesting to be a fly on the wall in middle- and upper-middle-class households to see the parents' reactions if their children came home with this same program. When I showed my community college program to a professor in graduate school, he just shook his head, sadly. When I asked one upper-middle-class parent for another research project what she would say if her daughter did not want to go to college, her reply was, "Dr. Gorman, excuse me, but that is a stupid question, that is not going to happen in this *neighborhood*." She went on, "In this neighborhood, parents ask each other in which college is your child attending; attending college is just *assumed*" (Gorman 1998a, b). The word "assumed"—a very important cultural capital assumption—came up over and over in middle- and upper-middle-class neighborhoods. For those of us from City Line, college attendance was far from "assumed," though, and for those who did attend college, CUNY was very often the only real possibility, although a couple of my close friends attended Queensborough Community College.

Cultural capital comes in many forms for different social classes. For example, I can remember being very embarrassed in SSS when I raised my hand excitedly that yes, I did have an almanac in my house. When I told the class that the almanac was ten years old, my teacher seemed to lose interest in my comment, prompting a few of the other students to start giggling. I remember the pain of that moment like it was yesterday. Working-class kids lack access to the kinds of cultural capital that middle-class kids take for granted. In one of my own classes at a community college, I showed my students a video concerning the effects of social class on college attendance. When the video depicted middle-class and upper-middle-class parents paying upward of $500 for an hour of SAT tutoring for their children, my students laughed and called them nerds. It is not easy trying to break through students' attitudes based on the cultural capital they do or do not bring to the classroom.

After my first year at community college, I was offered an assistant production position in a printing firm in Manhattan. That would have meant, however, that I would need to finish community college at night after work. To a working-class kid, the opportunity to get a "real" job (instead of "book learning") was too alluring to turn down. Besides, Professor A. thought it was a good idea to accept the position. After all, his role, ultimately, was to help us get our first job in the field. One week later, though, I knew I had made a mistake, and quit my job to return to finish my second year full time at Community College. The person who helped me get the position never spoke to me again.

Why did I quit? It just did not feel right. I was 19 years old and working in the middle of Manhattan, and I lacked the confidence necessary to take on such a position at such a young age. This theme—lacking self-confidence—is one that will come up over and over in this socio-autobiography, and in many stories that working-class people tell. Indeed, when I did well in high school, I attributed this to it being "only" a vocational high school; when I did well in community college, I attributed this to it being "only" a community college. Not till later, when I was promoted to supervisor in a large printing company, and after doing well at a four-year college, did I start thinking that *maybe* I was pretty good at tasks I set out to accomplish. Yet, even then I said to myself, "It was only a CUNY four-year college." Subsequently, I questioned the graduate school that accepted me (rated 14th in the nation at the time), my dissertation (even after four articles were published from it), my first two academic positions, tenure, and promotion. Lack of confidence is something

I fight against every day. It is a part of growing up working class that someone from the middle class would have a difficult time understanding; that is, the feeling of never being good enough. As Sennett and Cobb (1972, p. 186) said, "no matter how much he [a working-class person] knows 'the system is rotten,' he has to fight a doubt about himself first to be able unreservedly to fight the world."

While I was at NYCCC I met new friends, and interesting and caring professors, and I gained knowledge and skills that prepared me for lower-level production management jobs in the printing, publishing, and advertising industries. Nevertheless, as you can see from Box 3.1, the program did not prepare its students for four-year colleges (even though the program stated otherwise). Obviously, I was still on the "track" to a lower-middle-level, technical/vocational career. One could argue that capitalism needed people who were trained for the new economy, an economy that was still transitioning from a manufacturing- to a service-oriented base. That was exactly (dare I say) the function that NYCCC filled. Thus, I obtained a lower-level, white-collar position in a large full-service printing corporation after graduating. Therefore, I was not really experiencing upward mobility in any real sense, I was just filling the new types of "working-class" jobs available for those with a two-year college degree. A high school degree might have been good enough for a relatively similar kind of job after World War II, but from the 1970s on a new "worker" was required, one who needed more than a high school degree but less than a four-year degree. I had more education than my parents, but not enough for real upward mobility.[9] Nevertheless, I did have a job coming out of community college that paid a fairly decent wage for the day, and more money than I would have had without the degree. Many of today's working-class students do not have that opportunity. In working at one of the largest printing plants in New York City in a lower-level middle management position, I learned about the planning, scheduling, and tracking of in-house printing jobs. It was a reasonable entry-level job in what could have been a long career in the printing industry—if not for the next round of life events.

One more person would interrupt my working-class job trajectory. Professor A. constantly reminded his students to continue their education after community college. Specifically, he recommended that I (and a few others) continue my education at a four-year college after graduating—Baruch College. There, he said, I could major in business and marketing, the logical step after the graphic arts program at NYCCC. Baruch College is a highly respected four-year college in Manhattan within the CUNY system. As a bonus, most of my community college credits would transfer if I entered with an associate's degree (even if there were not equivalent courses at the four-year college). This policy, along with open enrollment and free tuition, was one of the many attempts by CUNY to help working-class and lower-middle-class students in New York City acquire a college education. Without these policies, I would have never attended college. I transferred to Baruch College to major in marketing and advertising as a night student.

The experience was very different from life as a regular day student. At NYCCC I would sit in the lounge between classes hearing the latest songs playing on the jukebox, or listening to some guy with long hair play the guitar while singing Don McLean's "American Pie." It was 1971, but the sixties had not ended yet. At Baruch, my purple suede, fringed jacket stood out in contrast to the pinstripe suits that the typical night student wore. And what happened? This working-class young man dropped out of Baruch College after just six weeks. I had a (lower) white-collar job in a large printing plant—what else could I need? I promised to return after a semester or two, but that would not happen for another seven years, and only after the life-altering event of divorce.

I got married during my early college days. It is a social fact (see Durkheim 1982 [1895]) that the younger someone gets married, the greater the chances of that marriage ending in divorce (Pew Research Center Report on Marriage and Divorce 2010). When I got married, the tendency was for working-class couples to marry earlier in life than middle-class couples, and also more often. Hence, my marrying my first wife at 21 led to our splitting up at age 25 and divorce at 26. Two working-class kids, lacking college credentials and middle-class careers, took on adult responsibilities too soon. Today, middle-class couples are more likely to marry than working-class couples, and the two groups get married at about the same age. According to research, working-class couples, especially women, put off marriage until their economic future looks secure.[10] This data reflects a major change in demographic trends. Then, I imagined that adult life would entail marriage, kids, and an apartment or house. What else was a working-class guy to do? When my marriage ended, I diverted from this intended track.

This event was the biggest "turning point" in my life. Sociologists (starting with Elder 1985) have focused on the social turning points in people's lives. Although I was badly shaken by the divorce (calling for multiple Valium prescriptions), there was a silver lining: I now had the opportunity for what we called in my old neighborhood a "do over." In a fit of anger and rebellion, I decided to do something radical (for a working-class person, that is): to go to a four-year college and do a little traveling. I wanted to do some of the things that middle-class kids get to enjoy and that I missed out on. Where did I get the idea to go back to college and travel? Why not just hang out at the local bar, or get into drugs or gambling? I will explore that question later, because there are different ways to rebel: some move you forward, while some do not. For whatever reason, I decided to apply to Queens College—the "jewel" of the CUNY system—to major in psychology, inspired by the textbook belonging to my high school shop teacher and a couple of electives I had taken at community college.[11]

One particular incident had occurred the previous summer that made me realize I needed to go back and hit the books if I wanted to return to a four-year college. While hitchhiking across Canada and then back home through the northern states, I was staying at a youth hostel where a few people were discussing World War II. I decided to interject a comment about how Germany became divided (I'm not sure where I picked up that "fact"). One fellow, a history major, laughed at me and made me and my comment look foolish. When I got home and looked up the fact, I realized he was correct. I decided that would not happen again. Being in command of a body of knowledge, or just being confident in being able to accomplish a goal, was something I desired from a very early age. There is a scene at the end of the movie *The Beast from 20,000 Fathoms* (Warner Brothers 1953) where the "good guys" need someone who is a good shot to shoot a poison dart from a rifle to kill the monster. They find someone who can shoot a rifle and ask him, "Have you ever used one of these [guns]?" He replies, "I pick my teeth with them." I was floored by this scene as a kid. It may sound silly, but I remember to this day how much I was impressed by someone who was that confident in himself. Even as a kid, I wanted that confidence, I just never knew how to express the feeling. In addition one of my shop teachers in my freshman year at Edison said that as a child he would buy a new tool when he had enough money. I remember thinking, "Wow, he probably knows a lot about all those tools and what they can do." And when working for the large printer, I felt empty because I could not understand or participate in the entire process. Marxists would call that alienation.

My lack of self-confidence in my academic abilities almost kept me from applying to Queens College. As the first semester approached in February 1979, I spent a significant amount of time in the local library catching up on English grammar and ninth- and tenth-grade mathematics. I spent many hours at Queensborough Public Library and at home reviewing books on mathematics, English, and the natural sciences. I could be found going through these books during lunch breaks at work, on the subway and buses to and from work, and in the remaining hours at home. When I would read a column in a local newspaper, I would sometimes reread it two or three times to make sure I understood it. If only I had listened to my guidance counselor at high school and taken trigonometry, I would have fulfilled the three-math-course sequence required by Queens College at that time. More than 11 years after I took algebra and geometry, I had to take trigonometry. These are the kinds of roadblocks that ultimately keep many working-class adults from returning to complete a college degree. Sometimes, it is too late to make up for the effects of early tracking, especially with work and family responsibilities. Granted, I was saving money by living back in my parents' apartment, but I still debated whether it was worth returning to college at the age of 26. In spite of these doubts, or because of them, there was something inside me that wanted to "show them" I could do it (without fully understanding who "they" were).

According to Willis (1981), working-class kids "penetrate" the dominant ideology of America: that anyone can succeed if they just work hard enough. The problem is that working-class kids' repertoire of cultural capital only allows them to respond in ways that will reinforce social class relations. In brief, working-class kids become working-class adults because they put down, rebel against, and resist the academic environment. However, I embraced it! I had already had a taste of (community) college. One could also argue, as Bowles and Gintis (1976) and others do, that capitalism contains the seeds of its own destruction by requiring workers who have new types of knowledge (or at least workers who are aware of and question social class relations). Also, I had a decent grammar school education, a friend or two who had graduated from a four-year college, an older brother who had intellectual interests, and a few counselors who, rather than "cooling me out" (leading me away from academic subjects), pushed me to continue my education. The trajectory of this working-class kid, which my social structure had plotted, was being challenged by the "agency" inherent in my social life. Keep in mind, though, that social structure does not wither in the face of agency. These forces are constantly interacting to shape one's future.

In my first semester at Queens College, I took two courses: Introduction to Philosophy and Introduction to Sociology. I took only two courses because I was still working full time during the day in the printing industry. Then, I started to take more psychology courses, but there was something about the theories and explanations in psychology that just did not seem to satisfy my interest in human behavior. So, I looked through the college catalogue, and when I came to the social sciences, and sociology in particular, I stopped to read the course offerings, remembering that I had dropped my first course in sociology in community college (I had thought it was boring—I keep this in mind each time I stand in front of a classroom). This time, the course offerings spoke to me and my current interests in social inequality and social justice. In Introduction to Sociology, we read Marx, and in a course on families, we read Lillian Rubin's *Worlds of Pain: Life in the Working-Class Family*. I was hooked! Later on, in my first tenure track faculty position, I sent Rubin a copy of a paper I had written confirming some of her findings, modifying, and questioning others. She was kind enough to respond to me with a nicely worded note. Thank you, Lillian Rubin.

Something was taking place at Queens College for which I was not prepared—I was doing very well in all my courses, especially sociology, and even in the ones I had worried about: English and trigonometry. Additionally, my sociology professors were making comments on my papers such as "well thought out," "nicely written," and "thank you." Yet, rather than appreciate the feedback, I started thinking that maybe Queens College was not that good a college—low confidence strikes again.

It was a difficult decision to continue my education. Again, my lack of confidence in my academic abilities is the key to understanding my quandary. If you are wondering why I would feel this way, then you probably have not really faced the self-doubt that a blue-collar/working-class background can create for young people. Above all, lacking confidence in different parts of daily life played a central role in my life as a whole. It is the prototypical, central concept in this book. As I went through Queens College, I found my confidence building, especially on graduating with honors and winning the Sociology Award for Academic Excellence. Still, that feeling of inadequacy has stayed with me all through my professional life.

Graduate School

After graduating Queens College at the age of 29, I had to decide my next move—I could pursue a Master of Social Work (MSW) or a PhD in Sociology. Already 29, and with many friends already making a pretty good living on Wall Street, I decided to attempt to acquire an MSW. To try for a PhD at the age of 29 and spend another six to eight years in school seemed too daunting. An MSW could be completed in as little as two years. The effects of social class, falling "behind" others, and being out of sync with those my own age were continuing to influence my decisions. So, I applied to a few of the "big-name" schools in the Tri-State Area, and was accepted at New York University, Columbia University, and the Hunter College School of Social Work (CUNY). Hunter was considered as good, or better, than the marquee names for social work across the country. Of particular interest to a working-class person, it was available at CUNY prices. Even after my success at Queens College, I still had doubts about whether I could cut it at Hunter, though, fearing that sooner or later I would be "found out."

The program at Hunter was described as having a bio-psycho-social approach to understanding human behavior. However, the social side of human behavior seemed to me to be given only a cursory examination. Therefore, after some deep soul searching over whether I was more cut out to be a social researcher than a social worker, I decided to leave the program after one semester. Also, one of the professors there had told me she did not like the way I had organized a paper for her course—just as I had always thought, I could not cut it. Walking along Atlantic Avenue near my parents' apartment, I started to cry. There were fewer and fewer avenues open now for me to acquire that body of knowledge I so needed to prove that I was "worthy."[12] Social work is a demanding and rewarding profession, but I found that the "hands-on" approach was not my forte. Could it be that my family (and working-class culture in general) did not foster an environment whereby certain abilities—such as the open discussions, negotiations, and feelings necessary for a successful career in social work—were developed? I am not sure, but it is clear that I was better at reading, analyzing, thinking, and writing than I had ever thought I could be.

During a short respite when I worked at another manufacturing firm as a scheduler, I changed course again and decided to apply to PhD programs in sociology. More importantly, I still possessed a radical streak that had me thinking I wanted to have some of the same experiences as people in the upper middle class. It might not sound very radical for someone to apply for a PhD, but it was for a 30-year-old working-class guy from City Line. Of course, my future classmates would likely be those upper-middle-class kids who went straight through high school into college and then on to graduate school. Nevertheless, I was willing to take a chance to see what that world was like.

An incident as a planner and scheduler at a printing firm in Manhattan helped motivate me to make my next decision. On one particularly hot and humid August Thursday, the owner of the business and his son—who had been hired at a huge salary even though he had little experience in the printing field—waved to the rest of us in the office as they went out the door, heading to the Hamptons (an upper-class beach resort on Long Island) for the weekend. This meant that not only did I still have to go home that day on the hot "A" train, I was going to have to come back the next day on the hot "A" train to finish work for them while they luxuri-ated. I went home, bought plane tickets for Europe, and gave my two-week notice to my boss the next day. It certainly helped my cause that I was living back home with my parents; I am almost sure I would not have been able to do this without their support and kindness—and also, maybe, with-out some of what I learned at Queens College about social inequality.

NOTES

1. See the demographic tables in Chapter 1; and see Kruse (2005) and Woldoff (2011) for some of the latest research on white flight.
2. Crockett's (2015) book of 12 serious/humorous stories about growing up in that time and place contains a similar account.
3. See the series of reports from UCLA's Civil Rights Project: Orfield (2016).
4. The demographic tables in Chapter 1 describe the educational levels for that time and place.
5. See Komarovsky (1962); Rubin (1976); Halle (1984); Lareau (1989); Gorman (1998), for discussions of various aspects of the lives of the work-ing class in this respect.
6. Tichy (1973) discusses the organization of different types of cliques found in high schools—some cliques allow interaction with non-members, and some do not.
7. An update: Thomas A. Edison High School was highlighted in a *New York Post* article (Linge 2015) pointing out recent changes to the school's cur-riculum and equipment—making it now a reputable "technical" high school in New York City. I was very happy (and proud) to read of the

improvements, especially to the school's reputation. It would be an interesting study to see how Edison graduates fare today in the job market and college attendance as opposed to my graduating class. By the way, Thomas A. Edison Vocational and Technical High School has changed its name to Thomas A. Edison Career and Technical Education. As I hypothesized in a graduate paper from a symbolic interactionist perspective, a change in name may prompt a rise in some students' self-esteem.

8. Interestingly, NYCCC now offers two-year and four-year degrees and is called New York College of Technology. It would be interesting to study which students are in the two different programs. As a sociologist, I would be fascinated to investigate these two "tracks" and the kind of careers to which they lead.

9. Bowles and Gintis (1976) also make this argument.

10. Cherlin (2014) has an insightful discussion of the changes that have occurred concerning social class and marriage.

11. When I got married at age 20, my parents had to give written permission, but my wife, who was only 19 at the time, did not have to get any parental signatures. It must have been assumed that women mature sooner than men. Also, the voting age at that time was dropped to 18, the age at which many young men were marching off to Vietnam.

12. Sennett and Cobb (1972) discuss the search for meaning and dignity by the working class.

CHAPTER 4

Previous Research on Education and The Hidden Injuries of Class. My Educational Career Compared

This is not the first time I have written about the hidden injuries of class that Sennett and Cobb so eloquently portrayed. In the early to mid 90's, I conducted research into the effects of social class on parents' attitudes toward education. I found a large segment of the white, working class bitter, angry, and lashing out at those whom they perceived to be "looking down" on them—college-educated, middle- and upper-middle-class, white-collar workers. It shows how the hidden injuries of class experienced in childhood and adolescence curdle later as an adult. What follows is a reprint of that research that was published in the *Journal of Contemporary Ethnography* (Vol. 27, No. 1, April 1998, pp. 10–44). It will be interesting, following the article, to then apply those research findings to my own experiences and educational career, and put into sociological perspective the educational system at that time and place.

SOCIAL CLASS AND PARENTAL ATTITUDES TOWARD EDUCATION: RESISTANCE AND CONFORMITY TO SCHOOLING IN THE FAMILY

Abstract
This study investigates the impact of social class on parents' attitudes toward their children's education. The results suggest that two concepts—resistance and conformity—are central to understanding parental attitudes toward education and the process by which those attitudes are shaped.

© The Author(s) 2017   103
T.J. Gorman, *Growing up Working Class*,
DOI 10.1007/978-3-319-58898-8_4

The data indicate that the probability parents will conform to or resist the meritocratic ideology of acquiring a college degree to help ensure occupational success tends to depend on parents' social-class background and, concomitantly, on whether they have experienced "hidden injuries of class." A more inclusive sampling strategy proved useful in documenting the varied attitudes found among working-class and middle-class parents. The attitudes of parents toward higher education have the potential to influence their children's attitudes toward education, their children's chances of obtaining a college degree, and their own chances of returning to school. This research suggests that the family is an important site for cultural production and social reproduction.

The impact parents have on their children's educational aspirations and occupational success has long occupied center stage in the sociological literature. This body of research, consisting mostly of large-scale surveys, suggests that parents' attitudes toward education have a significant effect on their children's educational aspirations (Coleman and Hoffer 1987; Henderson 1987; National Center for Education Statistics 1982; Sewell et al. 1969). If the attitudes of parents toward their children's education are important, then it is vital to understand how these parental attitudes are shaped.

It is commonly argued that social class plays an important part in the formation of an individual's attitudes toward education. One problem with the survey research in this area is its inability to delineate the process by which social class affects an individual's attitudes toward education. A key question remains to be answered: Just why are there differences in attitudes toward education among social classes? To help answer this research question, I conducted intensive and lengthy interviews with forty middle-class and forty working-class parents (using a cluster-sampling technique) residing in a medium-sized city in the United States.

This study, drawing on the work of Rubin (1976, 1994), Sennett and Cobb (1972), Willis (1977), and Anyon (1980), suggests that two concepts—resistance and conformity—are central to understanding the process by which parental attitudes are shaped. The probability that parents will conform to or resist the meritocratic ideology of acquiring a college education to help ensure occupational success tends to depend on their social-class background and, concomitantly, on whether they have experienced "hidden injuries of class" (Sennett and Cobb 1972). This reformulation of some classic sociological and social psychological

concepts—which helps explain the attitudes of parents toward education by their class-specific experiences in their own family, at school, and
at the workplace—suggests a new way of understanding the process by
which social class affects parental attitudes toward education.

This study explores the attitudes that develop in response to the educational, familial, and occupational experiences that people in different
social classes encounter in a capitalist society. Families, as well as schools,
are a critical site for reproduction of educational aspirations; working-
class parents hold more diverse and more complex orientations toward
their children's schooling than previous research has reported. Middle-
class parents are much more homogenous than working-class parents in
their view of American education and its impact on occupational success.
A culture of professionalism drives the attitudes of middle-class parents
toward education.

LITERATURE: DISPARATE EXPLANATIONS AND FINDINGS

Social reproduction theories, which explore the mechanisms by which
social-class relations are maintained, have had some success in outlining
the processes influencing a child's aspirations but usually limit their analyses to the peer group and the school to the exclusion of the family
(Bourdieu 1977, 1984, 1988a, b; Bourdieu and Passerson 1977; Bowles
and Gintis 1976; Giroux 1981; Giroux and Simon 1989; Willis 1977,
1981). At the same time, intensive studies of working-class families have
not focused on class-specific educational attitudes and aspirations (Berger
1960; Gans 1962; Halle 1984; Howell 1972; Komarovsky 1962;
Komblum 1974; Levitan 1971; Rubin 1976; Sennett and Cobb 1972;
Shostak 1969). This study links both of these research traditions.

There are several competing explanations for the different ways middle-
class and working-class parents approach education. Kohn (1969) argues
that parents know from their workplace experiences the skills and education their children will need; working-class parents teach traits such as
conformity, punctuality, and obedience, while middle-class parents try to
instill other traits in their children such as independence, creativity, and
self-actualization. Using the same argument, Rubin (1976, 207–08) adds
that the working-class families she encountered were lacking educational
role models and information concerning college admissions, but were not
overly concerned because this meant that they did not have to worry that
their children would be lost to an alien way of life.

A more recent version of this kind of argument posits that working-class parents are actually raising their educational aspirations for their children based on the parents' reading of the changing economy (Weis 1987). The deindustrialization that took place in the 1980s has forced working-class parents to consider a college education for their children.

A different reason given for low educational aspirations among the working class is that working-class children see their chance of upward mobility as slim, given their environment, and choose to drop out of school, figuratively if not literally (Ogbu 1978; Willis 1977). Willis (1977) contends that dropping out of school is a "penetration" into the workings of capitalism and an act of "resistance." Resistance to schooling, however, only solidifies social-class reproduction; working-class children (and I would argue parents, too) ensure their place in working-class occupations by participating in acts of resistance to the meritocratic ideology of upward mobility.

Yet, another explanation, class-specific attitudes toward education, is based on presumed differences in cultural capital available to different social classes. For instance, Lareau (1987) looked at two first-grade classrooms in working- and middle-class communities. She noted that working-class parents, as well as middle-class parents, value education (although middle-class parents have higher aspirations for their children's educational attainment); however, because of their social-class position, working-class parents do not have the cultural capital (i.e., educational level, information, occupational prestige, flexible work schedules, kinship ties, leisure activities, socialization patterns, and linguistic structure) that is necessary for their children to succeed in school. This lack of cultural capital prevents working-class parents from participating in school affairs and, therefore, hinders their children's educational achievement and attainment.

Other research has taken a social-psychological approach to the impact of social class on the attitudes of parents toward their children's education (Sennett and Cobb 1972). Working-class individuals, from this perspective, are ambivalent about the benefits of a college education. These parents want their children to have what they did not have—a college education (Connell et al. 1982)—but disrespect the kind of work for which the college degree will prepare their children. In short, working-class parents must prepare their children for work the parents disrespect; this is the key to understanding the hidden injuries of class.

Most of the research on attitudes toward education has focused on the working class—assuming middle-class values to be the benchmark—and have come up with conflicting results. A series of British studies has documented the anti-educational feeling found in working-class homes (see Craft et al. 1972). Most of the work in the United States on working-class attitudes toward educational attainment, in general, has recorded the tendency for the working class to be sensitive to discussions regarding their schooling (Halle 1984; Howell 1972; Rubin 1976; Sennett and Cobb 1972). This kind of reaction is indicative of the hidden injuries of class.

By contrast, some research (British and American) has captured positive working-class attitudes toward education (Cave 1970; Komarovsky 1962; Lindsay 1969). This body of work shows that members of the working class are interested in education and seek information about their children's schooling (even if it only concerns job opportunities). Lindsay's (1969) study suggests that the greater the frequency of parental social contacts, the more likely they will not underestimate their children's future educational attainment. This theme has also been expounded elsewhere. For instance, Marsden (1962) found that working-class parents make decisions regarding their children's schooling based on the neighborhood children's opinions, whereas middle-class parents have a more broadly based network. Similarly, Kahl (1953) uncovered a pattern suggesting that a working-class child has a better chance of attending college if his or her father has friends who went to college. In fact, if Halle (1984) is correct in his assertion that working-class and middle-class families frequent similar leisure establishments and live in close proximity to each other, we should expect to find working-class families slowly raising their educational aspirations for their children.

It is possible that these conflicting research findings reflect the reality of different segments of the working class. Lillian Rubin (1976) described the working-class families she studied as living in "worlds of pain": unfulfilled dreams, boring social lives, miserable jobs, and marriages offering little personal growth. But as *Hard Living on Clay Street* (Howell 1972) portrayed, working-class lifestyles fall on a continuum from "hard living" to "settled living" families. Based on the data I collected, I will argue that some working-class parents do, indeed, resist the traditional means of upward mobility through higher education, while other working-class parents—those who have encountered fewer hidden injuries of class—take a more "middle-class" approach to higher education. The middle class parents will be seen, for the most part, as reproducing their culture of professionalism.

DATA COLLECTION

The sample for this study was drawn from an old, medium-sized, north-eastern US city (population: approximately 100,000). Old City (name changed to protect confidentiality) had been a magnet for immigrants during the nineteenth century; industries such as trade, transportation, foundries, lumber, and railroads dominated the landscape. These immigrants built and lived in ethnic enclaves that, to some degree, still exist today. (A few of these neighborhoods are part of the present study.) Some of the neighborhoods remain stable demographically while others are in flux. Many of the respondents are worried about crime, drugs, and racial minorities. Today, the area's three main employers—the public, service, and wholesale/retail sectors—keep the unemployment rate relatively low (around 5 percent). The county boasts a vast and prestigious higher educational system and has a large number of Ph.D.s per 100,000 residents. The large number of students in the vicinity give parts of the city a "college town" atmosphere (as well as pumping up the local economy). The housing ranges from single-family ranch and colonial style homes in the middle-class neighborhoods to two- and three-story (multifamily) row houses, many with top and bottom porches, in the working-class neighborhoods.

A stratified cluster-sampling strategy allowed me to use United States census tract data (indicating years of schooling completed and occupation) to select the census tracts in Old City that optimized my chances of finding middle-class and working-class respondents. The primary sampling units (PSU) were composed of census tracts of comparable demographic characteristics from which I randomly selected enough city blocks to complete my sample; I visited every census tract and spoke to Old City residents about census tract socioeconomic characteristics. When I did not attain the desired yield (five respondents) for a designated block, I resampled the balance of that block until I reached a yield of five respondents or ran out of dwelling units. I left an introductory letter at each dwelling unit and returned a few days later to ask the occupant whether she or he, or any other adult in the household, would like to participate in the study.

Previous research of this type has been limited to highly paid men (Halle 1984), convenience samples drawn from church registers (Komarovsky 1962), full "snowball" samples (Rubin 1976; Sennett and Cobb 1972), and samples with only a few cases (Howell 1972). Although my sample includes a few individuals who were drawn by means of a snowball technique, my sampling methodology was meant to ensure a fairly representative cross-section of working-class and middle-class residents of Old City. (See the Appendix to this chapter for a breakdown of the demographic characteristics of the sample.)

To minimize bias, I approached the respondents and conducted the interviews at different times during the week and, as much as possible, interviewed the respondents privately, free from the distractions of family life (a few interviews were conducted with the spouse present). Most of the interviews were conducted in the kitchen, dining room, or living room, but I conducted some interviews on porches, stoops, and in backyards. I interviewed only one parent from each family. Interviewing both parents simultaneously presents the potential problem of one person contaminating the other's responses, while returning at a second time to interview the other parent assumes that one partner has not spoken to the other in the interim. Although I was not able to determine differences in attitudes between a husband and a wife, I was able to sample men and women who differed on the experiences that affect attitudes toward education. Furthermore, I kept track of the respondent's spouse's (significant other) social-class and educational attainment to determine if a respondent whose spouse differed on the social-class indicator had different attitudes from a respondent whose spouse had a similar social-class indicator (Halle 1984; Komarovsky 1962; Oppenheimer 1982; Stacey 1990). Twelve working-class and three middle-class respondents had spouses who differed on the social-class indicator. Although I acknowledge the importance of investigating the intersection of race and class, I focused on one segment of the population—white working- and middle-class parents. I did, however, include a few non-white respondents because they were randomly selected.

Halle (1984) has argued that much of the research on working-class families has looked at families in the early stages of the life cycle, a procedure that almost guarantees a sample living in worlds of pain. My research—with equal numbers of middle- and working-class families at a similar life-cycle stage—was intended to address this criticism. (On preliminary examination, there was no discernible difference in the attitudes of parents toward education based on their children's ages.)

Each interview took approximately two hours to complete and was tape-recorded. I used an open-ended, structured interview schedule. All quotations in the text are verbatim, but some have been condensed for easier reading. At the end of each quotation in the text, a notation lists the respondent's age, gender, educational level, and occupation (a few respondents' occupations were changed to equivalent occupations to ensure confidentiality).

I found most respondents to be quite candid during the interviews. It may have been that they felt comfortable talking to a stranger. As one respondent commented, "It might be easier to talk to you because I don't know you." Another respondent's response to one of my questions came with this initial comment: "I have never said this to anyone before." The interactions might be akin to the proverbial stranger sitting next to you on an airplane who tells you his or her life story. It may have been that the respondents knew I was new to the area, did not know many people in the area, and would probably move away from the area after the research was complete. It may also have been that I spoke to the respondents at length about the importance of confidentiality in sociological research.

A few respondents felt "funny" having the interviews tape-recorded, but the uninhibited quality of the data suggest they overcame their initial feelings. To organize my data, I summarized the responses to each question on paper, transferred key parts of the summaries to a series of charts, and used the charts to identify patterns and deviant cases.

I had to be careful about how I approached the sensitive topic of the respondent's educational attainment, especially for some of the working-class respondents, since I represented, to some extent, the object of their anger. On rare occasion, one of my questions would provoke an angry response. For instance, one working-class woman asked me, in an angry voice, whether I "categorize people" based on educational credentials. Other working-class respondents, though, reported that the interview made them think about returning to school. Other forms of resistance to my presence were nonverbal—laughing, blowing sounds, and waving hands—and usually were in reaction to interview questions. Nevertheless, I believe that the interviews gave the respondents a forum for venting their feelings. I tapped into "hidden scripts" (Scott 1990) usually not meant for researchers (see Gorman 1994 for additional information concerning the field experiences).

My definition of social class is fairly consistent with much of the work on social-class differences (Halle 1984; Lareau 1987). I coded the respondent's social class on the basis of his or her occupation. Working-class parents in the sample held the following blue-collar/lower white-collar occupations: skilled, semi-skilled, unskilled laborers; transportation workers; and lower-level sales, clerical, and service occupations. Middle-class parents in the sample held the following white-collar occupations: professionals, middle- and upper-level managers, high-level civil servants, academics, high-level sales and administrative positions, and small business owners. Wright's (1978) conceptual model was used when an occupational status was ambiguous. Social class in this model is based on economic ownership and the amount of control over the physical means of production and the labor power of others.

Some caveats should be kept in mind. My research was conducted in a city; suburban residents were not included. Many of my respondents liked the city and the multicultural experiences it offers. I am quite certain that I would not find this attitude prevalent in the suburbs. It should also be kept in mind that the interviews were conducted during the ten-month period from November 1991 through September 1992. During this time, the United States was in the midst of an economic recession—affecting both blue-collar and white-collar workers—that prompted the media to carry stories extolling the benefits of riding out the recession by going to college or to graduate school. The economic conditions and media accounts might have influenced particular respondents to have had positive attitudes toward education. It has been argued that these changes in attitude could be an outcome of deindustrialization (Weis 1987).

FINDINGS: WORKING-CLASS PARENTS' ATTITUDES TOWARD EDUCATION: RESISTANCE

Sennett and Cobb (1972) argue that members of the working class experience hidden injuries of class (frustration, anger, and bitterness) during their search for dignity in a capitalistic society, because in such an economic system working-class people are denied their fair share of two key measures of self-worth—educational credentials and occupational prestige. The data of this study suggest that hidden injuries of class, in part, lead many working-class parents to reject higher education and upper-level white-collar occupations; there is a tendency to respond to an assault on one's dignity by lashing out at college-educated, upper-level, white-collar workers. The manner in which these parents respond to these indignities—resisting the meritocratic ideology of upward mobility through higher education—is based on their pride in working-class culture but nevertheless solidifies their own social-class location while laying the (negative) groundwork for their children's attitudes toward education.

Almost half of the forty working-class parents in the sample described worlds of pain (Rubin 1976) when they spoke about the "injuries" they experienced when interacting with members of the middle class in the home, school, and workplace. An example of the hidden injuries of class was related to me by a bridge painter. He said he was at a Christmas party with people he had nothing in common with. One guy [made the comment] that I didn't have to worry about work, that I did manual labor. That hit a spot there. Like I could go to McDonald's, there's no difference in what I did. It made me angry that he'd say something like that because here's a guy that got a college education that he's lucky to be making $16,000 a year and I could pull down $30,000 in six months and he's going to tell me there's no difference in what I do.

This man's response to his injury was to turn against higher education and college-educated individuals:

Still today I hold resentment for [people like this]. I call them "suits." I think they look down on me because I work with my hands and not sit behind a desk. I think this country would be in bad shape if everybody wanted to sit behind a desk. (age 34, male, unemployed bridge painter, high school degree)

As this man's comments suggest, members of the working class struggle to find dignity in a society that is quick to judge one's worth on the basis of income, educational credentials, and occupational prestige. The men and women in this segment of the working-class sample felt that they were more "work oriented"; white-collar, college graduates were seen as "pretentious." In describing his interactions (and injuries) with white-collar, college-educated coworkers, a maintenance worker said, "They have contests [among workers in the store] .... It doesn't involve [me] or the people that work on the docks." When asked how he feels about college-educated individuals, he replied,

The way I look at it if you want to have an easy life, have money in your pocket, and do no work, go to college. That aggravates me. College makes them feel above other people intelligence wise even though they just know a few fancier words, along with that comes the fine dress and the posture. They basically get in the way. If you took [us] and you took the people who went to college and you made two little separate cities, who's going to be living right? Who's going to build the houses and the plumbing? I am right. Let's face it, the college people need people like us more than we need them. (age 40, male, maintenance worker, some college courses in the army)

This parent rejected the notion that one needs a college degree to "make it" in America and is contemptuous of those individuals who hold college degrees and upper-level, white-collar occupations. Moreover, some working-class parents felt that middle-class, college graduates are "perpetual students"; they waste time and money in college just to get "a piece of paper" that does not guarantee a job. One working-class woman summarized these themes when she said,

> I have a niece who's gone through eight years of college for an MA in art and now she's a waitress. I baby-sit for professional people [a child psychologist] which I think have no common sense. They drive me crazy. They're book smart and life stupid. So they know everything about child psychology. I just looked at them [and how they were raising their child] and I was like, you're doing this all wrong. This is not common sense. (age 31, female, inventory clerk, high school degree)

For such parents, a college degree seems to be a waste of time because they know people who make as much or more money by using "common sense" as those with the "piece of paper"—the college degree. These working-class parents also thought that they were caring and down-to-earth, a (cultural) essence that separates them from middle-class, college-educated parents. It was not unusual for these working-class parents to criticize middle-class parents for putting careers ahead of family life:

> The doctor who makes $150,000 a year compared to the guy working in the same hospital buffing the floor for $6 an hour, [the doctor's] a father. The guy who's buffing the floor might be a daddy. Anybody can be a father, it takes someone special to be a daddy. (age 33, male, unemployed house painter, some community college courses)

This type of response alleviates some of the hidden injuries of class. The anger exhibited by some of the working-class parents in this study is symptomatic of the scars inflicted by their interactions with members of the middle class. This segment of the working class may have little respect for white-collar, college graduates, yet they realize they are in a constant struggle to win respect for their kind of work.

Analyzing the connections between the hidden injuries of class and parental attitudes toward education can also help us understand parental involvement in schooling. This segment of the working-class sample—those parents whose responses indicated they had experienced hidden injuries of class—reported being minimally involved in their children's schooling and were less likely to have college aspirations for their children (a community college, if any higher education) and more likely to proclaim the acquisition of common sense as equally important as acquiring a college degree. Consider the following comments from the clerical worker quoted above:

[My daughter's teacher] knows me [but] I don't bug her. I'm not like that. College isn't the only thing. I think if [children] have common sense they can accomplish anything. I think she'll probably go to college. I'm not going to push it. Two years of college—I'd be happy with that. (age 31, female, clerk, high school)

This is not to say that those in this segment of the working class do not value education; on the contrary, they put a high value on education—a good high school education, that is. They search for examples to reinforce their belief that high-paying jobs not requiring a college degree are still available. One working-class man said he was talking to a friend who had:

just bought 200 acres and a farm. He said he never went to college. I'm sitting on the front porch of his log cabin looking at 200 acres of land and I said to myself [with an exaggerated tone of voice and a touch of irony in his comment] god damn, he's a real stupid son of a bitch. There's a lot of education. Some you can't buy. (age 36, male, lawn maintenance, two years of college)

This man's beliefs, to some extent, reflect the uncertain position of the working class in a changing labor market. Today, with the economy continuing to change from a manufacturing base to a service economy, members of the working class seek out examples to sustain their belief and pride in "real work." Even though the media are filled with stories concerning the lack of high-paying blue-collar jobs, having a high income and/or knowing someone who did not attend college but who has a high income (or knowing someone who has a college degree and a low income) tends to reinforce in some members of the working class the belief that college is a waste of time and money.

NOTES ON THE HIDDEN INJURIES OF CLASS

Exploring certain aspects of the hidden injuries of class can help clarify the concept. What makes the accounts given by working-class parents interesting—and not explored enough by Sennett and Cobb (1972)—are the variety of settings where the injuries took place. Many of the injuries I found were directly work related. Consider the following comments from a secretary: "One boss used to belittle us. He was a pig. He said, 'I only hired you because you graduated from high school—it doesn't take a brain surgeon to work in a job like this'" (age 30, female, secretary/ clerical, AAS).

The injuries experienced at work may be carried over to other situations. For example, the bridge painter's comments cited earlier derive from his experiences at work; he reported how he felt interacting with college-educated, white-collar workers at a Christmas party and in the Navy. Other injuries occurred during the respondents' schooling:

> I hated school because I couldn't stand sitting there. I was a depressed teenager. School didn't fare me well; they just let me slip through the system. I never had anyone in school behind me pushing me. For two months, no one would ask me where were you for first period. Never went to class—went to one class. Nothing was ever done about it. They let me go from the ninth to eleventh grade without taking any exams. In high school we never had clothes, kind of wore the same pants every day—very depressing. I didn't even have a bra at one point to go to school with. [The] track kind of made you feel not important. Learned about drugs. Learned to skip school. They [Guidance] said the hell with me, let's put her through, eventually she'll drop out, and that's what I did. (age 35, female, part-time secretary, GED)

She now resents her college-educated coworkers, especially when they use "big words." This case represents an important aspect of the hidden injuries of class: they are felt by more than just males in blue-collar jobs. The pain even reaches into the lives of the children of working-class parents; a truck driver said the following:

> I took them out [of Catholic school] and put them in public school. Their social feeling of themselves wasn't too good. Cliquey school—very detrimental. Any friends they had always would look down on them, type of shoes they had, etc. I had them coming home crying, feeling real bad. Made us feel like a minority—tragic. (age 47, male, truck driver, high school)

Even standing in a line in a quiet bank is no guarantee that working-class resentment will not surface:

> I've walked into banks before and your yuppies look at you like you're the scum of the earth. I might be dirty. I said that to one of them. He's standing there in his suit, looking all pretty and shit. He's looking at me like I'm a

piece of scum. I said "you think you're so hot, you want to compare apples to apples buddy." He held out his paycheck and I showed him mine. He shut right up. I said there is nothing wrong with an honest day's work. (age 33, male, unemployed house painter, a few community college courses)

This account is an example of the many attempts made by members of a segment of the working class to assert their dignity in the face of the hidden injuries of class associated with structural (economic) realities. These injuries are the result of the interaction of social classes. Having middle-class contacts, then, not only does not guarantee that the working class will raise their educational aspirations (Halle 1984; Kahl 1953; Weis 1990), but it also may, in fact, increase working-class contempt for both the middle class and higher education.

Sennett and Cobb (1972) described the hidden injuries of class without talking about their genesis. What is it about the white-collar, college graduate that makes these working-class parents angry? This is not an easy question to answer, but three foci emerge from the interviews: middle-class language, middle-class clothing, and middle-class attitudes.

Several working-class respondents voiced their resentment at attempts by middle-class college graduates to showcase their language skills. Consider the following two comments: "My boss [is] very insulting. She talks with big words, and if you don't use a word right, she loves to insult people with that. [It makes me feel] very low" (age 35, female, secretary, GED). "My neighbors, they both went to college, talking to them, no matter how old I get, I feel like an awkward little teenager stumbling about [not] knowing what I'm talking about" (age 27, female, unemployed clerical, high school).

Indeed, it has been argued (Lareau and Lamont 1988) that a major effect of cultural capital and its contribution to maintaining class differences is its ability to exclude others. Teenagers are excluded from important conversations. Imagine the experience of continuing to feel that way as an adult; imagine how angry that experience may make one feel.

The middle-class, college graduate's manner of dress—especially the business suit—is another aspect of middle-class behavior that made some of the respondents angry. As noted above, one working-class man said, "I hold resentment for some people who wear suits. I call them 'suits.' I think they look down on me because I work with my hands and not sit behind a desk" (age 34, male, unemployed bridge painter, high school). Similarly, a working-class woman said, "A man comes in a three-piece suit and orders something and acts like he's better than you are. My job is not sitting behind a desk; I'm on my feet. I'm as good as he is?" (age 43, female, waitress, less than high school).

What is it about the business suit that irritates some members of the working class? I would argue that it has less to do with the suit per se than with what the suit symbolizes. Most working-class respondents have probably worn suits at different points in their lives but not to work. The business suit represents the ability of members of the middle class to command respect for their kind of work. The business suit in our society proclaims loudly that the wearer is involved in dignified work.

Finally, working-class parents complained about the attitudes that college-educated, white-collar workers have toward those without a college education. Which attitudes? Consider the following comments from a middle-class respondent:

> If you're asking whether I categorize people, I definitely do. If someone doesn't have a college education, I definitely view them differently, which is bad. I see them as a little bit less sophisticated. I see their views as a little narrower. They don't see the whole picture; sometimes I think they don't know what they are talking about because they're talking from a limited position, especially if they're talking about issues they haven't studied. (age 32, female, ex-counselor [not working outside home], master's degree)

In turn, working-class respondents reported they were aware of, and resented, this type of "pretentious" attitude. One working-class man said, "People who go to college try to look down on people who don't or haven't attended college" (age 33, male, unemployed house painter, some community college courses).

WORKING-CLASS PARENTS' ATTITUDES TOWARD EDUCATION: CONFORMITY

The other working-class respondents (approximately one half), by contrast, felt that a college degree is valuable. These working-class parents—the "confomists"—tended to have experienced fewer indignities related to their own schooling, their home life, and their workplace. Their accounts of their youth and adult lives, while not as glowing as the middle-class respondents, were somewhat upbeat: they enjoyed learning and studying in school, experienced a more settled home life, and had high self-esteem and future goals. For example, one man described his self-confidence during his schooling: "I was always confident; I never felt I would fail. I mean, my dad taught me in the sixth grade to read books [as soon as] I get them. There were times you don't have anything to do, you pick up a history book and read it" (age 35, male, carpenter, high school). Similarly, a working-class woman said, "I liked reading. I would read anything. I learned that there was a lot out there to do—doctor, lawyer, whatever. There is a possibility of doing it" (age 29, female, office clerk, presently in college at night).

A key to understanding this segment of the working class can best be illustrated by the following statement by an electrician:

> I want to keep on working [as an] electrician, eventually to own some property. I don't want to wear a shirt and tie to work, not have stress on me. I make $27 an hour. [I went] through an apprenticeship program and learn[ed] a trade they can't take away from [you]. (age 34, male, electrician, some college)

This man is able to resist the hidden injuries of the working class by drawing on the prestige associated with a "skilled" occupation. Interestingly, the attitudes of these parents toward education reflected their "settled living" (Howell 1972) arrangements: they were involved in their children's schooling: "I have been nominated for the school board. I want to know what the people that are in charge are thinking, and which direction they are taking the school and hopefully [I] can influence a little bit" (age 31, male, plumber, high school). Although some of these parents had mixed feelings toward higher education, they still wanted their children to acquire a college degree.

This group of working-class parents, in conforming to the ideology of upward mobility through higher education, did not resent college-educated, upper-level, white-collar workers as much as the other segment of the working-class sample. In fact, many of them either had some previous college experience or had just returned to college. One woman described how it felt to continue her education:

> At one point in my life, I actually saw my potential. I remember that moment. When I went to [a local four-year liberal arts college], I took a logic course and a Shakespeare course and I got As in both courses and I thought, I am smart, I really am smart. (age 36, female, health care aide, some college courses)

Some of these working-class parents, though, found it difficult to return to school. It is not easy to return to school once out of the competition; the working-class parents learned that lesson too late. One working-class woman is trying to finish her bachelor's degree at night while working at a full-time day job. She said, "Oh, I know I'm going to reach [my goal] at the cost of not paying so much attention to my kids. I really feel bad about that. That hurts" (age 29, female, clerk, currently attending college).

Many of the working-class respondents wanted to get a job and/or marry right out of high school for reasons related to their independence or financial situation but found out later that it was almost impossible to catch up to those who went to college immediately after high school. Nevertheless, studies that portray all members of the working class as living in worlds of pain have missed this segment of the working class.

VARIATIONS ON THE WORKING-CLASS THEME

There were a few working-class parents who did have negative experiences in school, at home, and in the workplace but still wanted their children to acquire a college education. For instance, one working-class parent said, "I'd love to see it, be a feather in my cap, be something [that would] make me proud, helping them get a better job than maybe I had. I started out as a gas jockey" (age 48, male, truck driver, GED).

These respondents are reminiscent of the working-class parents described by Connell et al. (1982)—parents who wanted their children to get a college education because their own schooling was deficient. Some other factors that offset the hidden injuries of class—prompting the working-class parents in the sample to become active in their children's education and to push their children toward acquiring a college degree— are having had at least one of their own parents work in a middle-class occupation and/or attain a college degree, or having a spouse with a middle-class occupation and/or a college degree. For example, one working-class man said that his college-educated wife had an influence on his educational attitudes, and a working-class woman implied that her early middle-class upbringing had an influence on her decision to return to college. One working-class man who initially said he did not care if his children went to college changed his mind in the middle of his answer when his college-educated wife entered the room. In fact, a few working-class parents—mostly the conformists—had mixed feelings concerning the benefits of a college education:

People have to go to college these days to make out or else he's going to wind up being a bum. If [my son] could get into some kind of mechanics thing without going to college he's going to make out well. I don't know if I would feel bad or not [if he does not attend college]. As long as he can survive and be happy. (age 38, female, clerk [currently not working outside the home], high school)

This woman's ambivalence could be interpreted to mean, in light of Sennett and Cobb's (1972) research, that she may want her child to "better himself" while not respecting the process (college degree) or outcome (white-collar job).

MIDDLE-CLASS PARENTS' ATTITUDES TOWARD EDUCATION: CONFORMITY AND THE CULTURE OF PROFESSIONALISM

The attitudes of the middle-class parents in the sample toward education are driven by what has been called "the culture of professionalism" (Bledstein 1976), in which the pursuit of higher education and a career are central to increasing one's social standing and wealth. The responses by the middle-class parents show how attitudes toward education are formed in an environment relatively free from the hidden injuries of class. In general, middle-class parents offered glowing accounts of childhood experiences and current occupational satisfaction. For most of these respondents, school experiences were reinforced at home by parents who were college educated and/or had upper-level, white-collar occupations. Professional and managerial occupations were held by other family members and friends, and the respondents' college education was seen by their own parents as a natural rite of passage. According to many of the middle-class respondents, their own parents assumed that they were going to attend college.

One middle-class woman, a policy analyst, said, "It was assumed—no question [laughs]. It wasn't a matter of would you go to college, but which college. It's not an issue [for my child]" (age 41, female, policy development specialist, master's degree). In turn, many of the middle-class respondents assume that their children will also attend college. A photographer for a local television station said, "I don't know if it [my child going to college] will mean anything because I assume he will. I think that I assume the same thing about them that I assumed for myself" (age 38, male, television news photographer, bachelor's degree). One middle-class man, a high-level civil service employee, even said,

Going to college would be sort of like a natural extension of things—I always thought [my son] would do that. I expected [him] to do that as much as I expected [him] to go from middle school to high school. The point I would really start getting excited is after college, after the bachelor's degree [when] they start picking fields that they really want to go further in. (age 40, male, high-level civil servant, master's degree)

Indeed, many of the middle-class parents thought that their children, especially in today's tight economy, should get at least a bachelor's degree for their careers and professions. In fact, college was not perceived by these middle-class parents as the setting where one must necessarily decide one's life pursuit. This attitude raises the educational ante: graduate school is becoming the setting where many middle-class careers take shape (see Collins 1979). How will these middle-class parents try to ensure that their children will go to college? One woman said, "I'll try to make it part of normal conversation" (age 43, female, teacher [currently not working], master's degree [working on doctorate]).

These accounts are quite different from the accounts of the working-class parents who not only did not assume they were going to attend college but actually assumed they were not going to attend college after high school. Furthermore, the working-class accounts usually followed gender role socialization patterns: working-class females dreamed of getting married ("I just wanted to get married and have kids") and working-class males planned to join the workforce ("I knew I was destined to be a worker"). In addition, the relative lack of information (see Lareau 1987) that working-class parents have concerning higher education hindered working-class youth. As one working-class woman said, "[There was no mention] of things like student loans were available. I wasn't aware and [my parents] didn't know either" (age 31, female, clerk, AAS).

Middle-class parents' memories of schooling were associated with all the amenities that can bolster self-confidence: getting good grades and "perks," being in the advanced track, participating in extracurricular events, having academically oriented friends, and having caring teachers and administrators. For example, a chemist remarked,

I like school a lot as a kid. I always did well. It was a college-prep high school. I got teachers who were pretty innovative. I knew I was going to go to college. I think I learned a lot and did extracurricular: ski club, math club, student council, national honor society. I can't think of one person I associated with in high school that didn't go to college. (age 34, female, chemist, bachelor's degree)

While working-class parents complained about events that left their basic educational needs wanting, some middle-class parents felt that a better education could have supplemented their current prestigious occupations.

In relation to careers, the middle-class response heard time after time was one of contentment: "[I want to be] doing what I'm doing right now—same thing—research, consultation work, working on meaningful studies and research in the field that I enjoy. I'm very content with what I'm doing" (age 41, female, academic/applied research, master's degree, working on a doctorate).

It is probably safe to say that most of the working-class respondents, especially those who have recently lost their jobs, would find it hard to believe that relatively young people could say they have "meaningful" jobs they "enjoy" and that they have reached their goals in life. There are the kinds of experiences—educational and occupational—found in a culture of professionalism that have an impact on the attitudes of middle-class parents toward education.

Whereas some working-class parents feared that they would pass their lifestyle on to their children, most middle-class parents feared that they would not to be pass their lifestyle on to their children. These middle-class parents, in conforming to the meritocratic ideology, hope to guarantee the same lifestyle for their children that they themselves had experienced: good grades, honor classes, high goals and aspirations, and a college degree.

It was a common belief among middle-class parents in the sample that one of the keys to guaranteeing a successful future for children is the involvement of parents in the children's schooling. Middle-class parents reported being very involved in their children's schooling, learning all there is to know to navigate the choppy waters of the bureaucracy of their children's schools. They felt that parents need to be advocates for their children, especially if the parents want their children to get an excellent education in an urban public school. One middle-class parent, a teacher, said,

> There are limited resources and the people who use the system work it to their advantage, leave the other kids in the dust. The case is that you get what you advocate for; you really have to be a strong advocate. If your kid is outstanding they're going to recognize him. If your kid is average, you have to be out there making sure you know what's happening. There's other kids whose parents never do that and who are left in the dust. If you're not there, your kid cannot get the same kind of education. (age 41, female, teacher, master's degree)

Middle-class parents have the credentials and confidence to challenge a teacher's decisions, a school's regulations and curriculum, and a school board's policies. Moreover, middle-class parents reported that they have social contacts with people employed in the field of education, which is not surprising given that school teachers and administrators live, for the most part, in middle-class neighborhoods. These social contacts give middle-class parents an edge in navigating their children's schooling.

As opposed to many of the working-class parents who wanted their children to acquire common sense, middle-class parents wanted to see their children embody the skills and attitudes related to the business world: communicative, quantitative, and interpersonal. In part, these attitudes are a reaction to both an economy changing from a manufacturing base to a service orientation and the fear of falling from the middle class (Ehrenreich 1989; Newman 1988), with some middle-class parents willing to make great sacrifices—time and money—to guarantee their children a college education. The parents felt that providing a four-year college degree was the least they could do to guarantee occupational success for their children:

> I feel it's an obligation of a parent [to send children to college]. If my children want to study, I will attempt to provide the funds to enable them to study. That is part of my function. My parents provided that for me. (age 38, male, lawyer, law degree)

This view reflects the strength of the middle-class "culture of professionalism" (Bledstein 1976) and the belief of this class in the benefits of a college degree. The possibility that their children would not attend college after high school was rarely acknowledged by middle-class parents. Consider the following comments.

In responding to the question, "How would you feel if your child(ren) does (do) not go to college?" a high-level civil service employee, after a few seconds of silence and with a shocked expression, said, "I can't imagine her saying it. I mean ... in fact ... she was surprised to find our college wasn't required. [She said] college isn't required? [I said] it is for you" (age 50, female, teacher/high-level civil service, doctorate). A former teacher responded to the same question: "That's not going to happen I don't see that happening. What I can see happening is [one of them] giving me a hard time about graduate school right away" (age 56, female, teacher [currently not working outside home], master's degree).

Some of the middle-class parents even felt it would be a sign that they had been a failure if their children did not acquire a college degree. For instance, a lawyer replied, "If they didn't go to college I would feel I failed. I'd go through all the reasoning. I didn't quite do the job; the expectation was that they would [go]" (age 44, male, high-level civil service, master's degree).

This man's comments reflect one of the hidden injuries of being middle class. It is this deeply held belief in the benefits of higher education that leads some of the middle-class respondents to judge people without a college education as unworthy of receiving a high income.

VARIATIONS ON THE MIDDLE-CLASS THEME

Although most middle-class parents wanted to see their children get a bachelor's degree, if not a graduate or professional degree, a small segment were beginning to question, if not the value of a college degree, at least the pursuit of a college degree from a prestigious institution: "Sometimes we say the kids [are] definitely going to go to state schools. [But] sometimes you see the networking that goes on in some of the other schools. We can't see paying the tuition that some other places charge" (age 34, female, chemist, bachelor's degree). It may be that the parents in this segment of the middle class cannot afford to send their children to a prestigious college and/or they do not think a college education gives one the advantage it once did. Nevertheless, they are interesting cases. These few parents appear to represent a slowly changing attitude among the middle class, brought on by a recession that affects white-collar as well as blue-collar occupations regarding the link between a college education and occupational success.

A NOTE ON GENDER DIFFERENCES

Some have argued that working-class adolescent resistance to schooling, while not gender specific, is more obvious, if not more prevalent, among males (McRobbie 1978; Weis 1990). Furthermore, it has recently been argued that adolescent resistance to schooling is related to gender and not social class (Davies 1993). Although I studied a broad sample of adults, the strongest forms of "resistance" to higher education I encountered were voiced by working-class men, and the most "conformist" working-class attitudes, even to the point of wanting to return to college, were more prevalent among women.

However, there were a significant number of working-class women who had contempt for white-collar, college graduates and a significant number of working-class men who wanted their children to attend college and acquire a white-collar job, so generalizations based on gender are not possible. In addition, middle-class men had highly conformist attitudes. It is possible that the discrepancy between my findings and those of Davies (1993) is related to the different populations we studied: working-class contempt—male and female—for white-collar, college graduates may not surface until individuals in the working class experience the workplace. Nevertheless, class and gender oppression do interact. One woman from the middle-class sample said, "I look back, I'll tell you a disappointment. No one told me when I was younger that I could have gone to law school and I'm very sorry about that. But my parents wanted my brother to go to law school" (age 56, female, retired teacher, master's degree). Although middle-class women reported few class-related injuries, women of both classes spoke of the hidden injuries of gender.

SUMMARY AND CONCLUSIONS

Due to the limited nature of the sampling strategy, most studies of social class in America have produced "either/or" results: working-class pain/no pain, working-class conformity/resistance, working-class valuing education/not valuing education, proletarianization of the working class/embourgeoisment of the working class (for exceptions, see Howell 1972; Komarovsky 1962; MacLeod 1987; McFadden 1995). Analyses of class-specific differences related to educational attitudes among parents have made significant contributions to the sociology of education (Lareau 1989; Rubin 1976; Sennett and Cobb 1972; Weis 1987; Willis 1977). These analyses, however, only highlight segments of the working class; some studies suggest the working class live in worlds of pain, experience hidden injuries of class, see their chances of upward mobility as slim, and resist the educational establishment, while other studies suggest that the working class value education and are raising their educational aspirations in response to a changing economy.

Working-class lifestyles are more complex than these studies suggest; a more inclusive sampling strategy proved useful in documenting the varied lifestyles and attitudes found among working-class parents. I found working-class parents who lived in worlds of pain along with working-class parents who lived settled lives. I found working-class parents who were not involved in their children's schooling along with working-class parents who were deeply involved in their children's education. I found working-class parents who rejected higher education along with working-class parents who conformed to the meritocratic ideology of using higher education to enhance their children's chances of upward mobility. I found working-class parents who wanted to pass their lifestyles on to their children along with working-class parents who did not want to do so. A distinct pattern emerged from the interviews: parents who experienced hidden injuries of class tended to harbor the most contempt for individuals with college degrees and/or upper-level, white-collar occupations. Working-class parents who live a more settled existence had a stronger commitment to higher education (with some being mildly ambivalent); this finding helps make sense of the conflicting research related to class-based educational aspirations. An understanding of the process by which hidden injuries of class affect the attitudes of parents toward their children's education is crucial for the social psychology of education.

Most of the arguments exploring the process by which attitudes toward education are shaped (Bowles and Gintis 1976; Kohn 1969; Rubin 1976; Sennett and Cobb 1972; Weis 1987) rely on the perception of the parents to the changing economy. Indeed, some of the working-class parents in this study did speak about the need for their children to pursue a college education in today's job market. This is not an easy issue, though, for parents whose self-esteem has been battered by the world of the college-educated, white-collar worker; such parents do not always respond to the vagaries of the economy. So even though local newspaper and television reports cite the statistical advantages of obtaining a college degree in a changing economy, these parents still insist their children can be successful by pursuing traditional blue-collar occupations and using a little common sense. Thus, in an attempt to restore dignity by drawing on culturally valued meanings of success, the resistance to higher education exhibited by many working-class parents helps solidify their social-class position and may ultimately solidify their children's social-class position.

Weis (1987) has argued that members of the working class are slowly raising their educational aspirations due to the deindustrialization of America. That indeed may be true for some of the working-class respondents in this study; nevertheless, many of them still reject higher education—while placing a high value on a solid high school education—and resent those who hold college degrees and upper-level white-collar occupations.

Other factors that differentiated the working-class respondents' attitudes were the social-class composition of the marriages and the social class of the respondents' parents. A wide spectrum of working-class lifestyles exists in the real world; one must use an inclusive sampling strategy to find them.

This study, unlike many previous studies of the working class, had a comparative sample of middle-class respondents. Middle-class parents were much more homogenous than working-class parents in their view of American education and its impact on occupational success. A culture of professionalism drives the attitudes of middle-class parents toward education. This study has documented the taken-for-granted attitudes that members of the middle class have toward education; they assume that their children will go to college, possibly graduate school, and make good lives for themselves. To guarantee that their children will be ready for college, middle-class parents will make great sacrifices and put a lot of time and effort into shaping their children's educational experiences, whether it requires giving their children subtle hints about the benefits of a college education or advocating for their children at the school site.

Still, even a few of these middle-class parents were beginning to question the validity of a college degree, especially lower middle-class parents whose responses resembled working-class responses to many questions. Does this particular finding give credence to Halle's (1984) argument that middle-class and working-class lifestyles and attitudes are slowly converging? Only in the sense that there seems to be a segment of both the working class and the middle class that are ambivalent about the benefits of a college degree. Ironically, at the same time some working-class parents are raising their educational aspirations for their children, some middle-class parents are ostensibly reconsidering their beliefs in the benefits of a college degree. Therefore, the focus should not be on whether the working class is becoming more like the middle class or vice versa but should be on how the effects of the depressed wages of the past twenty years drive some members of both social classes to reconsider their attitudes toward higher education. The other two groups—middle-class parents who have a nearly "religious" belief in the benefits of a college degree and working-class parents who have contempt for college-educated, white-collar workers—are steadfast in their particular beliefs, showing no movement toward the other.

This study has replicated, modified, and given new insight into certain aspects of social reproduction theory. Some researchers of working-class lifestyles have noted that the working class, in their struggle for meaning and dignity, become frustrated, angry, and bitter (Rubin 1976; Sennett and Cobb 1972), leading them to denigrate white-collar work and extol blue-collar work (Halle 1984). These studies did not, however, tie this resistance to a larger theory of social-class reproduction. Other writers have tied working-class resistance to social-class reproduction but limited their studies to adolescence and schooling (Connell et al. 1982; Everhart 1983; MacLeod 1987; Weis 1987; Willis 1977). Both of these research traditions—working-class family studies and social reproduction studies—contribute significantly to the field, but there has been little attempt to link them in any meaningful way. I have provided evidence suggesting that the family is an important site for cultural production (resistance) and social reproduction.

These findings do not minimize the importance of research into adolescent peer cultures. Adolescent peer cultures also are important sites of production and reproduction of educational aspirations. Children and adolescents produce and reproduce peer cultures inside and outside schools that reflect not only their parents' values but their concerns and reactions to how they are treated by educators on a daily basis, which strongly shapes their academic achievement and future aspirations (Corsaro and Eder 1990). In addition, the messages that youth get about education from families and peer cultures may be similar or dissimilar. Thus, family influence operates along with peer culture influence, and both can operate outside of school sites (Eckert 1989; Kinney 1993; Luttrell 1992; Rosier and Corsaro 1993).

Willis (1977) has argued that working-class youth partially "penetrate" the meritocratic ideology, recognize that their chances for upward mobility are slim, reject schooling, and accept manual labor—thus reproducing social-class relations. Although ambivalent about the future, many of the parents in the present study—middle class and working class, conformist and nonconformist—believe that high-paying blue-collar jobs are still available, and that it is still possible to achieve upward mobility through hard work. This study suggests, then, that working-class parents' attitudes toward higher education are based, in part, on their search for dignity in a capitalistic society. The injuries that many working-class parents encounter during that search—at school, in the family, and at work—lead them to reject higher education.

To think that resistance to schooling takes place exclusively at schools misses an institution equally important for social reproduction: the family. The attitudes of parents toward higher education have the potential to influence their children's attitudes toward higher education, their children's chances of obtaining a college degree, and their own chances of returning to school. The resistance and/or conformity of parents to the meritocratic ideology of using higher education as a means of upward mobility must be considered in any discussion of the relationship between the family and the school or any theory of social-class reproduction.

REFERENCES

Anyon, Jean. 1980. "Social class and the hidden curriculum of work." *Journal of Education* 162:67–92.

Berger, Bennett M. 1960. *Working class suburb*. Berkeley: University of California Press.

Bledstein, Burton J. 1976. *The culture of professionalism: The middle class and the development of higher education in America*. New York: Norton.

Bourdieu, Pierre. 1977. "Cultural reproduction and social reproduction." In *Power and ideology in education*, edited by Jerome Karabel and A.H. Halsey. New York: Oxford University Press.

———. 1984. *Distinction: A social critique of the judgement of taste*. Cambridge, MA: Harvard University Press.

———. 1988a. "Social space and symbolic power." *Sociological Theory* 6:14–25.

Bourdieu, Pierre (as recorded by Loic J. D. Wacquant). 1988b. "Towards a reflexive sociology: A workshop with Pierre Bourdieu." *Sociological Theory* 6:26–63.

Bourdieu, Pierre, and Jean Claude Passerson. 1977. *Reproduction in education, society, and culture*. London: Sage.

Bowles, Samuel, and Herbert Gintis. 1976. *Schooling in capitalist America*. New York: Basic Books.

Cave, Ronald G. 1970. *Partnership for change*. London: Ward Lock Educational.

Coleman, James S., and Thomas Hoffer. 1987. *Public and private high schools*. New York: Basic Books.

Collins, Randall. 1979. *The credential society*. New York: Academic Press.

Connell, R. W., D. J. Ashenden, S. Kessler, and G. W. Dowsett. 1982. *Making the difference: Schools, families, and social division*. Sydney, Australia: Allen and Unwin.

Corsaro, William A., and Donna Eder. 1990. "Children's peer cultures." *Annual Review of Sociology* 16:197–220.

Craft, Maurice, Johm Raynor, and Louis Cohen, eds. 1972. *Linking home and school*. London: Longman.

Davies, Scoff. 1993. "Exploring class reproduction through cultural resistance in Ontario high schools." Paper presented at the annual meeting of the American Sociological Association, August, Miami, Florida.

Eckert, Penelope. 1989. *Jocks and burnouts: Social categories and identity in the high school*, New York: Teachers College Press, Columbia University.

Ehrenreich, Barbara. 1989. *Fear of falling: The inner life of the middle class*. New York: Pantheon.

Everhart, Robert B. 1983. *Reading, writing, and resistance: Adolescence and labor in a junior high school*. Boston: Routledge Kegan Paul.

Gans, Herbert J. 1962. *The urban villagers*. New York: Free Press.

Giroux, Henry A. 1981. "Hegemony, resistance, and the paradox of educational reform." *Interchange* 12:3–26.

Giroux, Henry A., and Roger I. Simon, eds. 1989. *Popular culture, schooling, and everyday life*. Westport, CT: Bergin and Garvey.

Gorman, Thomas J. 1994. *Social class and parental attitudes toward education: Resistance and conformity*. Ph.D. diss., State University of New York, Stony Brook.

Halle, David. 1984. *America's working man*. Chicago: University of Chicago Press.

Henderson, Anne. 1987. *The evidence continues to grow*. Columbia: NCCE.

Howell, Joseph T. 1972. *Hard living on Clay Street*. New York: Anchor.

Kahl, J. A. 1953. "Educational and occupational aspirations of 'common man boys.'" *Harvard Educational Review* 23(3):186–203.

Kinney, David A. 1993. "From nerds to normals: The recovery of identity among adolescents from middle school to high school." *Sociology of Education* 66:21–40.

Kohn, Melvin L. 1969. *Class and conformity*. Belmont, CA: Dorsey.

Komarovsky, Mirra. 1962. *Blue collar marriage*. New York: Vintage.

Komblum, William. 1974. *Blue collar community*. Chicago: University of Chicago Press.

Lareau, Annette. 1987. "Social class differences in family-school relationships." *Sociology of Education* 60:63–72.

———. 1989. *Home advantage: Social class and parental intervention in elementary education*. London: Falmer.

Lareau, Annette, and Michele Lamont. 1988. "Cultural capital: Allusions, gaps and glissandos in recent theoretical developments." *Sociological Theory* 6:153–68.

Levitan, Sar A. 1971. *Blue collar workers*. New York: McGraw-hill.

Lindsay, Catherine. 1969. *School and community*. London: Pergamon.

Luttrell, Wendy. 1992. "Working-class women's way of knowing: Effects of gender, race, and class." In *Education and gender equity*, edited by Julia Wrigley. London: Falmer.

MacLeod, Jay. 1987. *Ain't no makin' it: Leveled aspirations in a low-income neighborhood*. Boulder, CO: Westview.

Marsden, Dennis. 1962. "Education and the working class." In *Linking home and school*, edited by Maurice Craft, John Raynor, and Louis Cohen. London: Longman.

McFadden, Mark G. 1995. "Resistance to schooling and educational outcomes: Questions of structure and agency." *British Journal of Sociology of Education* 16:293–308.

McRobbie, Angela. 1978. "Working class girls and the culture of femininity." In *Women take issue*, edited by Women Studies Groups CCCS, 96–108. London: Women's Studies Group.

National Center for Education Statistics. 1982. *High school and beyond.* Washington, DC: National Center for Education Statistics.

Newman, Katherine S. 1988. *Failing from grace: The experience of downward mobility in the American middle class.* New York: Free Press.

Ogbu, John U. 1978. *Minority education and caste.* New York: Academic Press.

Oppenheimer, Valerie Kincade. 1982. *Work and the family.* New York: Academic Press.

Rosier, Katherine Brown, and William A. Corsaro. 1993. "Competent parents, complex lives." *Journal of Contemporary Ethnography* 22:171–204.

Rubin, Lillian Breslow. 1976. *Worlds of pain: Life in the working-class family.* New York: Basic Books.

———. 1994. *Families on the faultline: America's working-class speaks about the family, the economy, race, and ethnicity.* New York: HarperCollins.

Scott, James C. 1990. *Domination and the arts of resistance.* New Haven, CT: Yale University Press.

Sennett, Richard, and Jonathan Cobb. 1972. *The hidden injuries of class.* New York: Vintage.

Sewell, W. H., A. O. Haller, and A. Portes. 1969. "The educational and early occupational attainment process." *American Sociological Review* 34:82–92.

Shostak, Arthur B. 1969. *Blue collar life.* New York: Random House.

Stacey, Judith. 1990. *Brave new families: Stories of domestic upheaval in late twentieth century America.* New York: Basic Books.

Weis, Lois. 1987. "The 1980's: Deindustrialization and change in White working class male and female use cultural forms." *Metropolitan Education* 5:82–117.

———. 1990. *Working class without work.* New York: Routledge.

Willis, Paul. 1977. *Learning to Labor: How working-class kids get working-class jobs.* Aldershot, England: Gower.

———. 1981. "Cultural production is different from cultural reproduction is different from social reproduction is different from reproduction." *Interchange* 12:48–67.

Wright, Eric Olin. 1978. *Class, crisis and the state.* London: Verso.

	Middle	Working
Gender by Class		
Male	20	18
Female	20	22
Age by Class		
20–30	2	5
31–40	23	25
41–50	12	9
51–60	2	1
Education by Class		
Less than high school	0	2
GED	0	2
High school graduate	2	10
High school + vocational training	1	2
Some college (any course work)	1	20
Associate degree	2	2
Bachelor degree	11	2
Graduate degree	23	0
Family Yearly Income by Class		
Less than $12,700	0	6
$12,700–$20,000	0	0
$20,001–$30,000	1	11
$30,001–$40,000	5	9
$40,001–$50,000	7	7
$50,001–100,000	21	7
$100,000+	5	0
Housing by Class		
Own home	35	24
Rent	5	16
Marital Status by Class		
Single	5	0
Married	29	35
Separated	1	3
Divorced	5	2

(continued)

(continued)

	Number of Children in the Family by Class	
	Middle	Working
1	7	5
2	18	17
3	6	10
4	4	1
5	2	3
6+	3	4

	Age of Oldest Child in the Family by Class	
	Middle	Working
Less than 5	7	5
5	3	3
6–12	15	16
13–17	7	7
18+	8	8

A COMPARISON OF MY RESEARCH TO MY OWN EDUCATIONAL CAREER

When thinking back to my own parents' attitudes toward education, there are two distinct orientations that shine through. First, my parents wanted me to do well in school—elementary school and high school. The passing grade at SSS at that time was 75 percent, and any grade of mine lower than a 90 percent was looked upon askance by my parents. With a stern warning, my mother would say "Wait till your father gets home"; never mind that he had dropped out of school in the tenth grade. That is probably why they wanted me to do well in school. To be sure, on many nights during elementary school, my mom would have me redo my homework if she deemed it too sloppy. Keep in mind that this was a Catholic school where, at that time, neat penmanship was next to godliness. Interestingly, she later found little problem with my attending a public high school where penmanship was not as valued. When I asked my son's first-grade public school teacher about his poor penmanship, she reassured me that I should not worry, since he will probably use a computer for the rest of his life. If only we had known then what we now know, it would have made my life much easier, because my poor, left-handed writing was looked upon suspiciously.

My home lacked the kind of cultural capital which was found in many middle-class homes (no one ever read to me as a child), and which has been documented by researchers (see Lareau 1989) as being necessary to prepare for college and foster academic excellence. It is true that a number of my working-class friends attended Catholic—college preparatory—high schools in New York City, but it is difficult to pull apart those who went to those schools for religious reasons from those who attended because they were college preparatory schools. In that time and place, I would guess that quite a few attended those schools because it satisfied the parents' religious proclivities, and because those schools were seen as more orderly and disciplined (with racial overtones involved, too, as most public high schools in New York City were viewed as poor because there were too many non-whites in attendance). In like manner, my wife recounts her (working-class) mother not liking the idea of her attending college—until her mom visited St. Bonaventure in the Southern Tier of New York State, and saw a statue of the Virgin Mary as they entered the campus. My parents were even unaware of the existence of the "technical" (college bound) track in my high school, which would have given me a chance of (and an understanding of the importance of) attending college. Basically, they assumed the opposite of what I found to be a significant pattern among middle-class and upper-middle-class parents: that I was not going to attend college. This may come as a shock to some middle-class readers, but where were my parents going to pick up those attitudes toward education? They had not attended college, my older brother had not attended college right out of high school (he attended Queens College as an adult), and there were just one or two individuals from the neighborhood who had, in fact, attended college.

When I applied to a college after high school—a vocationally oriented community college, at that—my parents were supportive; the program was for only two years, it was a commuter school (with no housing bills), it was *free*, and it was a *vocational* program. Previously, I noted how shocked middle-class parents would probably be if they were told their children would spend four to five periods of high school, and most of their children's first two years of college, in vocationally oriented courses. Well, it would be as incredulous for my parents to find out for how much time middle- and upper-middle-class parents invest in their children's education (as found in my study) to get their children into the best schools—from pre-school up to and including college.

Eventually, middle-class parents (tend to) help their children pick out and pay for Advanced Placement courses, help them write their personal essays, pay for college consultants to craft the perfect college entrance letter, pay for SAT preparation courses (which can cost $500 an hour in Manhattan), and then, ultimately, pay for room and board for four years at the top colleges in the United States (today approaching $60,000).

This is where talk about being from Mars and Venus is appropriate. My own parents' "resistance" to (higher) education first reared its head when I decided to return to school to study for a bachelor's degree in sociology at Queens College. Then, my pursuit of an MSW was able to mitigate some of my parents' concerns, but the extra two years of schooling it would take did not totally sit well with them. They really didn't understand fully what a career in social work meant. When I decided to leave the MSW program and start a PhD in sociology, it left them totally perplexed about my future plans. In fact, to the day my mom passed away, she would still tell anyone who asked her about me that I was studying to be a social worker. Being a social worker had some meaning to them: my dad was in the hospital a few times for his alcoholism, and my mom had to deal with social workers when she had to apply for food stamps and SSI (Supplementary Security Income) benefits later in life, when my dad's drinking started to cut into the number of days he could drive a taxi, and therefore their income. In time I tried to explain what a professor does, teaching a few courses for two or three days each week across two semesters each year, doing research and service to the university. My dad replied, "Why don't you get a real fucking job?" That was not the reasoning of Dr. Huxtable on *The Cosby Show*. After receiving my first full-time, tenure track position, however, my father was very proud, repeating over and over "My son is a professor." He was a good man, underneath all the alcohol.

In retrospect, it is very apparent that a number of people in my surrounding environment had mixed feelings toward education. Just recently, a fairly close relative of mine said to me, after I told her about my current career, "What do you want me to do, give you a medal?" At first I was taken aback; I had let down my "academic guard"—I had forgotten they were *working-class* family members. Even my own mom finally had to admit to her reservations about academia, when I was explaining to her the significance of one of my early research papers. She tried to look interested, but finally asked, "What good is any of that?"

My previous research pointed out that many members of the working class are very sensitive about their lack of higher educational credentials. This social fact continues to be part of the hidden injuries of class (Sennett and Cobb 1972). Remember, my mother-in-law attempted to talk my wife out of applying to college altogether (see Rubin 1976 for a discussion about this kind of behavior.). In contrast my father-in-law, a production line worker for Kodak, had supported my wife going off to college. Interestingly, he had had some contact with people at work who had sent their children to college, an indirect means of acquiring cultural capital.

And he knew that the people who had "good jobs" (as he would say) had attended college. He wasn't exactly sure what those jobs were about or the precise connection between going to college and acquiring those jobs, but he nevertheless supported my wife's application. Today, some of my relatives still laugh and talk about being "a lifetime student" when they find out that one of my sons is "still" pursuing a PhD in physics. One relative in particular loves to tell the story of one of his friends who, even though he taught at a local Catholic high school, had not finished his bachelor's degree, as if to convince himself of the uselessness of a college degree. In addition, when my mother-in-law visited my wife at work, seeing the usual bevy of people typing away on their computers behind cubicle screens, she asked, "Why isn't anyone working?" They were "working," but they weren't "working" in a way that she knew from her working-class position as a cashier in a department store. She did, however (as did another working-class relative), keep extensive paper records of her daily activities, like if she had worked as a clerk in an office. This attitude, disrespecting (and for some working-class individuals respecting) white-collar, college-educated workers, was highlighted in my research (also see Halle 1984; Lareau 1989). Recent research suggests that many members of the working class still aren't convinced of the benefits of a college education (See Longman 2017). That could possibly be because of the cost now associated with a college degree. Nevertheless, the data indicate the continued financial benefits of a college degree (if not the effects of college on the overall development of students; see Feldman and Newcomb (1969), and Pascarella and Terenzini (1992), for the best summaries of the research in this area).

The attitudes my parents held toward education was reflected in their overall orientation toward life. My mother was very sensitive to anyone she thought was "looking down on her." This manifested itself in a number of ways. One particular incident stands out in my mind. When I moved out to Stony Brook, Long Island for my graduate studies, my mom looked around at the (upper-middle-class) neighborhood and wondered out loud, "Where is everyone?" She then speculated that "they must be peeking out their windows at us"—being very "snooty" people. As pointed out in my research, members of the working class look for examples in their own lives to support their attitudes toward the middle class in general, and toward higher education in particular (with stories about college-educated people only able to get jobs driving taxis, for example). These attitudes can again be explained by the lack of confidence among working-class individuals, which motivates them to lash out at higher education and at the kind of work in which the middle class are involved. Ultimately, however, these attitudes can come back to haunt them, in that they and their children may not attend college. Thus, upward social mobility is thwarted, keeping social class relations unchanged.

I have argued elsewhere (Gorman 1998a, b) that there are a variety of settings and situations where these injuries take place—involving clothing, language, and interactions with middle- and upper-middle-class individuals. In my research, a sensitive topic for members of the working class concerns the "big words" that college-educated people use. These words are another illustration of the middle class really only being "book smart" and "life stupid," as a few working-class respondents noted. A related, but little-studied, area of working-class life is the conversational error known as a malapropism—misusing a word that sounds the same as another word. Without a doubt, the character held up as the working-class hero of malapropisms was Archie Bunker in the 1970s television sitcom *All in the Family* (set in a working-class section of Queens, NY). In my own working-class social world some family members and friends would, on occasion, use a variation on a word or phrase. While they all are not technically malapropisms, they are examples of the working class misusing and mispronouncing words. One relative spoke about "sapeenies" (subpoenas), while another liked to take "Tabit-d" (Tavist-d) for a cold, and my own mother would say that she "bunked" (meaning "bumped") into someone on the street. It wasn't until I was 26 years old that someone corrected me on that one. And in my neighborhood, if a girl was thought to be sexually active with more than one boy, she might get a reputation of being a "who-a" (whore).

How can we explain the use of malapropisms and other misuse of words among some members of the working class? On the one hand, it could be as simple as the different educational experiences of the middle and working classes. It could, on the other hand, be a product of the working class's infrequent use of certain words and phrases. These explanations may have some merit, but my research (and life experiences) suggests that malapropisms are just another method by which some members of the working class sometimes show their disrespect for "book learning" and white-collar work—sort of like giving the "elite" a poke in the eye. People who mispronounce words are actually, in their own way, making fun of and fighting back against those college-educated individuals who use "big words" because even when their errors were pointed out, working-class family and friends would continue to misuse those words. We started to hear more about white working-class resentment during the 2016 Presidential election, but I discovered it in the early 1990s.

Those in the working class rebel, in different ways, against an educational and economic system that has put them well behind others (for a discussion of resistance theory, see Willis 1981; Macleod 1987). They feel as if they played by the rules and worked hard at difficult jobs, but they have not seen the same income and benefits as others who, just because "they have a piece of paper" (a college degree), seem to live better lives.

A couple of working-class respondents in my research voiced such opinions. One man in particular asked me, "When did the rules of the game change? When did it become a requirement that one needs a college degree in order to live a decent life?" Indeed, the most pernicious aspect of the effects of social class on people's lives may be what it keeps hidden from them. Much of what I have discussed in this book, in fact, is about the hidden injuries of class. Again, how were we supposed to know what it would really take to attain upward social mobility? A friend of mine from the old neighborhood recently said to me that he "didn't know there was a race taking place."

Going to the right schools, and living in the right neighborhood matter only in a society where working-class ways of life have been devalued. My aunt, who had a chance to interact with the upper-middle and upper classes (in her job as an office manager in a large corporation), always talked about feeling somewhat inferior to them at work-related gatherings. Why? She felt inferior because "those people" had college degrees, and could speak about topics and issues that she knew little about, such as the new paintings being put up in the office or the favorite pieces of literature being discussed at cocktail parties. Even members of the working class who rise up into the professions, such as the professoriate, talk about feelings of inferiority when surrounded by a majority of middle-class colleagues (see Ryan and Sackrey 1984; Dews 1995 for a discussion of academics from the working class).

The current recommendation for women to "lean in" at work is based on the belief that women lack the confidence necessary to break the glass ceiling. The working class face the same problem, and working-class women have to fight especially hard. Yet, leaning in is not easy when lacking self-confidence. Quite often, the response when facing dominant others is to "lean back," with a less successful outcome. And (resistance) research has suggested that the working class respond not by leaning in, nor leaning back, but by moving directly *against* the socially approved ways of attaining success, thus reproducing their social class position. When Willis (1981) found that boys understood that the system was not working for them, they did not work twice as hard to get by; instead, they goofed off, had laughs, threw spit balls and erasers at teachers and the like. Sad, but true. Their stock of cultural capital contained only those types of responses. How could it have turned out any other way? I see my own educational career as a possible alternative to this kind of bitterness and resistance. Nevertherless, it is not an easy task to choose an alternative to resistance—working-class anger and frustration are real and I feel them myself sometimes. They have to be harnessed and funneled properly.

Even the way members of the middle class dress has been seen by the working class as another way they are 'looked down' upon by the middle class. As I found in my own research on working-class attitudes, some of the people in my old neighborhood called anyone who had a white-collar job a "stuffed suit." That was a put-down, a way of saying that those people may have better-paying jobs, with higher status and prestige, but in reality they are just self-important. Being "real" was a cherished value in the old neighborhood. You have to be able to explain to yourself and to others why you have the job and the lifestyle that you do.

My own journey, as noted previously, has been marked by a lack of self-confidence. When I found out that Edison was a vocational high school I felt secure; when I found out that NYCCC was vocationally oriented I felt better; but when I went to Baruch College at night and found students in suits, ties, and holding briefcases, I dropped out; and when I heard that Queens College was considered the jewel of the CUNY system, I worried, although I knew it was still a CUNY school. It was a feeling similar to the saying attributed to Groucho Marx: "I wouldn't want to belong to any club that would have me as a member." However, when I got divorced, I started to take a different attitude toward higher education and my future: I did get angry, but instead of getting involved in drugs, crime, or scapegoating other groups, I decided to go back to college. Yes, I fought back, but in a socially approved manner, thus leading to upward social mobility. Is that selling out? Well, you have to be in the game to help fight it. Why did I take that approach? There were many factors: by then I was 26 years old, my brother had started a college program and was interested in politics, a couple of friends were attending college (later in life also), more people in general were going to college, and we were working class, not poor, so we had some contact with the middle class (the job I took after community college put me into contact with college-educated coworkers).

Nevertheless, it is not easy to tame your anger after experiencing the hidden injuries of class. For example, one particular professor at Hunter criticized a paper I had written for her class. Instead of seeing this, as I should have in a professional setting, as a learning experience, I packed my books and left the program so angry that I cried while walking down Atlantic Avenue. It was an "aha" moment, but my (working-class-based) conclusion at first was, "I knew it, I don't belong here." I wondered whether all the previous professors who had such high praise for my academic work—including the professor in charge of the Social Policy program at Hunter College, who begged me to stay—had been wrong. Structure and agency are constantly shaping and reshaping our constraints and opportunities.

Many professors at Queens College had written very positive comments on my papers; a few of them had even written "thank you," and as a college professor now, I know what they mean. This encouraged me to apply for a doctoral program in sociology. It was a very difficult decision. It would take an awful long time to complete such a program, and I was already 30 years old. Yet, life is funny sometimes. My divorce had given me a bit of a controlled "what the hell" approach to life for a period of time—I had even hitchhiked across the country and back with just a small shoulder sack. So I applied, and two graduate programs in sociology accepted me with funding: the University of Indiana (ranked about 8th in the country at the time) and the State University at Stony Brook (ranked 14th). The director of the program at Indiana called me a couple of times to see if I was interested, but a few of the Queens College faculty told me that Indiana was quantitatively oriented, which was not what I preferred. I think helping Dr. Patricia Kendall put together an author and subject index for a book on Paul Lazersfeld had impressed both universities. She thanked me in the acknowledgments page in her book about Paul Lazersfeld right after she thanked Dr. Robert Merton, probably the most renowned sociologist alive at the time! What a boost to my confidence that was—she even told me I should have been awarded a PhD just for the research I had conducted on graduate programs in sociology.

So I began a Ph.D. program in sociology at Stony Brook University on Long Island, N.Y., which was more of a shock culturally than academically. On July 4, 1984, I moved to the suburbs for the first time in my life. There was not a person to be found on those upper-middle-class streets on that Independence Day, when the streets of City Line would have been rocking, literally, with stoops filled with people and tables full of food. And where the heck were the sidewalks?

During my first semester I had the chance to take a class in sociological theory with one of the nicest individuals and a living legend in sociology—Dr. Louis Coser. For the final paper for his course, I chose to compare Karl Marx and Max Weber. Receiving a poor grade on that paper could have sent me packing, back home again. When I saw the graded paper in a pile of papers in the mail room in the Department of Sociology, I noticed that at the top of the page he had written these words: "SOLID PAPER." That moment, more than any other, sent me in a career direction that I could never have predicted just a few years earlier. A few other graduate students had dropped Coser's course because they found him (his name) too intimidating, but I found him to be such a nice human being. So I thought, if one of the leading social theorists alive at the time (if not *the* leading social theorist along with Merton) said my paper was solid, then maybe I could get through the program.

During my time as a graduate student, I took a year off from sociology to complete the requirements for the New York State Certification in Social Studies (grades 7–12). It was a way to investigate, first hand, many of the concepts and theories in the sociology of education. Furthermore, I thought it might come in handy as a back-up career if I did not finish the PhD. Oh yes, that lack of self-confidence is tough to escape. While completing my student teaching (in a better high school than I had attended), I interacted daily with the "cool" kids. To my surprise, in this upper-middle-class community, those who were considered cool were the high achievers (Regents level and above). It would be interesting to see what my old buddies from Edison—or my old neighborhood—would think about that social fact.

After a stint as an assistant and then associate professor at Queensborough Community College and Queens College (a joint appointment), I am now based solely at Queens College—and I am still trying to prove my worth. It is a difficult task to make up that time spent pursuing a career in the printing industry. (It was a pleasure to teach at a CUNY community college; it gave me the opportunity to give back to the community in which I began my studies in sociology.) And I don't know if I would want to—those years gave me a working-class perspective that helps me interact with many of my students and provide them with good examples in my lessons. The effects of social class are ongoing: I am still about ten years behind where I should be in academia given my age (see Ryan and Sackrey 1984; Dews 1995 for problems that academics from the working class encounter). Now, during advisement, I tell my students to "reach for the stars" (the title of the handbook I had at Queens College as a student). Truly, I can tell them that I stood in their shoes (and sat in their seats). It is very satisfying, and not a cliché at all, to try to give back to my community, to help my students believe in themselves, as a number of people in my life have done for me.

CHAPTER 5

Friends, Girlfriends, and Sports: The Injuries Escalate and Become Personal

FRIENDS

After schooling, peers and friends—male and female—constitute most of a young person's social world. Yet, for some working-class youths—such as myself—it can be a time when the effects of social class "injuries" escalate, and get personal. In *The Hidden Injuries of Class* (1972), the authors posit that "The 'putdowns' adolescents practice on each other have this same motivation: if a kid can make a witty crack about someone else that makes the other feel inept or bumbling, he stands out" (p. 65).

In City Line and Ozone Park, one's friends were determined mostly by the block in which one lived. Since I grew up on 76th Street, most of my friends were from 76th Street. Still, as previously mentioned, those boundaries included only the kids I befriended from 76th Street between 101st Avenue and 97th Avenue (refer to Map 1.2). The children who lived on the next block, 76th Street but between 97th Avenue and 95th Avenue, were considered to be our rivals. That may seem strange to someone from the suburbs or a small town, where one's main friends may be kids from various parts of town. Interestingly, the Census Bureau defines a block differently from the way most people in my old neighborhood would. For example, I lived on the block that included the east side of 76th Street and the west side of 77th Street, as defined by the census. However, to us our "block" included the east side of 76th Street between 101st and 97th Avenues, and the west side of 75th Street.

© The Author(s) 2017
T.J. Gorman, *Growing up Working Class*,
DOI 10.1007/978-3-319-58898-8_5

143

You could make other friends at school, but those kids, for the most part, were not the ones you hung out with for any length of time after school, on weekends, and in the summer. My friends from SSS and Edison were secondary to those from 76th Street. Nonetheless, it was my friends from school, especially high school, who helped me reshape my identity and leave behind some painful experiences. Just going around the corner to 75th Street allowed me to leave behind a couple of painful "friendships." That might not be possible in a suburban/rural environment—going around the corner may not be much of a "move" at all—but in that time and place it was very rebellious. One of my friends from 76th Street, who later followed me to that same block, told me he was surprised by my change of scene, and that I should have talked to him beforehand.

At first I had just two friends: a boy who lived two "doors" (row housing) from me and a girl who lived four doors away. They lived on the same side of the street as me, and that turned out to be a good thing, because I wasn't allowed to cross the street yet. The boy moved around the corner, a universe away; and the girl started hanging out with other friends on other blocks. She was my first big crush, but I was way too shy ever to tell her. A couple of my "friends" would tease me about her no end.

As time went on I developed a number of other friends on 76th Street. Remember, this time period corresponded to the peak years of the baby boom. What this meant, on a day-to-day basis, was that there were plenty of kids on each block, but they were stratified by age and sex. Back then, in that place, parents did not plan "playdates" as they do today. (Even the idea of a playdate back then makes me laugh; there were also few, if any, day care centers, and almost no one went away to summer camp because there were more adults at home during the day back then, usually mom.) If you wanted to play with a friend, you went to his house (usually on the same block), rang the bell, and asked if he could come out to play. That was known as "calling for someone." I had a few older friends with whom I spent a lot of time, six friends who were younger (by a year or two) and two who were exactly my age. All were boys; we only started "hanging out" with girls around the age of 14—a little later than in other groups in the area. My older brother, by seven years, hung out with a group of four or five guys who were approximately seven years older than me. Across the street, four or five girls of around the same age stayed together, and the same was true for my side of the block: four or five girls, a year or two older than me, hung out on my stoop. By the way, "hanging out" has no particular definition—just two or more kids sitting or standing around listening to a radio, or talking (rapping), and/or smoking. When I hung out with any one of my older friends, all was well. When I played stickball or slapball with my older friends and others, all was well, However, when I just hung out with two or three of my older friends (and maybe six or so "little kids," a year or two younger), all hell would break loose. Or, I should say, the "rank-out sessions" would start. Let me explain.

Rank-out sessions were vicious and brutal, and left a lasting mark on my self-confidence. How this "sport" began is not quite clear, but once it started it became, over time, our "go-to" activity. There have been a number of attempts to explain the urban game of "the dozens," whereby two participants (young and often male) square off and try to one-up each other with clever quips, such as "Your mother wears combat boots," to which the retort might be "Your mother is like a doorknob, everyone gets a turn." Onlookers are sometimes recruited to keep score, which often reflects the reactions of the audience. Everyone knows that such quips don't reflect reality, but it will help a participant's score if he or she can elicit groans, gasps, and the occasional "oh shit." Ground rules are usually set before the match as to what topics are fair game; "no mothers" may be one, and other reality-based comments are frequently taboo.

Our rank-out sessions had no such rules. In fact, the closer you got to another person's inadequacies or faults (individual or family), the higher you could score. Those "faults" included dead parents, drunk parents, economic hardship, athletic and educational failings, or any disability of any member of the family. The more you could really hurt your opponent, the better. One of the reasons for the popularity of this pastime was the age differential between the older kids in the group and everyone else. Being older, they were able to come up with very clever quips and responses; this gave them status and power in a neighborhood that offered little of either. Over time, the rank-out sessions took on a life of their own, and became part of the everyday experiences of all the kids in my group on the block. When I was hanging out with just one of my older friends we got along fine, but when two or more of the older kids found each other, they would show off, verbally pounding the younger kids. For example, one July 4, one of the older friends shared with me the fireworks my father had brought home. Afterward, this "friend" actually said, "Don't think I am going to be nice to you later because of this." In fact, most of my older friends always seemed to hope I would do something wrong so they could use it against me, such as the time I ordered the wrong size board for my train set at a local building supply outlet. It took a strong constitution not to let their exaggerated laughs bring me to tears.

In earlier years we played different sports all day and night, or I would just play stoopball by myself. However, the rank-out sessions made me dislike leaving the house, especially since the daily scene of my mother dragging my alcoholic dad from the car played out for all to see (he worked nights and came home during the day, and sometimes stopped to show the boys who were playing, say, stickball in the street his pitching acumen). Having my "friends" across the street laughing at the events unfolding around my alcoholic father would have been just too much to take if I had been hanging outside with them. Those memories are ingrained in my mind and are still painful. And in a way, I believe that learning how to entertain myself in my apartment—playing electric football, or baseball using a rolled-up piece of tin foil and a pencil, playing with my model trains or stamp collection, tropical fish or plastic dinosaurs, or just throwing a rubber ball up in the air and catching it—gave me the time to be creative (it felt like my little world). A number of experts today have warned about the lack of creativity among young people because the kids are too overscheduled and constantly stimulated (Coles et al. 2001). In fact, my brother also started staying in the house most of the time. He once quipped that when my father was drunk and at home with him, he would make believe he was in a prisoner of war camp. On many days I would leave the house after my dad came home, because staying there was no picnic for me either.

The verbal attacks on me and my family covered a wide range of areas: how I made an error as a 9-year-old in little league to allow the winning run in a championship baseball game; how much talking my mother did in the gate; how hot it was in our apartment; how pale my sister's skin seemed (from staying in the house too much, although others might see that as a plus); how much time my brother spent in the house; the size of my head; and so many others. Yet, of course, the main target was my father. Once, when one of the older kids (who I later caught stealing stamps from my stamp collection) was in my apartment trading stamps with me, my toddler sister came into the living room holding a bottle of whiskey that my mother had hidden from my dad, and said, "Bisky, my daddy drink." My heart sank, because I knew that event would become a killer story against me in the future. People also knew that my father's drinking was causing financial problems for us. My "friends" accordingly loved to tell the tale that my dad received $10,000 as a compensation package when he left Bordens and subsequently drank it all away in a short time.

When we were teenagers, a couple of friends came up with a nickname for me: Goon. Apparently this was based on my long, lanky posture

(I never really figured it out). What I can report is that by this time many of us were starting to "go out" with girls, and some kids (among them those who came up with the nickname) were not as successful at first. So when I think back, it is very clear who should have been called a goon. That might sound defensive, but those rank-out sessions were devastating for my self-esteem and self-confidence. Furthermore, my section of City Line seemed to have significantly more negativity than other parts of the neighborhood. True, the older kids were instigators of much of it, but they liked to hang out with the younger kids just because they themselves lacked self-confidence, coming as they did from "hard-living" families.

I understand now that these were attacks by older kids who were look-ing to feel better about themselves in a neighborhood where there was not much to feel better about. Some urban analysts have argued that "the dozens," as practiced in poor and working-class neighborhoods, repre-sents a necessary safe outlet for pent-up frustrations and anger and/or preparation for a hostile society (see Jemie 2003 for a full analysis of the dozens). Granted, those are reasonable explanations. Nevertheless, I believe a stronger argument could be made that our rank-out sessions reflected the lack of self-confidence found among poor and working-class youth. In fact, if those rank outs function in any way, it is to keep the poor and working class recipients of put-downs from gaining the self-confi-dence that is vital to experience upward social mobility. Only now, through the eyes of a sociologist, can I see the rank-outs for what they were—a way of temporarily bolstering low self-esteem for the perpetrators.

In the previous chapter, I contended that self-confidence is a key vari-able in understanding the *Worlds of Pain* (Rubin 1976) experienced by many members of the working class. What better way to reach for a little dignity (Sennett and Cobb 1972) in a capitalist society that has stripped some people of their dignity, than to keep others from moving upward and onward? Correspondingly, sociologists such as Rubin (1976) have shown that the reason some working-class parents may not want their children to attend college is the parents' own fear of losing those children to an alien way of life. Misery just may love company.

Many of the rank-outs were directed at the spot where the working class is vulnerable: our parents' economic status and educational failures. And interestingly, they were specific to that time and place- low income families, intact families, and alcoholism. Even our athletic achievements, something that might just allow members of the working class to escape from their day-to-day lives, were up for redefinition. You can claim total victory over your opponent if you can knock him down in one of the only areas that provides social status to a working-class boy. Granted, we also made fun of each other in school—both elementary and high school—but the rank-outs did not go for the jugular. In school a few friends called me "Tom the Bomb" or "Geeter Gorman"—because I once mispronounced guitar as "geeter." We might even say something nice to each other. But on my block, we never patted each other on the back for a job well done, because it might work against us later. Today, when I see movies where (male) friends help each other and have each other's backs, I wonder if that actually happens in real life or whether it's just a Hollywood fantasy. Many of us were on the SSS baseball team that won the Catholic Youth Organization (CYO) Tyro Championship in Brooklyn in 1968. I helped turn a key double play (I played third base) with the bases loaded and one out in the bottom of the final inning; this play allowed us to win the championship, and finally made up for my error as a 9-year-old. (I also got a hit with the bases loaded that allowed us to tie a game we needed to win or even to qualify for the championship game; and I led the team in hitting the following year, 1969, which garnered me "most improved player" of the team that year.) That is a good example of my point: my "friends" should have been there to support me after the error I made at 9 years old and not seen it as another chance to put me down. And we should have patted each other on the back for our hard-earned championship win. We were happy, but there should have been much more celebrating than there was. Middle-class and upper-middle-class kids compete, of course, but they compete differently. Their self-confidence is already high.

It is a travesty, too, that working-class kids lack the kind of support (readily available to middle-class kids) to help them achieve and reach their full potential. Some of my friends did well in school, going to Catholic (college prep) high schools, while others had obvious skills in writing, drawing, athletics, and music. One of the guys was an excellent football player and could, with a little active coaching, have become.... We will never know. We never acknowledged in each other these potential skills and talents. Actually, a few of my "friends," I believe, were quietly rooting for others to fail so they could have a good laugh, like the time someone from another block slapped a bag of potato chips out of my hands on the corner of Drew Street and Liberty Avenue.

One of the problems I had with my mean older friends was the fact that I matured, socially, too quickly. It was necessary for survival to learn how to defend oneself during the verbal rank-out bouts, but let me be very clear, I *hated* them. This was not because, being somewhat quiet, I was a favorite target for the older kids (and I had a family background ripe for exploitation), but because I was a serious kid and thought that the entire exercise was "childish." Yes, at the ripe old age of 11, 12, and 13, my thinking was, "I can't wait to grow up, so I won't have to put up with this type of behavior." You might think this mature approach would have served me well, but the reverse was true: I would have been better off, and had more status in the eyes of my peers, if I had been just as "childish" as everyone else. Much as I wanted to grow up and escape all my problems, that wasn't possible. This was not just the usual longing by children to have the perceived opportunities and privileges of adulthood, such as buying beer without being "proofed." Mine was a wish not to be a child. It is really sad that social class can have such an effect at the individual level at such an early age.

This is not to say that a corollary cannot be found in middle-class culture, but there are significant differences. Middle-class youths do not have to pull each other down; they succeed by doing well in school and in extracurricular activities. The typical middle- and upper-middle-class youth knows full well that their friends are going to do well in life—the goal is to do better. Middle-class kids have the self-confidence necessary to fend off feelings of not measuring up to their peers. Signs of success are all around them. Middle-class youth compete with each other, comparatively, but they try to succeed by being better than their friends at activities that will matter later in life such as schooling, not tearing them down because they lack self-confidence.

As I got a little older, I began to see a return to spending time practicing hitting a rolled-up piece of aluminum foil or a sock with my sister's broom in my parents' bedroom. Two key incidents immediately come to mind that reinforced the value of practicing one's craft. First, during a game of stickball (against the side wall of Associated Supermarkets), I was hitting against a well-known (older) fire-baller and connected with one of his best fast balls. The ball traveled over the pitcher's head, over the fence belonging to "Frenchy Son of a Bitch", over the back of the weed-strewn old diner on the corner, and into the gas station that faced 75th Street and 101st Avenue. My teammate (another older friend) watched the ball sail over the wall and cried out, "Oh Mama." As we walked over to the gas station to try to find the ball, with my teammate teasing the pitcher about the distance of my shot, I did not utter a word to the other two players—as if to say, I have arrived. (I never understood how "Frenchy Son of a Bitch" got his nickname because, while he yelled "son of bitch" at us every time we hit the ball into his yard, he was Italian.) The second incident occurred in the middle of 75th Street where I was playing touch football against the above mentioned teammate. On one particular play, I ran a "down and out," and my future baseball coach threw a beautiful pass that I hauled in for a touchdown. My older opponent could only say, obviously embarrassed, "Now he thinks he's Homer Jones" (a wide receiver for the New York Giants in the late 1960s and early 1970s). These two incidents remain as vivid to me today as if they had happened yesterday. Why? It is probably because they marked, for a young working-class boy, the beginning of my growing confidence—a confidence that I had been almost totally lacking. Doing well in school was another way, throughout my life, for me to show that I had the "right stuff," but doing well in sports started to give me some street credibility in my working-class neighborhood.

You might be wondering why I continued to put up with all the negativity. In fact, one of my best friends once said I should just tell one of the bullies to "fuck off" and punch him in the nose (I sometimes still wish I had). The ways to combat the negativity were few. My father told my mom, who had started to become aware of the rank-out sessions, to let me fight my own battles. Yet, I finally had enough of the putdowns, and I had enough friends from SSS to give me the opportunity to leave 76th Street and go around the corner to hang out with other guys on 75th Street. There is nothing like having social connections, or, as we say in sociology, social capital. This may not seem like a big deal to the uninitiated, but it could have been seen as a traitorous act, putting me at risk for further abuse. Such is the way working-class city life operates. If you are familiar with urban friendship networks, then you know this move took a certain amount of courage and agency on my part. Contrast this with a middle- or upper-middle-class environment, where a child may escape from their friends by being driven to other parts of town, doing well in school, and/or going to an out-of-state college.

On 75th Street, I made some new friends and got reacquainted with others. Remember, one of my first friends had moved to 75th Street when I was very young and I had hung out there for a brief period, only to have my front tooth broken in a football game. A big fellow jumped on me and my mouth bounced off the concrete when I collapsed to the ground, cracking one of my two permanent front teeth in half (giving my friends more ammunition during rank-out sessions—"toothless Tom"). When the boy's mom slammed her front door in my mom's face, my mom did not let me go back.

At this later time, the atmosphere I found on this new block, with new friends, was quite different from what I was used to. The emphasis, as it had been on 76th Street when I was younger, was on sports: stickball, touch football, and, one of my favorites, wiffle-ball (I was one of the best hitters in wiffle-ball and stick-ball on 75th street—a boost to my self-confidence). When not playing sports in the street, we played sports-oriented board games such as Strato-Matic baseball and football, hockey, and electric football. And instead of seeing me as a traitor to my block, a few of my friends seemed to respect that I had started hanging out with another group and some of them followed me to the new block, little by little. Lo and behold, one of these older kids eventually stopped coming around because rank-outs were not as welcome on that block. We were all getting a little older (14–15) and that maturity might have started to put a dampener on his favorite game of putting others down. There was some good-natured teasing, but it was usually confined to sporting events, the kind of quips one might expect among friends—like when I was the first big "loser" in a card game: I had a King and a 2 in a game of "Acey Deucey," but I pulled a King and lost 50 cents. Attacks on someone's family finances and "dysfunctions" were minimal, although there were still some "ranking" based on educational failings. Interestingly, if you failed a course and had to go to summer school, that was seen as a badge of honor—another indication of being "cool," although failing too many courses could make you susceptible to rank-outs. Overall, however, the atmosphere was very different than on 75th Street, which just reinforced my belief that the negativity on my own block *had* gone beyond the pale.

By the time 75th Street and 76th Street finally combined and we all moved around the corner to hang out on Drew Street (the Brooklyn/Queens border), ranking out had just about stopped. At first, the guys on Drew Street were our football rivals. As the 1960s turned into the 1970s, however, most sports-related activities ceased as we grew our hair (see Photo 5.1), listened to rock and roll, worried about the Vietnam War, experimented with drugs, and hung out with and went out with girls.

Most of us were now 17 and 18 years old and our attention started to turn to the opposite sex, as well as what we might want to do after high school. I was finally becoming a young adult, and enjoying it. Hurting other people did not completely stop, however. One of the guys from the group was "tripping" on LSD one night, but a few of his friends—as a joke—put him in front of a mirror and accidently freaked him out. On another night a younger friend was tied to a pole and whipped by a couple of his friends—again, as a "joke." Neither of them returned to the group.

Photo 5.1 Author after a concert in the mud in 1971—long hair, sex, drugs, and rock and roll

There was one particular bully who lived on 76th Street and who gave a few kids trouble, including myself. Of course, the older kids would encourage him to pick on some of the others. He was big and about my age. He and I had had one or two fist fights when we very young, but as I grew older I started to think that fighting was silly. That is not a good philosophy to have when there is a bully on the block, however. Furthermore, it is a radical departure from what my father wanted me to do. He came home on a number of occasions and told the rest of the family tales of knocking out other guys in the bars he frequented. My early maturity was sometimes misinterpreted as "punking out." Of course, this just gave my older "friends" even more ammunition to use against me during rank-out sessions.

Bullies are found across classes. Recent research on the effects of bullying suggests that the victims are more likely to experience anxiety, depression, and low self-esteem (see, for example, Doheny 2015; Drum 2011). This research also indicates that bullying is an attempt at jockeying for social status within a group. In fact, bulling quite often takes place in front of peers—this is how one's social status rises (Sennett and Cobb 1972). On top of this, research has shown that living in dysfunctional family settings is stressful and can be harmful to children's future health (Feletti et al. 1998). Is it any wonder, then, that I have experienced low self-esteem and anxiety during my life? A therapist once said to me, after hearing my life story for the first time, "I am surprised you took so long to come to see me."

There is without a doubt a testosterone-laced attitude surrounding the kind of behaviors I have been describing: rank-out sessions, bullying, and "punking out." True, there are "mean girls" and "Queen Wannabees" (Wiseman 2002), and I do not doubt the pain this must inflict on the girls who are their targets. The main difference I can report, however, is that bullying and putdowns among the males in my neighborhood were carried out in face-to-face interactions, sometimes with your opponent yelling insults right in your face, spittle and all. Supposedly, it is a "manly" thing to insult someone to their face. Talking about someone behind their back and the "cold shoulder" approach that researchers have found among "mean girls" was not the way the boys in my neighborhood were "mean."

Interestingly, when I began to attend high school, the distance (geographic and social) between the school and my neighborhood gave me an opportunity to create somewhat of a new identity (Kinney 1993). Two incidents immediately come to mind as examples of the flexibility of identity formation in different institutional settings. The first occurred one day in gym, during my freshman year, when the seniors were playing a game of basketball and they needed an extra player. They asked me if I wanted to fill in for the player who had to leave (I was just watching them play). Basketball was not my best sport, which was true for many of my friends in the neighborhood. Every once in a while, however, I would surprise myself (and others) with some decent play, although I was very inconsistent. As the game progressed, I had just a few opportunities to handle the ball; not surprisingly, since the other players were mostly seniors and knew each other. As the game was coming to an end there was a loose ball and, for the first time, I got my hands on it. I saw that the gym teacher was about to blow his whistle to stop play, so I dribbled across court and, at the whistle, launched a running hook shot from the foul line that hit nothing but net. The other players were stunned; one of them said, "Oh smack, who is this guy, Jerry West?" (a great player for the LA Lakers in the 1960s). Here is a little secret: I was stunned, too. Nevertheless, after that I was a hot property for basketball games at Edison, more than at any time in my old neighborhood. You see, after the shot I walked around as if I did that every day. Yet, back home I was experiencing a somewhat different reality while playing certain sports.

As the saying goes, though, "You have to know when to hold them, and know when to fold them." My time to exit tackle football in my neighborhood came after one particular play in which I made a great (if I do say so myself) over-the-shoulder interception. On returning the ball up the field, however, the other team's fullback hit me so hard that the ball must have stuck to me as I hit the ground, because I didn't fumble. I crawled off the field on my hands and knees, and I couldn't walk properly for a week. You were still supposed to "walk it off" in our social world; I couldn't do that, and that prompted our team's quarterback to get mad at me for leaving the game. Anytime I get together with my friends from the old neighborhood, that play is invariably one of the topics of conversation, providing everyone with good laughs.

The second example that comes to mind occurred in the lunchroom at Edison when I was a sophomore. One day, another student put a pat of butter on my seat when I went to get my lunch. I came back and sat down, and incurred a large stain on the back of my pants. As this was an all-boy's school, your "manliness" was a key asset—I knew that if I did not respond in a certain way, the next few years would be hellish. Another kid, somewhat overweight, was constantly being bullied by others, and in a similar incident someone had put a cup of coleslaw down his back. He had done nothing to retaliate, and he suffered for the next four years. As the howls of laughter from the surrounding tables died down, I walked over to the perpetrator, pushing him as he stood up. He slipped and fell and everyone in the lunchroom started chanting "Fight, fight!" A teacher broke up the minor altercation, but the other fellow said, as usual, "After school at the mailbox—3 pm." All day, I played out in my mind how I would fight this guy. When school finally ended I waited for him, but, to my delight, he looked at me and kept on walking with his friend. My friends raised my hand and patted me on the back. Later that year, the fellow I was supposed to fight—whom I had eventually befriended—told me he had kept walking that day because he thought the other guys who were there with me were going to help me fight him. They were not— they just wanted to see a good fight—but I now had a reputation (briefly) as a bit of a tough guy.

Those two incidents helped me survive my four years at Edison. Even though they were somewhat out of character for me, they provided a boost to my self-confidence. Doing well academically, in turn, also added to my high school years being a very positive experience. All in all, our identities are flexible and as varied as the institutional settings we inhabit (as the symbolic interactionists would argue). Moreover, there can be a "carry-over" effect, in that my newly developed high school identity had a slight effect on my neighborhood identity, since a few of my neighborhood friends attended Edison. Here is what is significant about all of these stories. Middle-class kids garner respect, self-esteem, and confidence by getting good grades and getting into good colleges. As a working-class kid, my self-confidence was still being shaped by how well I played sports and how tough I was perceived to be.

Girlfriends

Throughout this book, I have been careful to highlight elements of my social world that are class-specific and those that are not. Most young men go through a period of awkwardness vis-à-vis young women, but it is chiefly the class-specific lack of self-confidence that added to my inability to feel comfortable around girls while maturing (see Photo 5.2). Some of my close friends, I believe, suffered from the same affliction.

Growing up on 76th Street, there were a number of girls I had a "crush" on. One girl in particular, whom I saw as some sort of goddess, lived on my block. She went to the same grammar school, SSS, and when I was between the ages of 10 and 12 I would wait for her to leave her house so I could catch up with her on her way to school, and—just maybe—talk to her. My young heart, so full of new feelings, finally forced me to tell one of the other kids on the block that I liked her. That turned out to be a very bad move. As you can probably guess, he used this information to verbally torture me (and her) when she walked past our group in front of the garage on the corner of 76th Street and 97th Avenue. (She remembers that I used to just put my head down when my friend made

Photo 5.2 Author's confirmation, St. Sylvester, sixth grade—author looking quite awkward standing between two female classmates

fun of me.) One day, I mustered up all the nerve I could find and approached another girl I liked. Having planned for days what I would say to break the ice, I told her not to pay any attention to my friends' comments. Then, I asked her if she wanted to go around the corner to Angelo's (the candy store) to get a soda (actually, I think I specifically mentioned a Yoo-hoo). Unfortunately, she said she had just had a soda with her lunch. That shouldn't have been a big deal; I wasn't the first guy to be rejected by a girl (and perhaps she had just had a soda with her lunch). Nevertheless, I made a big mistake: I told my "friend" about the incident. Why? I think I still believed that one day he would come around to supporting me. This is the kind of heartbreaking event that, in a Hollywood movie, would lead to the rejected boy's friends coming together and helping him work through the experience. That, I am afraid, is not how the groups of which I was a part dealt with these kinds of situations. I was tortured even further by a couple of the older kids, making me feel even more awkward around girls. Surprisingly, another woman from my old neighborhood, who went to SSS with me, mentioned on a social media website recently that she had had a crush on *me* in elementary school. "OMG," I responded. "Now you tell me." I had never entertained the thought that any girl could have had a crush on me.

When I turned 13 years old, I built up the courage, helped along by one of the only kids on the block my age, to ask a girl out. It was very common in that time and place when a boy really liked a girl to "ask her out"—just a "cool" way of asking her to "go steady." Especially in my group, there was little dating of a number of girls simultaneously, as is sometimes portrayed in movies and on television. Admittedly, one might go out on a few dates, but then it would be time to "pop the question": Will you go out with me? If the girl said yes, the boy might then give her his high school ring to wear around her neck on a chain, or, if he had a few more bucks, actually buy her a piece of jewelry, usually an ankle chain, to symbolize their newly formed status as an "item." This practice is interesting in the context of working-class neighborhoods in that time and place. Was this ritual practice for an early marriage, since we weren't going away to college? Or was this a practice by young people of a certain social class who were trying to maintain a sense of order, stability, and control in an unstable social world? Some experts have argued that going steady protected the reputation of women as monogamous, relieved the emotional strains of the dating scene, and provided a ready-made date for every weekend. It might also be a way to prepare young adult couples for marriage earlier than in middle- and upper-middle-class neighborhoods. For middle- and upper middle-class students planning for college, getting this serious with any one person that early in life would seem odd. In any case, this is how the boys and girls in my old (working-class) neighborhood coupled and uncoupled in the late 1960s and early to mid-1970s.[1]

In the summer between the seventh and eighth grades (1966), there was a girl I befriended who lived a couple of blocks away (pretty far for our friendship networks). I asked her out, and gave her a little heart on a chain that I found in my house. During that summer, we sat on her stoop (of course); played handball a block or two away, against the wall of a medium-sized supermarket—Bohacks; and hung around a nearby public school playground—P.S. 214. A friend who was my age had asked out another girl who lived near 214 at the same time. My "girlfriend" and I spent the summer with this "couple," trying to keep away from my other friends from 76th Street, especially the older ones, because we knew they would be nothing but trouble. As you can probably guess by now, they would search for us newly blissful couples and tease us. Of course, I now understand their behavior to be the kind to expect from those who have their own problems with self-confidence, but are trying to hide that fact. This particular girl really liked me, though, and told my older friends to get lost. I think she hinted one day that she wanted me to kiss her, but it was not to be—my self-confidence had not improved that much.

In the summer of 1968—that incredible time of major social and political events, with the "whole world watching Chicago"—I was busy helping my SSS baseball team win the CYO Tyro Championship, as discussed earlier. We were also busy starting to pair up with some of the girls on 75th Street. Our relationships with girls were not of the Hollywood type, going to dances and such, though others from the neighborhood did go to dances and "cruised" the streets in their cars. In fact, one of the stories in Crockett's (2015) book about growing up in our neighborhood concerns a hilarious incident at Rockaway Beach where a group of friends try—awkwardly—to "pick up" girls. Fresh from my successful attempt at asking a girl to go steady two years earlier, my confidence was starting to build (even "making out" with a girl during a game of spin the bottle). Then one night, after a Mr. Softee ice-cream vanilla milkshake, I popped the question to a girl I liked: Will you go out with me? "No," she answered. She was very kind in explaining that she did not want to be "going out" with just one person, but it didn't matter, my self-confidence around girls was shattered once again. You start to reconstruct your own biography at a time like that; maybe going out with a girl two years earlier was a fluke. Yet, there was more bad news to come—a story went around that she was "shocked" when I asked her out, and that she almost smashed her Mr. Softee cone in my face. Two of my older "friends" could be heard laughing all the way down the block when they found out about this incident. Again, looking back, it is easy to see that their laughter must have been an attempt at hiding their own problems with the opposite sex; neither had a girlfriend at that time. Still, it hurt me, badly.

There were also a number of major changes in our family around this time, including my father losing his job at Bordens in 1969 and the passing away of my maternal grandparents. Bordens was consolidating and moving out of New York City. These were the early rumblings of the earth-shattering changes we have seen in the economy, going from a blue-collar, manufacturing base to a white-collar, high-tech, and information age.

Yet, it was nothing compared to the biggest change for me: moving from 76th Street and City Line to 106th Street between Liberty Avenue and 103rd Avenue, deeper into Ozone Park. The move to a new area, about a mile and a half from my old neighborhood, gave me the opportunity to meet some new people my own age. In my mind, I also thought we had moved up in status, because there was a few feet of space between the houses on the block (see Photo 1.4). In the nine months I stayed with this new group around John Adams High School, I started to change. In keeping with the times I had grown my hair long, purchased some new "groovy" clothes (including a purple fringed jacket, purple pants, purple shirt, and two-tone purple shoes), started listening to "hard" rock music (such as Led Zeppelin), and experimented with marijuana. Markedly, these new experiences and people, whether deemed positive or negative, had a profound positive impact on my self-confidence.

Subsequently, just by chance, I saw a flyer tacked on a telephone pole, announced an upcoming bazaar at my old church, St. Sylvester. When I met a few old friends there, it was apparent that they had not yet moved on to some of the interests I had recently acquired. Then, I ran into two girls from the old neighborhood—a life-altering meeting. The three of us walked around the bazaar, playing a number of different games of chance. One of the girls lived right next to one of my best friends, but I had never really noticed her before that night. Someone had told me my best friend's sister liked me, not this new girl with blonde hair. To my delight, it started to become clear subsequently that this new girl actually did like me. One night, while leaning against a car across the street from her (row) house, I said (after practicing the lines for about a week), "I don't come 30 blocks for nothing, you know," and then I asked her, "Will you go out with me?" Lots of planning went into those words, although I admit, they're not worthy of Hollywood. My heart was pounding, and she said, "Yes." As was customary, I gave her my high school ring (off my shaking hand) to wear around her neck on a chain. My journey home that night on the Q-8 Green Bus was sweet. How did we celebrate? The next day we went to a Mets game at Shea Stadium—no one can accuse me of not being a romantic. We sat and kissed at the game—a little too much of a public display of affection, in fact. I was feeling on top of the world.

Some of my older friends tried to make fun of me again, but this time other boys and girls were also pairing up on Drew Street, so these "friends" were being left behind in Cupid's dustbin. If it sounds as if my level of self-confidence went up and down like a roller coaster, you are correct.

That is what it is like growing up working class—you are never really certain if you are good enough, smart enough, or attractive enough. The evidence against you might be just around the corner. Besides, hanging out with more and more girls, and heading toward our 20s, seemed to mitigate the amount and kind of in-your-face rank-outs that had made my life miserable just a few years earlier. Additionally, it was a time of peace, love, and getting high; the kind of behavior that characterized my early life did not fit into the zeitgeist. Correspondingly, one of my friends left the group after a while, as he was no longer able to live off ranking out others. That left only one of my original older friends as part of the group, who believe it or not became a very good friend of mine. After going out (or going steady) for four years, my girlfriend and I were married in 1974. I was only 20 and she had just turned 19.

Much research in sociology (start with Laslett 1973, and Census Bureau data) has shown that the younger the age at first marriage, the greater the chance of divorce. My first marriage reflected that social fact. Although the average age of first marriage in 1974 was lower than today, my girlfriend and I were still very young when we married. In 1970, the median age of first marriage for men was 23.2 years and for women was 20.8 years (in 2010, the figures were 28.2 and 26.1 years, respectively, according to the US Census). My first wife's family, like mine, was working class to the bone: her mother stayed home raising five children; her dad went out to work, as a longshoreman and then, like my dad, driving a taxi. Their oldest daughter, the woman I married, worked during high school summers to help support her family financially, and went straight into the workforce on graduating from high school. None of the five children attended college (My ex-wife attended community college later in life). To use a phrase their dad was fond of, they were all "good people."

It is impossible for me to conceal my ex-wife's identity from anyone who lived in that neighborhood at the time. Therefore, I am duty bound by sociological ethics not to discuss much about our relationship. And there, indeed, are two sides to every story—and every relationship. So, all I am really able to discuss are my own foibles. Actually, I want to make one point relevant to our discussion here: coming from a fairly dysfunctional family, I wanted everything in our relationship, marriage, and apartment to be perfect. That, of course, is impossible in reality, but I was young, came from a "hard-living" working-class family, and thought that perfection was possible in a relationship. I cringe, sometimes, when I think about how I tried to make our world perfect. Yet, sociology has allowed me to look back and understand what happened. In fact, I once suggested to my ex-wife that she read Rubin's (1976) *Worlds of Pain: Life in the Working Class* to help her understand the processes by which our lives unfolded. It was a time when the economy was changing, gender roles were changing, styles of marriage were changing, and the sexual revolution was in full swing, leaving two unsuspecting working-class kids unable to figure it all out.

In the previous chapter, I noted that the only reason I attended college was because of the tenacity of my high school shop teacher. At NYCCC I learned what it took to get started in the graphic arts industry as an entry-level production coordinator/planner. When I graduated community college in 1973, my fiancée graduated high school in the same year. So, what do working-class kids from a working-class neighborhood do at that point in their lives to announce their entry in adulthood? They get married. Both sets of our parents had gotten married young. So, why not? Indeed, working-class youths do not have the benefit of the extended adolescence that middle- and upper-middle-class culture offers. The young woman I married was the girl next door; well, next door to one of my friends. We did not meet enough people, or enough different people, from whom to choose to marry. Going to college means that the years in which to find oneself are extended into the early 20s, allowing middle-class youths the opportunity to meet many different members of the opposite (or same) sex. And today, adolescence is extended further, into one's late 20s, by attending graduate school. Similarly, a close friend of ours also got married at a young age to someone from the neighborhood and experienced the same outcome: she was divorced after a few years of marriage.

Other than the few people we had met in our new jobs, there were not many in our social world who could have stepped up and warned us about the consequences of our decision. It was not that unusual in a working-class neighborhood to get married at that age. Then again, I would not have listened to anyone uttering such a warning anyway. After all, many working-class individuals see college as a waste of time and money; as not living life in the "real world" (see Rubin 1976; Gorman 1998a, b). In contrast, marriage is one of the sociological signposts of having entered adulthood.

As it is for many people, the divorce was devastating emotionally. What was I to do now? The break-up of my marriage shook the world I thought I knew, the things I wanted to do, and the places I wanted to go. As a matter of fact, even work seemed meaningless: I quit my supervisory job at the printing plant where I had worked since graduating community college.

To be sure, my self-confidence took another beating, too. This is when one older friend of mine started to help me through my fog. He would come to my parents' apartment, where I was living after the separation, and drag me out to some club, where I would at least sit and listen to some music, have a few "cold refreshments," and watch other people dance. A few of my friends from the old neighborhood helped me smile again as well. In fact, I started to feel so much better, I thought about going back to school. Coming out of a local pub one night, a good friend of mine commented that he thought I was the "intellectual type." It is funny how sometimes, even little comments such as that one can have an impact on one's self-confidence (and one's career). A symbolic interactionist would not hesitate to remind us of that important perspective. It was one of those "aha" moments—I recently reminded him of that very important social exchange and how important it was for me. I remember thinking for the first time that maybe I was intellectual.

Boys' and Girls' Values

If one were interested in the values found among my friends in City Line and Ozone Park at that time, the following would have to be included: being tough, loyal, real (not phony), athletic, and being funny/cool. Notice that status was not so much built on schooling, clothing, or money, or, I would even argue, to some degree, "looks"—the kinds of values you might find in a middle- or upper-middle-class neighborhood. As a matter of fact, the norms and values found in this working-class neighborhood I understand to be a response to a *lack* of money, clothing, and self-esteem. Indeed, in my own research, working-class men and women spoke about their economic problems, but were proud to be working class, "good people" who appreciated/valued the little things in life (not like those who have money and are stuck up and snooty; see Gorman 1998a, b). Of course, in a working-class neighborhood working hard was valued highly (though knowing someone who could get you a job or a good deal was also valued). The values found in City Line played out in normative behavior such as smoking, using drugs, drinking alcohol, fighting, being sexual at a young age, playing loud rock music, pursuing athletics, spitting, cursing, having long hair, having a cool car, and, importantly, not appearing to be too smart in school.

It is true that at that time a smaller percentage of young people attended college than today. Yet, as you can see from the demographic tables in Chap. 1, a much larger percentage of middle- and upper-middle-class young people from other neighborhoods in Queens did attend college at that time. So, what *did* we do while we should have been studying for our SAT exams? Well, we tried to be "cool" and "street smart." The following may be described as the working-class kids' guide to accomplishing those goals.

In the first place, if one wanted to be considered cool, one needed to smoke—particularly Marlboro's. Oh, how I wanted to smoke; but to no avail. When I tried smoking for the first time, I almost died. Well, not quite, but I was not ready for the intense burning in my throat and lungs. Then, I tried to smoke, believe it or not, cherry-flavored cigars. They were brutal! For some reason, though, smoking pot was a different story. Somehow, that smoke went down more smoothly. After moving away from 76th Street in October 1969, I had already tried smoking pot by the time I returned to my old hangout in mid-1970. As a result, my claim to being cool was somewhat saved. Furthermore, when I moved away I made friends with a group of peers whom were up on the latest music—such as Led Zeppelin, Ten Years After, and Iron Butterfly. This knowledge helped increase my "street cred" when I returned to my old "hood." Even the first concert I attended—Blood, Sweat & Tears and Buddy Miles at Madison Square Garden—branded me as somewhat unique. Being seen in this manner was new to me, and irritated at least one of my friends. Notably, he finally left the group, seemingly not able to survive in an environment that was not suitable to the kinds of rites and rituals that had favored him in his younger years. Yes, the times *were* changing. Still, standing on the street corner smoking a cigarette had a certain coolness that I would never attain.

When it came to consuming alcohol, I found I could keep up with the rest of the group. I could drink beer—lots of beer. A six-pack of Pabst was no obstacle for me to overcome—when it was not considered a "hipster" beer. Coupled with one or two cheeseburgers on club from Nathans (after having had dinner at home), I could drink most of the night without getting sick. When one of my friends came home from boot camp at Paris Island, SC, we bought approximately 50 cases of Pabst Blue Ribbon beer from Crystals Supermarket on Liberty Avenue. Word got around the neighborhood about the party, and young people from the across the neighborhood came, even if they were strangers to us, just to take a six-pack of beer. That party is one of the tales always told when we have a reunion. The one positive effect of our "drinking" environment was that it kept some of us from going too far into the drug culture. And my ability to hold my liquor significantly raised my score on the coolness scale. Consuming vast quantities of beer also gave us license to express our repressed emotions, with one friend actually punching a hole in the wall of another friend's basement. These are early indications of the pent-up frustrations of growing up as alienated working-class kids, the kind of frustration that can develop into anger and bitterness when entering adulthood and the opportunities for social mobility fade. Oh, by the way, we still were not studying for our SAT exams.

Drug use varied by individual, but let me be very clear: drug use was rampant in my old neighborhood. A few people even turned to dealing drugs. Pot was, by far, the drug of choice for most of us, but some others did venture in "harder" drugs—uppers, downers, LSD, and, for a select few, heroin. As one friend recently commented, "people did not acquire nicknames such as 'groggy' for nothing." Someone else on social media talked about Forest Park (Queens) back then being a drug supermarket. When a couple of my friends started to experiment with LSD, I backed out—I held a tab of "Yellow Sunshine" in my hand, but decided against it, since I'd had a bad "trip" one night smoking pot (I thought I was swallowing my tongue). Who knows how I would have reacted to LSD. One friend had such a bad trip one night that he never returned to our group. On another occasion, a friend of mine who was tripping on acid, or thought he was, climbed the Unisphere in Flushing Meadow Park, at the site of the 1964 World's Fair. Unfortunately, one or two of our friends started using heroin, became addicted, and eventually (even after methadone treatment) died. One of them I knew well and he was a great person. He treated me kindly and always had a big smile for everyone. I was told that he is buried in Potter's Field, a cemetery on an island in New York for those whose bodies were never claimed—that bothers me to this day. In contrast, to show the extent of naïveté still prevalent among some members of our group, one friend bragged about his brother having a "drawer full of grass" in his house. When we went to investigate, we found just that— his brother had ripped up a chunk of honest-to-goodness, real grass from Shea Stadium the day the Mets won the World Series in 1969.

Even though my neighborhood was situated geographically between two gangs—OZ (Ozone Park) and F and P (Fountain and Pitkin Avenues in Brooklyn), being cool in our group had little to do with physical toughness. For instance, while playing a more rugged form of touch football (stopping the guy) in the back of Anchor Bank on Liberty Avenue, one fellow on the other team (an ex-Marine) took on four of us in a fight after he didn't like the way one of us blocked him—he won the "fight." Be that as it may, that does not mean that it was okay to be seen as a "pussy." Some friends still talk about who had whose backs during the few confrontations we had with other groups. That is a funny way to put it for me, because I always felt that, except for maybe one person, almost no one had my back (I do remember a few "knives" in my back, though, when I was younger). Using "curse" words was ubiquitous—and was a poor substitute for being really tough. From what I have heard, there was only one true gang fight in which our group was involved. Wouldn't you know it, I missed it, because it occurred during the time I was hanging out with another group of young people near John Adams High School. The fight was with some members of OZ, but ended quickly when one of our group recognized one of the other group's members—another benefit of social capital.

There were some key areas where I picked up some cool points on Drew Street. First, I had a girlfriend and people just assumed we were having sexual relations. Second, I had really long hair (see Photo 5.1). I knew quite a lot about rock music, and I attended more concerts than just about anyone else in the group, for acts such as The Who, Led Zeppelin, Ten Years After, Blood Rock, The Doors, Alice Cooper, Grand Funk Railroad, Paul McCartney, John Lennon (the One to One Concert), Creedence Clearwater Revival, Steppenwolf, Janis Joplin, Blood, Sweat & Tears, and I went to the Concert for Bangladesh featuring George Harrison, Bob Dylan, and Eric Clapton. These were held at such venues as Madison Square Garden, the Brooklyn Academy of Music, the Forest Hills Tennis Complex, and the legendary Fillmore East. In fact, I had to sleep out at Madison Square Garden and Shea Stadium for a couple of those concerts. Many in my group were still listening to just The Doors, The Beatles, and The Rolling Stones. (Or, as someone mumbled one night, the boors, doodles, and tones or some such—an old inside joke about one of my older friends, who was so angry one night he mispronounced the names of The Doors, Beatles and Rolling Stones).

So as time went on, I came out fairly well on these indicators of coolness. Don't get the wrong idea, I was far from being "Mr. Cool." It is just that I was finally pulling myself up from being so uncool and it seemed to me to be quite an exciting new identity.

SPORTS

It is pertinent to discuss the importance of sport and leisure activities to our lives in City Line after touching on our relationships with the opposite sex. Sport dominated our lives until our late teenage years: playing it, watching it, discussing it, simulating it in board games, and debating it (and even flipping baseball cards and attaching them to our bicycles with clothes pins). Is it any wonder girls took second place to sports for many of us? Is it possible that we let sports dominate because we lacked girlfriends until our late teens? Possibly. Nevertheless, when I think about growing up in City Line, the first item that comes to mind is sports. I cannot overemphasize that fact enough. It may be part of growing up in many places, but there is a distinct experience of playing sports in an urban, working-class environment. It was a way for working-class kids to experience acclaim and confidence.

The games in which I participated were played, mostly, on the block with kids from just that block and in the streets, dodging traffic, with someone watching for traffic and yelling out loud, "car." Some streets had one-way traffic, but my block (76th Street) had two-way traffic. Many games were played with a rubber ball, either a Pensy Pinky that cost 10 cents or, if you had hit the jackpot, a Spalding (pronounced spaldeen), which cost 25 cents. Most games were age and sex segregated; very rarely would one find older kids playing with younger kids, and never, I mean never, playing with girls. The Pensy Pinky was good for games where the ball may be lost down a sewer, whereas the more expensive Spaldings could be reserved for games such as slapball, punchball, boxball (some people called it Chinese boxball, I don't know why), stoopball, or kings. Playing stickball, where one pitches the ball at a strike zone box against the wall of the local supermarket, or at a handball court in a playground, one could easily use (and lose) a few rubber balls. Stickball in the street, where a pitcher threw the ball to the hitter on a bounce, was a game made for losing rubber balls, especially if the batter "pulled the ball" just a little. I lost a ball over the houses on 75th Street one day after I started hanging out on that block during a stickball game, prompting one of the players to tell me to go back to my own block. It was not a good beginning to a new life. One of the fathers on the block, however, went on to the row of roofs and threw down a basketful of balls, and I lived for another day.

If the ball did go down a sewer, all was not necessarily lost—it could be fished out with a coat hanger. That was an art. Broom handles became bats, but later on we actually had a dollar or so and bought a few official stickball bats. Remember, we were working class, we were not poor. That is an important social fact to keep in mind. Our dads (and sometimes moms) made decent wages in that time and place. Blue-collar workers, with limited skills and education, could make a living wage; some families struggled or lived week to week; but there was little of the concentrated poverty that we see in some cities today—see the demographic tables in

Chap. 1 for median income levels. The balls were so prized that the owner would sometimes "call chips" on one: that meant the person who lost the ball had to pay the owner or buy a new ball himself. This rule was almost never enforced—everyone lost a ball at one time or another—but it set up an eye-opening example of class conflict in a seemingly working-class neighborhood. One day I lost a ball that belonged to a guy whose family owned a local store. He rang my bell and asked my mother for "chips on the ball." She said, "Get the hell out of here, how dare you ask me for money?" My mother was quite the feisty one.

All the games we played were influenced by the urban setting, and the traffic. Stoopball, stickball, and boxball are games shaped by the urban density of working-class neighborhoods. They are invariably played where there is concrete. Also, all of our "leagues" were of the "pick-up" type—there were no managers, mentors, coaches, umpires, or referees. This led a friend of mine, in a feat of mathematics and engineering, to mark out a 100-yard football field using a yardstick in the middle of the street, from one end of the block to another. He also created a playbook for *each position* on our football team that we had to memorize. Those are just a couple of illustrations of the important role sports played in our lives.

There were a couple of grass fields (although mostly rocks) about a mile or so to the south of us near the Conduit Highway. We also played a number of tackle football games on a patch of grass between the two sides of this busy highway. One time, a friend who was a very good football player—a linebacker—had to be wheeled off this grass segment by paramedics. He was one of the working-class kids in the neighborhood who, with a little bit of extra training that an upper-middle-class family would have provided, could possibly had made it to a top college on a football scholarship. When I made the CYO All-Star Team in my final year of playing baseball, I had the opportunity to play on a field on Long Island which had an infield without rocks, real dugouts, water fountains that worked, and lights for night games—my reaction was "Wow, I never knew those kinds of places existed." I had to adjust to catching pop-ups against that lighting background. I was modest, but it did wonders for my confidence. That game was one of the first inklings I had that other kids grew up and lived out their lives under very different material circumstances. Having to buy the cheap seats at both Shea and Yankee Stadiums also illustrated to me that there were class differences related to sports. Likewise, the fact that I had to take a number of subways and buses to get to big league games (instead of being driven to them by parents from the suburbs) hinted at an unequal playing field—no pun intended.

The big differences between middle-class and working-class worlds of play and leisure revolve around the different reasons for participating. My friends and I played various sports for the love of the game. We did not participate in sports, as is found among more and more middle-class enclaves, to build our résumé, to acquire a scholarship, or to live out some parent's painful childhood memories.[2] There were no playdates—and that is the way it is today for most working-class children, according to Lareau's (2003) research. There were no "helicopter parents," constantly hovering over their children's activities. Incredibly, there were only two or three parents present to witness our SSS Tyro baseball team win the CYO Championship in 1968. And, for that matter, those parents were there because we needed more than the two cars that belonged to the coach and manager of the team to ferry us to and from the field in Highland Park. Compared to today, consider the following: there is not one photo of me in my baseball uniform in the six or more years I played organized baseball for SSS. Today, visit a sports field in a middle-class neighborhood when a soccer league begins to play and you will see professional photographers in attendance, ready to put your child's photo on just about anything you desire: coffee mugs, can openers, and book markers. As Eitzen (2011) noted, there is a new definition of what it means to be a good parent. Keep in mind, though, that as far back as Seeley's et al. (1956) research in Crestwood Heights, middle-class parents have been involved in helping to schedule their children's activities. But, today, that orientation to child rearing has been taken to extremes (Coles et al. 2001). Middle- to upper-middle-class parents feel the need to show others that they are very involved in their children's lives.

Looking down the suburban street in which I now live, I see a number of basketball hoops. Living in an urban setting, we did not have a single basketball hoop in a back or front yard to play a game we loved. We had to go to one of the school-yard playgrounds, usually P.S. 214 to play basketball. And when I played in the house by myself (because of weather or the pangs of rank-out sessions), my activities were shaped by the crowded railroad-car rooms, whether it was hitting a sock through the rooms, throwing a rolled-up piece of tinfoil into the kitchen garbage bag, or throwing the football from my mom's bedroom to my own in order to dive on my bed to catch it. Coupled with playing stoopball in the confined gate of a two-story row house, is it any wonder it felt claustrophobic, and had me asking my father: "Where does the concrete end?" (Recently, I purchased a fairly expensive basketball hoop set, which I located in our driveway, for one of my sons. This would have been something I would have only dreamed of when I was young. How did my son celebrate? By "playing" basketball on the television set using a computer-simulated game.)

Some sociologists see sport as the new opiate of the masses, especially for the working class(es) (see Eitzen 2011; Guttman 1978). As a general illustration, just take a look at soccer (football) matches in Great Britain, or all the hoopla and betting connected to the Super Bowl. In particular, these sociologists argue that much could be accomplished in the social world with all that time, money, and energy currently devoted to sports. Fair enough, but other sociologists are coming around to realizing that sport can be a site to challenge, resist, and possibly change social structure (see the discussion below). Sport may not have given my group of friends what we needed to overturn the existing social relations, in the sense of experiencing a revolutionary social epiphany, but it at least kept us from sliding further into the social abyss (drugs, crime, and gambling) that can come along with growing up in a neighborhood like ours. I will have more to say about sport and social class and my own research in the next section.

Sports Research

In 1998, I submitted the grant proposal in Box 5.1 to study parents' involvement in their children's sports-related activities. The study was awarded a City University of New York Grant.

Box 5.1   Grant Proposal

Theories of cultural production and social reproduction, which explore the processes by which social relations are produced and reproduced, have focused their analyses on the peer group, school (Bowles and Gintis 1976; Willis 1981; Macleod 1987), and more recently, on the family (Gorman 1998a, b). Early studies in this theoretical approach examined the cultural practices of individuals within the context of capitalist social institutions, and highlighted the processes by which their actions produced and reproduced social inequalities. But, as others argue, the cultural practices of people can alter (resist) traditional social relations. Yet this resistance to traditional social relations can, quite often, take a form that, ultimately, can reproduce traditional social relationships.

For instance, Willis (1981) showed how working-class males' resistance to schooling solidified their social class position. While peer group, school, and family, obviously, are important sites for any

(continued)

Box 5.1   (continued)

exploration of social production and reproduction, one institution central to understanding the processes of cultural reproduction and social reproduction has long been relegated to the periphery of sociological analyses—sport (for a discussion of core and peripheral specialties within sociology see Cole 1983). The focus of this project is to deconstruct that process.

Although there is a substantial literature on the sociology of sport, it is still seen, often, by many sociologists, as not worthy of serious scholarly study, and not as an integral part of social organization. Note the dearth of advertisements for leisure, popular culture, sport specialties in the American Sociological Association's Employment Bulletin. (In fact, when I recently told a colleague I wanted to undertake a scholarly investigation of sport and social class he said, "But what about your career.")

Scholars who have studied sport have, until recently, approached it from a "social-system, social-role" perspective (for example see Watson 1977; Oliver 1980; McGuire and Cook 1983). For example, Berlage (1982) said

> children's sports serve several functions for the family. They provide for total family participation in a world of age segregation, where many of the socializing functions of the parent for the child have been taken over by other agencies such as the school. Sports enable parents to take active part in the socialization of their children within a formalized activity. Sports help the parent to socialize the child in the values of hard work, competitiveness, and teamwork. (p. 46)

Indeed, one topic of interest among these sociologists is "socialization and sport" (for excellent reviews see Coakley 1993; McPherson 1988). As Coakley (1993) notes: "The goal of these studies is usually to identify: (a) sources of social influence and other factors that lead a person to participate in sport, and (b) the developmental outcomes of participation itself" (p. 171). Although the "social system, social role" perspective still has a following by many sports sociologists, a number of studies taking a critical and/or interactionist approach to the study of sport have appeared

(continued)

Box 5.1   (continued)

(for example see Gruneau 1983; Donnelly and Young 1988; Messner 1990; Adler and Adler 1991; Curry 1993; Birrell and Richter 1994). This body of research attempts to investigate "the social construction of identity, the dynamics of participation decisions, or the meanings underlying sport participation" and "the related issues and the connection between sport practices (including patterns of individual involvement and participation) and processes of subordination and oppression" (Coakley 1993:574). Few of these studies, however, focus on parents and how their approach to sport within a capitalist economic system helps produce and reproduce social relations. That will be a critical concern in the current research project.

Parents have been shown to have a significant influence on their children's participation in sports (for a review of this research, see Lewko and Greendorfer 1988). Most of these studies, however, showed how the impact of various members of the family affects the children's involvement in, and retirement from sports, and how this involvement builds character and patriotism, promotes social mobility, reinforces cultural norms and values, teaches social control, and relieves anger and hostility. But a key question still remains: What is the **meaning** of sport to parents of children in organized youth sports programs? The meaning of sport to parents and their response to that imputed meaning is crucial for understanding how social class, racial and ethnic, and gender relations get produced and reproduced. Parents **are** important players in the socialization process, but this social fact should not keep us from using a critical/interpretative approach to the study of the socialization of children by their parents.

This is the first phase of a larger project designed to understand the impact of parents' attitudes toward sport on the production and reproduction of gender, racial and ethnic, and social class relations. This initial phase of the study will explore questions that add to the existing literature on socialization and sport: What are the different meanings of sport to working-class and middle-class parents? Do middle-class parents have a more instrumental orientation (a means of upward mobility through résumé enhancement) toward their children's involvement in sports? Which group of

(continued)

Box 5.1   (continued)

parents—middle class or working class—puts more of an emphasis on winning? Fine (1987) found that middle-class parents, more than working-class parents, emphasize to their children the importance of winning baseball games, while Watson (1977) found that working-class parents have a more instrumental approach to baseball than middle-class parents.

My own research (Gorman 1998a, b), however, suggested that middle-class parents are more instrumental—goal oriented—in their approach to education. The data suggest that members of the middle class tend to value schooling more for the credentials schools offer, whereas members of the working class tend to value schooling more for the applicability of the course content and the learning opportunities schools offer. It may be that middle-class parents do not emphasize the outcome of their children's sporting events because these parents have "won" elsewhere in life and use sports just as a means to enhance their children's chances of upward social mobility, whereas working-class parents emphasize the importance of their children winning at sporting events to alleviate some of the hidden injuries of class (Sennett and Cobb 1972).

Watson (1977) focused on parents' orientation to sport. In an attempt to expand Kohn's (1969) research on social class and values, Watson found that middle-school parents are attracted to little league baseball as a means of attaining and maintaining middle-class values (adaptive, cooperative, self-directed behavior—"getting on with others"), whereas working-class parents are attracted to little league baseball for its training in integrative (conformist) behavior. Yet, in my own research I argue that, more often than not, middle-class parents exhibit "conformist" behavior; working-class parents tend to be more "resistant" to social institutions (such as education). In addition, Watson analyzed the data from a functionalist perspective, conducted only brief interviews with the parents, looked at only one sport, grouped all sales and office workers into the working class, and focused mostly on social class to the exclusion of gender, race, and ethnicity. His findings also need to be tested to see if they hold for different contexts (other sports, different ethnic/gender

(continued)

Box 5.1   (continued)

groups, other regions—urban/suburban). This research project will also update Kohn's research on social class and conformity.

Oliver (1980) studied the family's orientation to social mobility through sport by racial and social class categories. He showed how race and social class interact to produce various parental orientations toward the belief in social mobility through sport; blacks more than whites believe in the chance of social mobility, but there were significant class differences in the beliefs among black families—upper-middle-class black families did not hold these beliefs as much as working-class and poor black families. This research also relied upon a social systems approach and did not show variations by gender.

My data will suggest how racial, ethnic, and gender social relations are produced and reproduced, in part, by parental orientation to sport and how those variables interact to produce various outcomes. Indeed, research has found (see Lewko and Greendorfer 1988) that fathers may play the most important role in the socialization of children into sports, but these studies did not explore the meaning of sport for parents—men and women—of varying social class and racial/ethnic groupings. Likewise, parents' orientation to sports may be as much gender related as class related, and may be mediated by race and ethnicity (early proponents of resistance theory were criticized for neglecting the effects of gender). It may be that men, regardless of social class, have more "romantic" athletic aspirations for their children (especially for their sons to be professional athletes).

Foley (1990) and Fine (1987) explored the meaning of sport, and how it contributes to the production and reproduction of gender, ethnic, and social class relations. Foley (1990) found that high school football games in a small Texas town were sites where social relations (social class, race, and gender) get produced and reproduced. Although he found instances of resistance to the hegemonic processes involved in social reproduction, he concluded that there were too few in number to challenge the capitalist elite group that were in control of the town.

Fine (1987) used an interactionist approach to show how participating in little league baseball helps boys construct a definition of "masculinity." According to Fine, reproduction of gender roles

(*continued*)

Box 5.1 (continued)

does not go uncontested; boys interpret and transform the messages sent by peers, coaches, and parents to suit their immediate needs. Although a classic in the field, his sample only included white, middle-class boys living in suburbs who participated in organized little leagues. What about other contexts? What about the meaning of sport to parents? This is the task of the current research project.

The study of the attitudes of parents toward sport is crucial for advancing our understanding of the relationship between parents, sport, and social reproduction. In fact, this study will add to the general understanding of the processes by which social relations are produced and reproduced. In conjunction with my research on parents' attitudes toward their children's education, I will show how resistance theory can be used, in general, to understand the utilization of social institutions by different social groups (race/ethnicity, class and gender), thus producing and reproducing social relations.

The meaning of sports to parents may vary according to the type of sport (baseball, football, etc.), organization (organized or not, school-related or not), and region of the country (urban, suburban, or rural). The study of the processes by which social class, race and ethnicity, and gender interact to produce various outcomes within different contexts is a daunting but manageable task. I am going to begin this large research project by undertaking the following research project. Initially, I plan to interview forty middle-class parents and forty working-class parents of children playing in organized soccer and baseball youth leagues in Queens County, New York City. (In another research project, I explored the attitudes of forty middle-class and forty working-class parents toward their children's education. In this research I showed how intensive interviewing can be used to understand the meaning of education for parents of school-age children.) The sample will contain an equal number of male and female parents; I will interview only one parent from each family. Queens County has many opportunities for boys and girls to participate in organized youth sport. I plan to interview the parents of children on four teams in each sport (two for each social class) in

(*continued*)

Box 5.1 (continued)

two neighborhoods. These two neighborhoods are differentiated by social class and race/ethnicity. Social class will be defined by occupational category (see Halle 1984; Lareau 1989; Gorman 1998a, b). The sample will break down as follows:

Baseball		Soccer	
Working Class	Middle Class	Working Class	Middle Class
2 Teams	2 Teams	2 Teams	2 Teams
20 Parents	20 Parents	20 Parents	20 Parents
(10 Male/	(10 Male/	(10 Male/	(10 Male/
10 Female)	10 Female)	10 Female)	10 Female)

The league offices will be contacted to ask for help in arranging the interviews and to become familiar with the social organization of the league. If the league officials decline to help me contact parents, I am prepared to approach parents directly to arrange the interviews. The interviews will be conducted before, during, and after both the practices and games, or at the parent's residence. I hope to conduct as much of the research as possible at the playing fields to capture the "richness" of the data.

In this phase of the research program I will be exploring the attitudes of parents whose children participate in either organized baseball or soccer. This will give me the opportunity to compare and contrast a traditional American sport (and one where there is some existing research on parental attitudes toward sport) with a sport that, upon initial investigation, is populated in New York City by many newly arrived immigrants. Interestingly, many of the soccer leagues in the surrounding suburban communities seem to be populated by a different mix of people with, hypothetically, different attitudes toward their children's participation in sport. Comparing the results from this initial project with the results from a suburban population is being considered for the second phase of the research program, along with studying the attitudes of parents whose children participate in other sports such as basketball and lacrosse.

(continued)

Box 5.1 (continued)

The interviews should take approximately one hour to conduct and all the interviews should be completed during the summer months of 1999; the interviews will be tape recorded, transcribed, and analyzed. The interview schedule will contain questions such as the following:[3]

1. Is there anything that you personally like about sports? Why?
2. Is there anything that you personally do not like about sports? Why?
3. Were you ever active in sports? Why?
4. Did your parents encourage you to participate in sports? Why?
5. Are you still active in sports? Why?
6. Why do you like your child(ren) to participate in sports?
7. Why do you like them to participate in baseball/soccer?
8. How long would you like to see your child(ren) participate in sport in general and this sport in particular?
9. Do you encourage your child(ren) to participate in sports? How? Why?
10. Is there anything that you like about organized sport for children?
11. Is there anything you dislike about organized sport for children?
12. What do you think should be the purpose of organized sport for children?
13. What do you think should be the purpose of local unorganized sport for children?
14. Is there anything you would like to see changed in sports to make them better for children?

RESULTS

What did I find when I interviewed middle- and working-class parents at their children's youth activity leagues? The first thing to remember is that the sample is somewhat biased: all the parents interviewed were attending their children's games. What this means is that I would not hear from any parents who had chosen not to attend their children's games. That is very important to remember when trying to put these parents' comments in perspective. As I had found when interviewing (1998a, b) parents about their attitudes toward their children's education, there were significant class-specific responses concerning their attitudes toward their children's participation in youth leagues. Middle-class parents approached their children's participation in sports with an instrumental concern. They liked the competitive nature of the environment. One middle-class parent said, "They better learn it [the competition]. It has a direct parallel with business." Similarly, another middle-class parent responded, "I understand the economy. It's [sport] a motivator." What is interesting about these remarks is the conscious attempt by middle-class parents to mold their children's future through their participation in sport. Kohn's (1969) explanation of how different workplace experiences translate into different approaches to child rearing seems mysterious and unconscious, but Lareau's (2003) research suggests a more conscious attempt by middle-class parents to influence their children. She called it "concerted cultivation." It is obvious that these parents, as Lareau has argued, are very aware that their child-rearing practices have a focused goal: to prepare their children for middle- and upper-middle-class positions in commerce, industry, education, and healthcare. They see sport, then, as a résumé and college application builder. As one parent put it, "You are not here [at the field] to play." These parents understand that sport can help their children be competitive—"They better get it [a competitive personality] soon." It will, as this parent said, "Give them a competitive edge at work." And it will, as another parent said, "help them focus and succeed." Some parents were very direct and brutally honest in their responses, with one parent commenting that "there are winners and losers in this society" and that sport "opens up avenues that can help them [his children] in the future." Middle-class parents wanted to give their children whatever they could to help ensure their success in life, hoping, I hypothesize, that if they threw as much and as many opportunities as they could their children's way, something would stick; thus reaffirming for them their status as good parents.

It quickly became obvious that working-class parents approach sports and child rearing quite differently. As if programmed by some alien entity, working-class parents spoke, almost in unison, as to why they want their children to participate in youth leagues. Indeed, most of the working-class parents said that they think sport "keeps their children out of trouble and off the streets." In contrast to middle-class parents, they were very concerned with giving their children something fun to do. Lareau (2003) has found that working-class parents do not plan their children's activities as much and as often as middle-class parents do. It is important to keep in mind that my sample contained parents from both classes who had already enrolled their children in organized youth sports leagues. So there were hints of an "instrumental" motivating approach even among a few working-class parents—but with a working-class twist. The working-class parents thought that by participating in organized youth sports, their children's self-confidence may improve, the kind of confidence these parents said they lacked as children (and that I understood all too well). These working-class parents stressed, consistently, their wish to keep their children away from drugs, gangs, and teen pregnancy. These are very different reasons to motivate children to participate in sports as opposed to the concerns of the middle-class parents— and one of the main reasons why many City Liners (especially boys) escaped those same urban problems. Sport may be the new "opiate of the masses," and it may have contributed to our "false consciousness," as Marxists argue. Nevertheless, at least we were still conscious when the dust settled from the 1960s and 1970s, and were able to go to college and start careers later in life (which many of us from City Line have done).

Working-class parents also had their children join sports leagues as a way for the parents to meet new friends and have "fun." It was a fun-filled event for both parents and children. This is another way in which the responses of the two sets of parents differed. The working-class parents spoke often about the "fun" aspects that youth leagues provide for their children. It was the second most cited reason, after keeping their children off the streets, for enrolling their children in youth leagues. For example, one working-class parent noted, "If he's [the son] happy, then I'm happy," while other parents said, "He loves it," "It gives them a social life," and "I look at this as fun." Undoubtedly, these parents, much more than middle-class parents, were emphasizing the "love of the game." Interestingly, when I interviewed working-class parents for a different research project about their attitudes toward education, I found a similar "love of learning" attitude, as opposed to the résumé-building tactics found among the middle-class parents. Also, these findings fit nicely with Lareau's (1989, 2003) work on class-specific tactics used vis-à-vis the educational system and leisure activities. They support my previous work on class-specific attitudes to education, including working-class "resistance" to the dominant ideology of using college and/or sporting activities for upward mobility. Consciously or not, working-class parents have once again voiced their displeasure at the effects of living in a hyper-capitalist economy on various aspects of their children's environment: schooling and youth sports leagues.[4] Unfortunately, their approach—emphasizing fun and the love of the game—will (most likely) not help move their children up the social class ladder.

Sport was for my friends and me all about having fun—whether informal play, games, or organized youth leagues. To us it would have seemed almost like a science fiction movie that parents at some other time and place would register their children in youth leagues in order to build their résumés, get them prepared for the competitive world of business, or even possibly help them win a scholarship. All in all, we did well to have played sports with minimal adult interference, with our own bags of cultural capital being filled with creativity, diplomacy, and even an improved sense of self. These are not, by themselves, going to provide enough of an advantage for social mobility vis-à-vis middle-class kids, however. There are too many other factors discussed in this volume that usually help explain how working-class kids get working-class jobs. And this now comes at a time when "getting a working-class job" will not be able to provide the working class with the income, benefits, and job security that it once did.

The data collected in this study would benefit from further analysis and "mining" for differences by gender and race. Yet, there can be no doubt that the differing class-specific responses to my questions speak to the need for further research on class cultures, and on the kinds of class-cultures that push parents to extreme child-rearing measures.

Beginning in the mid to late 1970s, the winds of change started blowing through working-class neighborhoods. The deindustrialization of the workforce that hit the working class hard, and disrupted the American Dream for the most vulnerable populations, whether they were white, black, Latino, or Asian (See William Julius Wilson (1996) for the classic work on this subject). The printing plant in LIC, Queens where 500 people worked (myself included) shut its doors for the last time in the early 1980s. It has now turned into a condominium in a neighborhood facing gentrification—a sign of the times. During the late 1990s the economic plight of the working class was becoming very clear to me, even if some in academia disagreed. Today, that type of analysis is taken for granted, with future economic conditions predicted to follow the same path—continued and wider social inequality.

Middle- and upper-middle-class parents are well aware of the economic situation and try to give their children every advantage: AP courses, internships, extracurricular activities, and scholarships. In light of the new economic reality, middle-class parents seem to think that if they throw enough "stuff" at a problem—including their children's participation in organized sports—something might stick that will give those children an upper hand. Indeed, they know the game has changed: hard work, and even a college education, can no longer "guarantee" success. My own research (Gorman 1998a, b) suggested that many working-class parents still hold to the belief that hard work and some "common sense" are "good enough" to give their children a shot at the middle class. That is the kind of attitude, brought about by their experiences in the social class hierarchy, that can lead to social class reproduction.

NOTES

1. See the recent work of Weigel (2016) for a social history of dating.
2. See Lareau (2003) for a discussion of class-specific differences in play—this difference informed my own interest in the sociology of sport.
3. Adapted from Orlick and Botterill (1977).
4. See Rifkin (2001) and Reich (2008) for a discussion on the hyper-capitalist economy.

CHAPTER 6

Social Structure and Culture: The Macro Context

Social Institutions

Family

Child Rearing

The larger (macro-level) social context of class-based injuries cannot be ignored. While the whole world was watching Chicago in 1968, I was worried that I would make an error in our CYO Championship game in Highland Park, Brooklyn. The social worlds in which I grew up—City Line and Ozone Park—seemed to keep the massive changes of the 1960s from infiltrating our little neighborhood; at least for a while.

Without a doubt, there was a significant difference in the 1950s and 1960s compared to today in the child-rearing approaches of parents, and their attitudes toward participation in their children's lives. It is worth repeating: Today there is a new definition of what it means to be a good parent (Eitzen 2011). Some of my students, who are parents, are astounded when I tell them that no one ever took a picture of me in a baseball (or football) uniform all those years I participated in organized sports. That is inconceivable to them because they know that many youth leagues today hire professional photographers to take pictures of their children just a few weeks into the season. Your child can appear on any number of items: book markers, cups, and magnets for your refrigerator. If you visit sporting events on weekends across the country, you will inevitably find more

© The Author(s) 2017
T.J. Gorman, *Growing up Working Class*,
DOI 10.1007/978-3-319-58898-8_6

parents on the field than children participating in the games. There seems to be a competition between parents as to whose children (and parents themselves) are involved in the most activities. Recently, there has been some movement against this kind of thinking, however. One community, ironically, tried to schedule a day off each week for parents, but could not find a day that everyone could agree on. Despite this small group of rebellious parents, the overscheduled child (see Coles 2001) is still a reality in middle-class and upper-middle-class neighborhoods.

This kind of hyper-parenting has not been found across all social classes, nevertheless. In an extension of her work on social class differences in educational attitudes, Lareau (2003) has found that overscheduling children mainly occurs among middle- and upper-middle-class parents. According to Lareau, these parents use a "concerted cultivation" method of child rearing, where conscious decisions are made to cultivate a child's interests. Eventually, this approach, shaped by the parents' own occupational experiences (see Kohn 1969), will endow students with the kinds of values and attitudes that will help ensure they go to "good" schools and, concomitantly, acquire interesting and high-paying careers. It might be considered the "hidden curriculum" (see Anyon 1980) of middle- and upper-middle-class families. Though that "curriculum" is not nearly as well hidden as schooling's own "hidden curriculum," it certainly helps determine how middle-class culture is produced and reproduced generation after generation.

According to Lareau (2003), working-class parents take a more "hands-off" approach to child rearing, which does not expose their children to the kinds of résumé-building experiences and contacts that will help middle-class children later in life. These findings also help explain the differences seen in children from different social classes at school, starting in kindergarten (and helps debunk the various "authoritarian" theories of working-class culture[1]). In a hyper-capitalist society, schools, especially those in middle-class and upper-middle-class neighborhoods, expect your child to be prepared from the first day. (I received a lengthy letter from my daughter's school on the third day of first grade stating that she was already behind in reading. She caught up with the rest of the class quickly.)

That there is not one photograph of me in any of the sports uniforms I donned is not surprising given the fact that I would not have wanted my parents to come to watch me play—and they would never have given it a thought, either. Having your parents watch you play was considered "sissy" behavior in my old neighborhood. One or two parents, besides the coach, usually were there to watch the game, but only because they were needed to transport the team, and that included when we won the

CYO Tyro Championship in 1968. Remember, this was a time when at least one member of the family—usually mom—was at home all day, but the expectations of what it meant to be a good parent just did not include attending your children's sport-related activities. What a difference a generation or two makes. Crockett (2015) talks about how our coach had recently been released from jail on manslaughter charges. That is an example of the "hands off approach," if I ever heard of one. Can you imagine that taking place in a middle- or upper-middle-class neighborhood?

The "hands-off" approach, Bourdieu and Passerson (1977) remind us, has its own cultural capital payoff. It may just be the kind of approach needed to give children the time to think, dream, and experiment with identities. For working-class kids, however, other factors come into play that tend to divert those resources away from what they could ultimately produce, in terms of academic achievement and well-paying jobs. The structural and cultural position of the working class—which includes few financial resources, lack of professional role models, and little information available about colleges and careers—works against and distorts the cultural resources that the "hands-off" approach provides. How does someone who plays with a chemistry set, microscope, and telescope actually become a scientist, and not get sent to a vocationally oriented high school and community college?

Lareau (2003) makes the point that the middle-class parents she studied were themselves raised by parents using a "hands-off" approach to child rearing. These parents learned from their own upwardly mobile careers what it takes to be successful in today's global economy. Therefore, it is worthwhile considering what the future may hold for children today. With social mobility slowing in the United States (OECD 2010; Economic Policy Institute 2012) and social inequality growing, this can only mean that in the future we will see fewer parents able to transmit their own success strategies to their children. Thus, class-specific child-rearing practices will continue to solidify social class positions, and contribute to growing social inequality.

Gender Roles
The family is on the front lines of producing and reproducing gender roles. Nevertheless, separating the effects of gender and gender roles from social class is difficult. How much of what my friends and I experienced as boys and girls was gender related and how much was related to social class? Obviously, there is some interaction between the two "variables." It all seemed so "normal," "natural." The boys played sports and the girls played hopscotch, jump rope, hit the stick, red light–green light, and, of course, played with their Barbie dolls.

We were growing up during a time of great social, cultural, and economic changes. Many of those changes seemed to come to our corner of world a little later than other places. Women were going on to pursue college degrees, working outside the home, and starting to fill jobs that had been historically a man's world, but these events were trickling down slowly to City Line and Ozone Park. It has been argued that social revolutions tend to spring from the middle and upper middle classes. That idea seemed to hold true for City Line. For many girls (and boys, too), going to college and pursuing professional careers came somewhat later in life. Indeed, some girls from City Line did finish their BA degrees as young women, and entered fields such as publishing, healthcare, engineering, music and the arts, and education.

In thinking about the girls in my old neighborhood, I should take a step back. To begin with, I remember that girls appeared very mysterious to me—and the Catholic school's tendency to separate boys and girls for many activities only seemed to make them even more mysterious. The girls always seemed to me to know something about life, love, and sex that I did not. I mean, I understood how my body worked (as well as any adolescent boy can), but girls' bodies and genitalia were incomprehensible. Any chance we had to take a peek at a copy of *Playboy* or, if we were really lucky, *Screw* that we might find in an abandoned lot only exacerbated our confusion. There were no formal discussions of the birds and the bees, especially in my house, where hugging each other and intimate discussions were out of the question, and I certainly was not going to get "sex-ed" in a Catholic grammar school at that time.

What were some of my most secretive questions about sex? It is still embarrassing to admit, but here goes. I remember wondering, after seeing a *Playboy* or two, what it would take to put a penis through all that hair a girl has "down there." Then one friend, whom I trusted, led me astray with some wild tale he said his mother had told him. He said a girl has a valve that "scum" comes out of if you touch it, and it is a guy's responsibility to put the scum into a "scumbag." Now, you must admit he had some of the pieces of the puzzle, but he'd scrambled them in his mind after his discussion with his mom. I must tell you, I pondered his sex-ed lesson for months. What was the purpose of all that effort? Another friend offered to tell me the purpose for a "Playtex," if I bought him a Mr. Softee ice-cream cone. That seemed a fair deal. After I bought him the cone, I found out he meant "Kotex" and not "Playtex." What a rip! I somehow knew what Kotex were used for; my mom used to send me to John's Pharmacy, around the corner, to buy them. Of course,

I would wait till everyone left the store before I grabbed the big blue box and ran up to the counter, looking the other way as I paid for the product.

To say that we had quite crude ideas about sexuality would be an understatement. For example, one night a member of the old crowd unfurled his knowledge about girls by telling us they are impossible once they grow "tits." On a different night, another old friend came up with a piece of information about women who are sexually intimate with other females: "If you gave them a nice big dick, they would go back to being 'normal.'" Finally, one friend came up with a plan, once and for all, to find out about female sexuality—he gave the girls in the group a questionnaire to fill out about their sex lives. It could be that he was a budding sociologist, but I am almost sure he did not use the data for scholarly purposes.

There was almost no place to get, once and for all, good, wholesome sex-ed. One day, the nuns at SSS sent me and two other classmates to Manhattan to pick up tickets for a movie my class was going to attend (*A Man for All Seasons*, Columbia Pictures, 1966). On the way on the A train, one of my classmates (who I believe had to repeat a grade in school at least once) said that even though he was Italian (while the other two of us were Irish), we were all after the same thing—"pussy." He said, "Girls really want to fuck as much as we do, you know." Holy cow, I thought to myself, really? It was my belief that it was a guy's job to chase girls and convince them to want to "do it." With all of these memories coming back to me, I can truly say I was mystified by girls.

Another time, one of the older boys in our group started running toward 101st Avenue and called back to the rest of the group that he had to go please some girl. I can picture him running down the block as if it were yesterday. The older boys laughed, but I was amazed. Was he telling the truth? How does that all work? Do girls really need sex that bad? I was very confused. Adolescence is a difficult time for almost all kids, but for working-class kids it is especially difficult, because to be considered "cool" means needing to act as if you understand all there is to know about sex. Middle-class and upper-middle-class kids can garner status through other means than being "cool," such as doing well in school, doing well on AP and SAT exams, and being accepted into elite high schools and colleges. Remember, being cool was very important in my neighborhood—the kind of cool that would attract the cool (attractive) girls. Additionally, my parents (like many working-class parents) were not "up" on the current "experts" in child-rearing techniques. And there was no one else I could ask about sex, when I knew that the older kids would just use my lack of information against me.

In my old neighborhood, few if any of us would have been considered a skilled "fighter," but one could also not be considered a "pussy" or a "punk." The girls had to be tough, too. When I was about 14 years old and we started to hang out with a few girls, one girl said, "I'm going to kick you in the balls." Trying to be cool, I replied, "If you do, I'll kick you in the cunt." She said, stunned, "*Gorman*!" That comment did not fit with my usual persona. She still went out with someone else and not me.

We heard about "women's lib" and we talked the talk, but we really had little idea what we were talking about (who did at that time?). Quite a lot of the discussion surrounding women's lib revolved around issues such as unisex bathrooms, burning bras, and the battle of the sexes, exemplified by the Bobby Riggs vs. Billie Jean King tennis match at the Houston Astrodome in 1973. Yes, most of the guys in the neighborhood mouthed the words that men and women should be given equal opportunities and be independent, but I think many of them thought that meant the girls should be able to show more skin, wear tube tops, and have sex with as many men as they pleased. It is also true that some sociologists (McRobbie 1978) would argue that that kind of sexualized behavior *did* represent working-class girls' resistance and rebellion at traditional gender role constraints. One recent social media friend, however, truly impressed me when she showed me a photo of her as a young girl with a particular toy I had myself: Astro-Base. A girl in the early 1960s playing with Astro-Base would have been revolutionary to me. In reality, though, a number of women friends have told me that there was not much for girls to do in City Line except fantasize about their knights in shining armor.

There could be a companion book to this one written by my female friends about what it was like to grow up in City Line at a time when traditional gender roles were starting to break down. My mom, like most on my block, was a stay-at-home mom. Some moms I knew did work outside the home, usually connected to the school or church. There were times when my mom did work outside the home: during World War II, and when she left my dad for a year. She worked in a bakery and spoke about it proudly.

The notion that a dad should be "helping" out around the house, along with co-parenting his children, had not made its way into our little corner of the world in City Line on any kind of scale. My mom did not expect much help around the house from any of her children either; she did it all. I am not sure how my mom and dad would have reacted if I (or my brother) had wanted to clean the dishes, clean the apartment, or do the laundry. A few men may have been somewhat involved with their families and children, but it was not until Betty Friedan (1963) named the problem felt by many "housewives" at that time that we, as a society, started to talk seriously about feminism. Studies today suggest that moms still spend as much time with their kids as moms did back then (Pew Research 2013). Men have moved more into the areas historically occupied by their wives inside and outside the home, but still lag far behind in the time put into all the household duties, including childcare (see Hochschild 1989). A few dads would occasionally show up at their (male) child's sporting events, but even then, there were usually only two or three fathers at our weekly baseball games. Basically, our dads' job was to go to work—and they worked very hard. After work, they would drag their bodies home past us kids in the gates and on the stoops. These were the men and women of what is termed the "Greatest Generation." If I close my eyes, I can hear my mother saying, "What good is a man if he doesn't work?" (notice she talked about work and not about sex). And at night, many of the fathers could be found on the stoops drinking a Piels beer (which along with Pabst was a real working-class beer at the time) while listening to the Mets or the Yankees on the radio, trying to heal their wounds—both physical and psychic— and prepare for the next day.

During my recent introduction to social media, a couple of women from the area voiced their anger at the attitudes from that time and place about women and the social roles that limited their goals and aspirations. It is important, of course, to keep in mind that social media forums are biased samples—those who are very happy or very unhappy about an issue are usually more likely to voice their opinions. One women, though, volunteered that she was not encouraged to pursue any career that would require a college education, and that her only choices were to get married and have children (after working, maybe, as a secretary). In fact, a very good female friend of mine actually got annoyed with me when I wanted to continue a conversation we were having about growing up in our old neighborhood. She was adamant: she wanted nothing to do with discussing what gender roles were like then and there. In her view they were that repressive.

I remember my sister's struggle to decide on her career choice after high school. What happened if my grades dropped was that my mom would try to placate my dad. If I slipped from a 98 to a 96 in some subject in elementary school, my mother would ask, "What happened?" This high standard was not used for my sister. This is not to cast a bad light on my parents (or my sister): my mom and dad were from another time and had certain ideas about the roles of men and women. In my classes at Queens College, stories such as these usually become "teaching moments," helping the students to realize the importance of time and place.

When I returned to college at the age of 26, my sister was 19 and I tried to impress on my sister the idea that she should go to college, too. I took her with me to a couple of my sociology classes. When she looked around the classroom, especially at the young women, I knew what she must have been thinking: What are these girls doing here? She must have heard our mother in her head saying that she would probably just get married and have children, so why should she walk around with "books under her arms." I now understand that it was partially my mother's own insecurity that fostered in her that kind of reaction to higher education. When I graduated with honors from Queens College, my mother was especially interested in the "pretty girls" who received honors and awards. When one who was not as "pretty" as the others received an award, my mother just nodded her head, confirming her beliefs about why some girls go to college. My sister was successful, though, in acquiring secretarial positions in a variety of organizations over the years. There were openings at that time and place for working-class young women with typing and stenographic skills, although my students are shocked to find out that it was a time when newspapers listed men's and women's positions separately.

The girls in my neighborhood, except for one or two I had crushes on, were virtually invisible to me until I was 13 years old. They would sometimes watch us boys play sports (stickball or football) in the street. They would jump rope, play with their dolls, do homework, and listen to music on small transistor radios—many gender-specific activities. At other times, their job was to hold our jewelry while we played stickball in the street; I still cringe and feel somewhat guilty about their "place" on the block. While hanging out with the guys on one of the stoops, one could peer over to the other stoop where a few of the girls would be studying and doing their homework. Sure enough, a couple would usually be doing stenography homework, drawing squiggly lines in their special "steno books," day after day, year after year, to prepare them for jobs as secretaries after high school. These were the social expectations for girls at that time, especially for the working-class girls in my neighborhood. If I tell this story to my students today, there are usually only a few who even know what I am talking about. Once or twice a (female) student had taken shorthand, or knew one of the shorthand languages (Pitman or Gregg) from her mother's experiences. If breaking through the "worlds of pain" described so elegantly by Rubin (1976) was difficult for working-class men, it was that much more difficult for working-class women. A few women from the old neighborhood did break through to get a college degree, sometimes later in life, sometimes an associate's degree. It must have been a long, strange trip. My sister never did make it back to school. (As you will hear in Chap. 7, a number of girls from the old neighborhood tend to blame themselves today for their career choices.)

RELIGION

To say that the Catholic Church was a dominant force in my old neighborhood is another understatement. St. Sylvester Parish boundaries, not coincidentally, overlap with City Line's boundaries almost perfectly. There was, to my knowledge, only one friend of mine who was not Catholic (he was Lutheran), and I cannot think of any friends who did not live within those boundaries. At that time of fire-and-brimstone Catholicism, having a friend who was Lutheran was disconcerting. Would he go to heaven? We were taught in our Catechism lessons that Jesus Christ built his one true church "on this rock." Ironically, my family moved into City Line from Canarsie, which was Italian and Jewish. There were few people who were not white, European, and Catholic, to be found in City Line.[2]

My mom and dad were not especially religious, but they wanted me to follow the dictates of the nuns and priests at SSS. They were married in a Catholic church and had all three of us receive the two basic sacraments of Catholicism: First Holy Communion and Confirmation (see Photo 5.2). Most of my friends' parents did not attend church regularly or belong to church groups, however. (The biggest problem posed by this auto-ethnography is to keep separate the effects of social class from the effects of other institutions, such as religious affiliation.)

Reflecting on my experiences at St. Sylvester School and Church, one word stands out above all others: fear. Whether my fear was consonant with the objective reality of those experiences can be debated, but let me be very clear here: even some of those who have mostly fond memories of that time and place tell horror stories connected to that school and church. What was it about SSS that frightened and worried me? Everything! I was afraid of missing 9 o'clock mass on Sunday; I was afraid of Confession and what the priest might say to me when I finished; I was afraid of what the nuns would say about my homework; I was afraid of getting hit by the nuns; I was afraid of being late for school; I was afraid of going to hell; I was afraid of asking a nun to for permission to go to the bathroom during mass—once I wet myself, and the feeling of the warm liquid running down my leg could have happened yesterday for its clarity in my mind. I was afraid of going to hell because I memorized the list of "condemned" movies (that I could watch when I was older) printed in the local catholic newspaper, *The Tablet*. Basically, I was afraid of everything. What was the cause of this fear? The answer to that question is the key to understanding the effects of my Catholic upbringing in a working-class environment.

A *New York Times Magazine* cover story (Tough 2014) can help shed some light on the connection between my social class and my fears in Catholic school. The article was about the reason some students, particularly working-class students, do not graduate from college, and noted the importance of the reactions of working-class and middle-class youths to their first failing grade. According to research on the subject, middle-class students have the ability, based on their high level of self-confidence, to take those first negative results with a grain of salt, whereas working-class students take the same kind of results as proof of their inadequacy. The results just confirm, for working-class students, what they had believed all along—they are poor students. That working-class youths internalize educational failures could be extended to other areas of their daily lives—and the hidden injuries of class investigated in this volume—such as sports, relationships with the opposite sex, and peer interactions, including rank-out sessions. The hidden injuries of class are sometimes spoken of as if they apply only to adults, but youth-oriented hidden injuries of class may, in effect, set up or add to those injuries experienced as an adult (through educational and/or work-related deficiencies).

Similarly, Steele (1995) has studied the effects of racial stereotyping on student achievement. According to the research, African-American students did not do as well on tests when they were told beforehand that race has been found to have a negative effect on academic achievement. Those African-American students who were not told anything about the effects of race on academic achievement did better on the same tests. In effect, African-American students' doubts about their own abilities become a self-fulfilling prophecy. Likewise, my lack of self-confidence based on other social class-related activities was reaffirmed, and further eroded, at SSS and the fears it instilled in me. Paradoxically, the rote learning of the basic three Rs (multiplication tables, spelling tests, sentence construction, and SRA reading cards) and strict discipline helped me later overcome a less than adequate academic high school experience.

How did I survive at a religiously oriented elementary school in the 1960s? I became a conformist.[3] In my eight years at SSS, there were only two or three times when the nuns yelled at me or hit me. I spent many hours each night making sure my homework was neat. Moreover, even my main liability, talking in class too much to nearby classmates, was described as being just a little chatty—a "Chatty Cathy," as one lay teacher once called me, after one of the first toy dolls that could "talk" by pulling a string on its back. In comparison, some other children (usually boys) were sent to the principal's office or smacked in the face. Except for the one occasion when a teacher hit me with a ruler and a couple of minor sideburn-pulling incidents, my life at SSS was violence free.

Being academically successful at SSS did not forestall my worries, nevertheless. There were still worries related to Catholicism: Was I going to heaven or hell? In the days leading up to my First Holy Communion, my thoughts were that maybe if I were to die immediately afterward, I would go to heaven. That is still one of my experiences that haunts me today—it is such a terrible thought for a 7-year-old boy to be walking around with in his head. Additionally, it was very common for me to reenact Sunday's Mass at home with all the Catholic paraphernalia laid out on the dining-room table, including my St. Joseph Missal and flattened-out pieces of bread for the communion hosts.[4] It is difficult to cleanse oneself of that kind of upbringing: I can remember once saying the entire rosary after I felt a lump under my arm, even when I had stopped going to church. There is no one example that can illustrate the importance of SSS for my early childhood experiences, especially for those not acquainted with what it means to grow up Catholic in that time and place, it was just an everyday reality and fear. Memorizing the answers found in our Baltimore Catechisms such as "Who made you?" and "Why did He make you?" took precedence over critical thinking skills. Preparing for college and careers took a back seat to preparing for heaven. In a community immersed deeply in Catholicism, this should come as no surprise.

The Christmas season brings back some good memories of those days, however, especially going to my friend's house to be with his family and other friends of mine, and to eat his mom's cooking. Yet, it also brings back memories of all the fear and worries associated with the Catholic Church. Even as a child, a small white plastic church would make me cry when it played "Silent Night." How have these experiences played out for me as an adult? Well, to please all the relatives involved, both of my marriages were conducted in Catholic churches (and that could only be the case for the second wedding after getting the first marriage annulled—for

$500). Then, to the consternation of some of those same relatives, we decided not to have our children (from my second marriage) baptized. Many in the two families saw that as blasphemy. My wife's nine siblings have had all their children receive all the Catholic Sacraments. Interestingly though, as far as I can tell, many of her siblings do not attend church any more.

As I have emphasized a number of times, while not the kind of education I would wish for my children, my schooling at SSS helped me in my future vocationally oriented educational experiences. It was for me (and possibly others in that time and place) the educational experience that, to some degree, compensated for my mediocre high school curriculum. This statement is going to put me at odds with a number of my old friends who attended the same school in the same period, and have spoken about the "hellish" years they spent there, not learning anything helpful for their academic development. Nevertheless, whether it was a "hellish" experience or provided a solid educational foundation to build on, there can be no doubt that school and church resonated loudly for many of us.

What did we learn at SSS? From the comments of some of my old friends, it is obvious that the lessons concerning "We are all God's children" missed the mark, as you will see shortly. It is quite ironic that many of the negative comments I have come across on social media about the old neighborhood concern the cultural practices of the new groups that now populate City Line. I sometimes wonder, though, how we must have looked to non-Catholics, when on May Day the entire school—all eight grades, three classes with 50 or more students each—marched through the streets of City Line dressed in our Sunday best, down McKinley Avenue, during the May Day procession. We would say the entire rosary while following one of the nuns. The nun on the loudspeaker would read the first part of each prayer (Hail Mary and Our Father), and then we would recite the balance of the prayer. From the perspective of the proverbial person from Mars, that had to look as if some sort of cult was trying to take over the neighborhood.

POLITICS

Any discussion of growing up in the time and place that I did has to address the political atmosphere, especially for the working class. During the years from 1966 to 1970, the Vietnam War was raging, Bobby Kennedy and Martin Luther King, Jr. were assassinated, and the whole world was watching the Democratic National Convention in Chicago. My older brother was thrust into the middle of the Vietnam War, halfway around the world, as others from neighborhoods like ours have been in the past (Appy 1993). He was drafted, but then volunteered for the Marine Corps. and service in Vietnam; he left in the morning to go to the draft board on Jamaica Avenue, and later called to say he was being sent down to Paris Island, South Carolina for eight weeks of training, from where he would be shipped to Vietnam. While was in Vietnam, my mom would cry when she heard certain songs on the radio that reminded her of him, especially "Jimmy Mack" (Motown 1967) by Martha and the Vandellas and "Homeward Bound" (Columbia 1966) by Simon and Garfunkel. At the end of his first tour of duty, he wanted to re-enlist for a second tour, which prompted my dad to smash his fist against a kitchen cabinet, pushing his knuckles farther back on his hand. My brother decided against re-enlisting, however, when my mom told him our (maternal) grandmother had just passed away. Unlike many others, he did come home after serving in Vietnam in one of the war's hot spots just prior to the Tet Offensive.

Two of my older friends had brothers the same age as mine who were able to avoid being drafted. Believe it or not, those two older "friends" had the nerve to make fun of my brother's day job in Vietnam—working in the post office. They knew nothing of the fact that after his day job, there were other opportunities where he saw some combat action. Again, it is apparent to me now that this was just those friends showing their insecurities. Sometimes, I wish I could go back to some of these moments to make them right. However, I am not sure how I would react. On the one hand, I would love to use my reason, and knowledge of history, to beat them into submission. On the other hand, I would love just to punch one of them in the face. It is not very professional or professorial to say that, but it comes from someplace inside of me that was formed before my professional career as an academic—somewhere from growing up working class. A professor once told me that I sometimes do not conceal the "seams" from my working-class background.

Some people from the neighborhood joined the service to help straighten out their lives, giving them a direction and help them mature. Where else does someone from this kind of neighborhood go for help? Could one go to a social worker or a psychologist? Not in my old neighborhood. My father, and other fathers I knew, would have said, "Get your shit together before I kick you in the ass." Fighting and dying in wars constitute one of the career tracks for poor and working-class men and women.

I cannot overstate my brother's influence on my political awakening— at first from the political right and then from the political left. Interestingly, our bedroom went from having conservative classics such as *None Dare Call It Treason* (Stormer 1964) in the 1960s to having a Sandinista flag on the mirror in the 1980s. Why did he become interested in national and local politics at such an early age in a neighborhood where that kind of interest was not fostered by any social institutions? Was it his way of blocking out the noise in our house? This is what we sociologists call "agency": that there are few, if any, guaranteed predetermined outcomes based on one's position in the social structure (whether it is because of free will or the inability to identify the other causes—or somewhere in between). The anti-war and left-leaning political opinions I developed during those days are still with me today. In fact, I am probably more of a "leftist" today. We were all, in our little part of the social world, looking more for laughs than wisdom. Sure, we sang "Street Fighting Man" and listened to The Doors and Creedence Clearwater Revival, drank beer, grew our hair long, took drugs, punched walls, and had sex (not in that order), but they were not the same kinds of countercultural reactions to the events of the 1960s that were occurring on many (middle-class) college campuses across the country. How could it have been the same? Not one of us ever went away to college during that time. A few of us took the subway to commuter (mostly community) colleges, where extracurricular student interaction is limited. We were copying what we had seen and heard others doing, but not for the same reasons. Indeed, one could argue that the working-class culture in which I was embedded produced a particular outcome: we experienced a working-class urban variation of that counterculture. Nevertheless, when I see photos of the Vietnam War or watch films and documentaries about it, I feel as if I missed something and should have been there. That is what growing up in a working-class neighborhood can do to a young man. To those who served then and now, I say thank you, but not to the politicians who sent them there, no matter what your politics.

By the time I turned 18 (1971), the war in Vietnam was starting to wind down, at least in the sense of the number of young men and women who were needed to serve. Everyone still had to sign up and receive a draft card—which some people burned in protest over US involvement in the war. However, a draft lottery was instituted to determine the number of new recruits required. This worked in the following way. Each day of the year was given a number, chosen randomly. The number you received was based on the month and day of your birthday. For instance, my birthday is July 15, and when that date was chosen from one basket, a corresponding number was picked from another basket. For me, that number turned out to be 359—with 365 being the highest number one could receive. The higher one's number, the lower one's chances of being chosen for the draft, therefore my chances of being picked to serve in the military were very low. In light of my opposition to the Vietnam War, I found this a fortunate outcome, especially given that there were few deferments (such as being in college) for those of us in working-class neighborhoods. For many young men, the draft lottery was a life-and-death roll of the dice. When the day came for the draft lottery the year I turned 18, my friend and I listened to the numbers being drawn on a small transistor radio, eating cold French fries, in a dreary cafeteria in an annexed building of my community college, where we'd just heard "Have You See Her?" by the Chi-Lites (Brunswick 1971). It was not a very glamorous situation or setting for such a monumental event. Luckily, the draft lottery system was discontinued the following year, and the entire draft system ended the year after that. Would I have served? Without the kinds of knowledge or connections (social and cultural capital) that one might find among middle- and upper-middle-class families, there was not much I would have been able to do to fight against Uncle Sam. I was at a Neil Young concert at Madison Square Garden when it was announced that the Vietnam War was going to be coming to an end. What a setting, what a party.

Anyway, I had grown up in a working-class neighborhood, where serving one's country was (and still is) valued. As for feeling guilty about not having served in the military during those years, I have to remind myself that feeling is a product of my social class background. Middle-class and upper-middle-class kids who attended Harvard during that time probably do not have similar feelings. Nonetheless, "The Ballad of the Green Berets" by Barry Saddler gives me goosebumps to this day, even though I was against the war.[5] Yes, I was changing: I can remember telling my girlfriend (while listening to a Led Zeppelin album on my family's furniture-style console stereo) that my politics were becoming clear to me, and they reflected the peace sign on my headband. With the Watergate scandal on the horizon and the youth culture movement glorifying "sex, drugs, and rock and roll" taking hold, my opinions were turning more toward an "anti-war" and pacifist political stance. My girlfriend's father started to think I was a communist; he was a Nixon supporter and was not happy when I started calling for Nixon to be jailed.

The United States, however, was moving more to the right politically. From Nixon to Reagan and then Bush, with a brief four years of Carter, a large part of the working class (Reagan Democrats) began to trade their hard fought benefits for a conservative ideology with a veiled promise to protect the working-class way of life (See the voting patterns for the neighborhood in the Appendix to Chap. 1). That veiled promise had at its core a demonized image of the "other." In reality, it meant tax cuts for the wealthy, an attack on unions, and a minimum wage that failed to keep up with the cost of living. Robert Reich (2016) has written prolifically on these matters. To make things worse for the working class, the country was moving quickly from a manufacturing- to a service/knowledge-based economy.

ECONOMY

We are currently in a period when economic inequality is front-page, headline news. Much of what is being discussed is about the time in which I came of age, post World War II. During that period, America witnessed a great expansion of economic democracy. It emerged from the war as the most powerful nation on Earth. In effect, the war economy helped lift the United States out of the Depression years and into the suburbanization of its major cities. It is still dealing with this earth-shattering transformation of society. For a number of returning men and women who served the nation, the G.I. Bill helped supply housing and educational opportunities, and a chance at making it into the middle class sometimes referred to as affirmative action for whites (Katznelson 2005). New types of neighborhoods sprung up: single-family homes in places such as Levitown, Long Island, with lawns, yards, and a car or two in the garage. Thus, anyone writing about the years prior to and after World War II has a responsibility to explain the social, political, and economic conditions that shaped my generation. Interestingly, some of my friends from the old neighborhood argue back and forth about the lack of initiative and hard work of current young people (especially in that neighborhood) without noting the importance of the economic and historical context. The new economic reality after World War II had a major impact on those of us growing up in City Line.

My father dropped out of high school in the tenth grade, but acquired a job in a Bordens Milk factory in Long Island City, New York, which provided, at that time, what we now call "a living wage." I am not saying we were well-off, or even middle class, but on his income alone we were able to afford an apartment, clothes for three children, utilities, food, and even a pizza from Aldo's each week (usually on Friday, because the Catholic Church forbade eating meat on Fridays). My mom would dress us up for Easter and Christmas. Granted, we would have been in immediate financial trouble if my dad had lost his job, but so would most working-class families of that time (and today). Families like ours did not have much in the way of bank accounts, insurance, or stocks and bonds. As many did, we lived week to week. Blue-collar work, however, was plentiful and we never went hungry, even with my mom not working outside the home, and my dad drinking away a big chunk of his paycheck each week, and we celebrated Easter, Thanksgiving, and Christmas with other family members. In addition, my dad would prod my mom to "give the boy some money" for my pocket. It made him proud that he could support us, given his lack of a high school degree. Actually, later in his life he would sometimes get mad that he, as he saw it, was still supporting me when I was attending college (and for a time after graduation). The working class sometimes want to see an immediate payoff for sending their children to college.

When we discuss social stratification in my SOC 101 course, I ask my students whether or not they would want to raise a family of five, today, on the income of one individual who had just a tenth-grade education. They look at me as if I'm from another planet. Then, to make the commonplace even more strange (as sociologists like to do), I tell them that my uncle, who had only a high school degree and had learned a skilled trade, printing, helped support a family of *seven* on just his income. As mentioned previously, they owned two homes, one in Brooklyn and a summer home in the Poconos. When he lost that job, however, the manufacturing-based economy was changing to a more service-oriented one, in which he found it difficult to find similar work. Finally, he got a job ordering printing services for a corporation in Manhattan—for less money than he had been making previously—a sign of things to come.

But, there were still a sense of economic optimism for many at that time: my fiancée and I started to plan a wedding one year before my graduation from community college. That is correct. We planned a wedding one year in advance without either one of us having a job. It was just assumed that we would find work; the notion of not being able to do so never crossed my mind. Even later in that decade, after we divorced, it only took me a matter of days after I left one job in printing to find another in the same field. That is certainly not the way the job market operates today. My twentysomething son is having difficulty landing his first full-time job, and I must admit it baffles me, coming from a time when the economic picture was stronger. Only after I reapply my sociological lenses does it make any sense. I try to imagine how it impinges on his self-esteem.

Many women in our neighborhood mostly worked in the home. Our generation started to see changes occurring, but it happened slowly (the data in the demographic tables on women's workforce participation was surprisingly high). My generation was torn between the old and the new, especially concerning gender roles. My own thinking (and my fiancée's) at the time was that she would work for a few years and then we would have children. The 1970s saw the beginning of wage stagnation, along with momentum from the feminist movement to motivate women to bring home a paycheck. In our neighborhood, women were involved with the church. In other neighborhoods—middle and upper middle class—women were becoming socially and politically involved.[6]

The younger generation, certainly, had different attitudes than their parents' generation. Without going into the question of whether there was a "generation gap" or not, let me just say that the gap, if any, would especially be found in men's attitudes toward women and women's roles. Some of the men from my father's generation could be found outwardly expressing their displeasure with "women's lib." On more than one occasion I heard a "Greatest Generation" husband say "That's your mother's job" when talking about housework, childcare, and food shopping. You could even, if you listened closely, hear some of these men saying, "Your mother did not take care" when talking about birth control and the arrival of an additional child. Were they just a product of their time?

CULTURE

Generations

In trying to sharpen my students' sociological imaginations (Mills 1959), I ask them to consider the impact of their generation on their lives.[7] Then I ask them to consider previous generations, including mine. It gives me a chance to talk about the 1960s, eight-track tapes, and the first generation of computers. It always turns out to be a lesson that is fun and entertaining, and one in which I think students really begin to understand what sociology is about. In like manner, I want to do the same for my time and place, because no matter how much the focus of this auto-ethnography/socio-biography is on social class, the (macro) generational context must be put in the foreground to give social context to the micro, day-to-day interactions.

The macro context is important to understand, especially given the events my friends and I experienced as baby boomers (born between 1946 and 1964) while growing up in the 1960s and early to mid-1970s. Being born in 1953 puts me in the middle of the baby boom generation. It is important, to be sure, to differentiate the early and later boomers: coming of age, say, as a 16-year-old in the early and mid-1960s was very different than coming of age in 1980. In the mid-1960s the economy was strong; by the 1980s stagflation had taken hold. My age group was located right in the middle of some important social, cultural, and economic events, but missed others. Specifically, my cohort came of age late in the 1960s, with its culture of sex, drugs, and rock and roll, but by 1970 (when I turned 17), many of the great battles for social justice were winding down. Gitlin (1987) has written a wonderful book about the 1960s, describing in great detail the defining events and trends of the early to middle years of the decade, many of which my age cohort missed: folk rock, the protest era, Bob Dylan, the full impact of the assassinations of John F. Kennedy, Martin Luther King, Jr., Bobby Kennedy, and Malcolm X, the Vietnam War, and the Democratic Convention in Chicago in 1968. That is not to say we were not alive: we were hanging out in City Line, but were somewhat protected from these events by time and class. The age at which one experiences these events can make a big difference. As I have said previously, the chaotic year of 1968 (when I was 15) found us firmly focused on winning the SSS Tyro Baseball Championship.

A friend of mine from the old neighborhood recently commented to me that she was surprised by the racist comments she heard from others who had lived through that time and place, given the fight for African-American civil rights. On the one hand, I agree with her, but on the other hand, I am not too surprised. You see, City Line is not that far, geographically and culturally, from the neighborhood portrayed in *All in the Family*. Of course, it is always dangerous to use any television show, designed to entertain to make a point in a serious discussion about working-class Americans, but words like "spic" and "nigger" were spoken with little hesitation in my social world. Our neighborhood did not learn some of the lessons coming out of the 1960s, or learned them later than in other places (feminism, for example). My brother's age group, the one that fought in Vietnam during the peak years of the war, also did not respond to the events of the 1960s as the children from middle-class and upper-middle-class homes did on campuses across the United States. In a way, it was as if we lived in a little bubble in City Line. We experienced the 1960s, for sure—music, long hair, drugs, and some members of the community going to Vietnam—but our embrace of the cultural and social revolution that accompanied those years was weak, especially for my group: I was 18 in 1971 (a year past the peak political battles, according to Gitlin 1987). In Chap. 7, we will hear from some of those ex-City Liners about how they perceive their old neighborhood. Some of the comments are eye opening and breath-taking.

All during this time, many of the residents of the surrounding area were happy and proud that organized crime members were living in their neighborhood. To this day, the residents talk about how safe they felt walking the streets when known gang members lived in and, some say, ran the area. Yet, a black person moving into the neighborhood was just not going to be tolerated. For many in the working class, defining people of color as the "problem" provided a sense of clarity: we may be working class, but we are whites, hard-working whites, not reliant on the government for any help (even though they did—GI Bill, Social Security, Medicare, and student loans). Attitudes such as these helped support the dignity of white working-class men and women (Sennett and Cobb 1972) and made them feel as if they were middle class. So, instead of seeing the common plight of working-class whites, blacks, and Latinos (which would have created a solid voting bloc, the kind Robert Kennedy was starting to build), my working-class neighborhood was trying hard to keep blacks and Latinos east of Lefferts Boulevard and west of the Earl Theatre and East New York.[8]

At the same time, we all attended Catholic Mass on Sundays not far from the Earl Theatre. "Blessed are the poor" stopped resonating for many after leaving the church doors. Instead, it was replaced by another saying, believed to come from the Scriptures: "God helps those that help themselves." This sometimes assists some people with mentally separating two disparate ideas (psychologists call this cognitive dissonance): racism and Christianity. That this quote is not in the Bible and is credited to Benjamin Franklin (and was probably to placate land owners) was of no import. The lack of contact between whites and "others" left us rather unprepared for the wider world. As an illustration, when a friend of mine had an African-American friend come over to her house to study together, my friend's mother inquired later about "what do *those* people eat at home." We all marched up the stairs in our crisp blue school uniforms for eight years in that Catholic elementary school, and we were taught to "Love one's neighbor as one's self." Let me tell you, we fell far short of that ideal in our day-to-day lives in City Line. Blacks and Latinos were seen as lazy, shifty, loud, and violent, and were to be avoided at all costs. Again, in Chap. 7 we will hear clearly from some residents of my old neighborhood about their beliefs that other cultures are weird, deficient, and dangerous, even though the "culture of poverty thesis" has been widely discredited within the social sciences. While this may be true for some (although not others), it is not surprising that growing up in that time and place shaped one's attitudes. The civil rights movement and the March on Washington in 1963, spearheaded by Martin Luther King, Jr., were light years away from our little world in City Line.

By the same token, the attitudes of the past residents now have to be understood in the context of the shrinking middle class, and lack of well-paying jobs for blue-collar high school graduates. The post–World War II economic boom, which gave my parents' generation a shot at a middle-class lifestyle, was over, and the attack on labor, the deindustrialization of the 1970s and 1980s, and the flattening of working-class wages had begun.[9] I grew up in that neighborhood, I knew the people, I understand their fears, but I am saddened that they blamed black and Latino workers—and nowadays, Muslims—for their problems.[10] We all (Blacks, Whites, Asians, and Hispanics) took the A train in the morning to work, but the powers-that-be did not.

Sex, Drugs, and Rock and Roll

The advent of "The (birth control) Pill" had a big impact on the way we matured and experienced late adolescent relationships. Nevertheless, many of the relationships in our neighborhood at that time were fairly monogamous ("going out" with one person at a time). That is, there was not much of the supposed "free love" of the 1960s on a day-to-day basis in the neighborhood. One of my old friends recently said that there was a lot of sex with very few kids to show for it—I quickly reminded him of the social/generational context in which we experienced teenage sex.

Keep in mind that this was a time where old and new norms guiding gender expectations came together. For example, my girlfriend's father sat us down to tell *me* that he would hold *me* accountable if his daughter "got in trouble." She said, "Hey, what about me?" I told him I understood, although there was no question in our minds that we wanted to "do it." Her mom and I also once had a fight about whether my girlfriend could wear a halter top—I was banned from their house until I apologized. Again, the sexual revolution that was (supposedly) rampant across campuses across the country did not make it fully intact into my old neighborhood. Even my own "progressive" ideas were also intertwined with notions about married life, such as that my wife should work (probably as a secretary) until we had kids. Did I ever think that she should go to college? Actually, I did, but not until we had been married for a few years. Some of these issues are discussed further in other sections. These issues, like many of the others in this volume, are highly interconnected.

There was, as discussed in Chap. 5, a significant amount of drug use in City Line, enhanced with some of the paraphernalia of the day—water pipes (sometimes filled with wine) and so on. Initially the "drug" scene in our section of City Line was alcohol based: most parties had plenty of beer. The images of young people sitting around wearing flowers and beads was not to be found in our social reality. We certainly experimented with drugs, but the atmosphere was not one of "peace and love." On the contrary, most of the people taking, say, LSD were not seeking some higher plane of wisdom, but rather escaping our social reality and having a good time. This is not insignificant sociologically. This kind of drug use reflected the underlying alienation that many of us were starting to feel about our futures. So, in a sense—an urban working-class sense—we did experience the 1960s. Unfortunately, we lost a few people when they started to experiment with dangerous drugs such as heroin; we did not have any of the support systems available to middle-class youths in middle-class families in middle-class neighborhoods. Our drug use took place on city street corners with little parental supervision. Neither were there college-based infirmaries or clubs to turn to for help, nor professional role models to remind us that it was not in our best (future) interests to continue on that path. I am reminded of something Jonathan Kozol has said (*Children in America's Schools*, PBS Documentary, 1996): that we should build an educational system so good that a poor girl (or, I would add, a working-class boy) wouldn't allow herself to be sidetracked from her goal of being a medical doctor by having children (or getting into heavy drug use) that she wasn't prepared for.

New York City was experiencing financial difficulties in the mid-1970s—I think of the *New York Daily News* headline announcing "Ford to City, Drop Dead." There was also an increase in crime and an infusion of drugs (see the demographic tables in Chap. 1). Howard Cosell famously announced—in so many words—during a World Series game from Yankee Stadium in the mid-1970's that the Bronx was burning. In contrast, the only real "trouble" we ever got into with the authorities was one night when someone called the police—from the 75th precinct, which had the highest level of crime in the city at the time—on us, just because a large number of us City Line, working-class kids were hanging out on the border between Brooklyn and Queens; I would estimate there were 50 of us (One of us also pulled a "false" fire alarm one night after drinking quite a few beers, scattering us to our respecitve homes). It made me mad; I said to one of the officers, "Listen to your radio—don't you have more pressing problems than hassling a bunch of kids standing on a corner?" A few of us were probably high or drunk, but I do wonder what would have happened if it had been today, if we had been black kids in a low-income neighborhood, and if I had uttered the same words to an officer. In the event, they took two people who got a little more mouthy with the officers to the police station, and just told the rest of us to go home.[11]

In the early 1970s, our group's taste in music was limited to The Doors, The Rolling Stones, and The Beatles. Ours was a specific kind of counter-cultural experience: we weren't interested in a particular sound, message, or philosophy, we just liked to jump up and down, and get drunk in some-one's basement to the opening licks of "Satisfaction" by the Stones or "The Soft Parade" by The Doors (and maybe have sex with someone later). It helped relieve some of the frustrations and alienation we were starting to experience as working-class young adults. Can you blame us? What did we have to look forward to: being IBM trainees after coming out of Princeton? Please.

The politics of the group (if we had any) was center-right. A few people supported Richard Nixon, and some even supported George Wallace because they "didn't take any crap from blacks." Those politi-cians were running on "law and order" slogans that were "code" for keeping blacks in their place. Nonetheless, that kind of politics played well in City Line, no matter how much weed we smoked.[12] Although many of our fathers were union members, there were fears that the Democrats were going to give their jobs to "undeserving" blacks. The last days of a strong labor movement and the working class as the domi-nant political force were upon us (Cowie 2010). Obviously, this was a very different response to the events of the 1960s than was found on col-lege campuses across the country. Sociologically speaking, then, we repre-sented a subculture not a counterculture. As a subculture, we bought into most of the norms and values of the larger culture. The 1960s are some-times painted with a large brush, presenting the youth of America with one stroke. When working-class youth in my part of City Line reached into their bags of cultural capital, they came up with a response that was a variant of the middle-class answer to world events (Willis 1981). There were, to be sure, baseball and football games to watch and play, giving an interesting twist to our hangovers. And there were still put-downs of each other, even if their extent had subsided over time. Did they disappear because we were getting older or because we were stoned and hung over? I'm not sure. At least the rank-outs had taken a new direc-tion. I told one of my friends at the time that my fantasy was to be lead guitarist and singer for a group called Vallo. I even knew the song with which I wanted to open my first concert: "Up Around the Bend" by Creedence Clearwater Revival. Only a handful of my friends still remember that, but, as you can imagine, it has come back to haunt me every now and then—I may have deserved that one.

The Good Times: Benefits of Growing Up Working Class

Some people from City Line will object to the picture painted here of my perceptions of growing up in that working-class neighborhood (about which more in Chap. 7). Part of the discrepancy, simply, has to do with the way we romanticize our childhoods. A couple of my friends on social media have mentioned that tendency. Their parents, when they had a chance, moved their families far from the old neighborhood; when confronted with this fact, my old friends acknowledged that in doing so, they were seeking a "better life." Nevertheless, as any sociologist who studies working-class culture will argue, working-class cultural capital does have its benefits (Bourdieu and Passerson 1977). When studies point to the benefits of middle-class cultural capital—independent thinking, for instance, helping middle-class students at school—it must be remembered that there is another side to that coin: working-class students' ability to take and follow orders can come in handy in certain situations, such as on the battlefield.

One of the benefits of growing up in a working-class neighborhood is the fact that there were always plenty of kids to play with. Equally importantly, the concentration of families on a block of row houses contributed to a rather (urban) "village-like" atmosphere (Gans 1962). Truly, summer nights felt as if there was one season-long block party taking place. By the same token, the block parties that were held—with the block cordoned off and each house offering tasty delights on a table—could not have existed without the input of a large number of families that related to each other in more than a superficial way. After a few "cold refreshments," a fist fight or two could be expected to break out at a block party. In fact, my last fist fight took place at a block party held on Drew Street around 1971. The fighting was limited to me swinging and missing and my opponent swinging and missing, too. Yet, just the sight of me putting up my hands led one father of a friend to say, "Did you see that Gorman go?" My dad would have been proud.

Yes, it was a community. Children could be seen running up and down 76th Street while their parents talked to each other across the fences and gates that separated the closely stacked two-story buildings. Then, the lights of the Mr. Softee ice-cream truck would turn the corner of 76th Street and 101st Avenue and break through the warm and humid night with that pleasing sound to every child on the street—"The creamiest, creamiest soft ice cream comes from Mr. Softee." Meanwhile, the Bungalow Bar ice-cream truck might have just left, or be down the street offering the children on the block different treats. I even have fond memories of listening to the clanking of the metal radiators at night in winter, and watching the colored lights on our windows celebrating the coming holidays.

As you got a little older, you could walk down the street to face the main thoroughfares of 101st Avenue and Liberty Avenue (as Queens turns into Brooklyn), where a plethora of mom and pop stores awaited you (one of the stores we liked to go to was actually called "Mom's"). Just around the corner from my row house stood, one after another on just one block, a series of stores (see Photo 1.3) that could compete with any modern-day shopping mall: John's Pharmacy, Mike the barber, Sevirolli's bakery (oh, those Italian ices), Angelo's (Frank's for the younger set) candy store, Associated Grocery Store, and (oh my) Aldo's Pizzeria. One of the workers at Aldos told me once after I had moved away from the neighborhood that he would make a pizza for my dad for free after he came out of the bar on the next block, just to keep him happy. My father would then bring it home, telling us how surprised he was that the workers at were so nice to him. I am smiling at those memories as I type.

Each night, my job was to go to Angelo's and buy my father a few packs of King Size Chesterfield Cigarettes and then wait for the *Daily News* to be delivered. When it came, the idea was you would pay 5 cents for the paper and then go home. But not me—I would order an egg cream (with no egg or cream, for those who grew up outside New York City) or a Lime Rickey and read the (usually losing) box scores of the Mets, Yankees, Giants, Jets, and Rangers. One night, after I had stayed home from school during the day because of an illness, I still had to go to Angelo's for my dad. The mom of one of my friends (from a block away) tapped me on the shoulder and said, "My son said you were not in school today. I am surprise to see you here." I slumped down from the twirling seat and made my way home. Everyone did seem to know everyone, and it was a small world. By the way, those jaunts to Angelo's took place each night around 8:30 pm. Can you imagine children, especially in middle-class suburban communities, doing such a thing?

As I got even older and was able to hang out with kids on other blocks, I could purchase the newspaper farther down Liberty Avenue (at Max's or Dave's) and eat greasy cheeseburgers on club at Nathans Bar and Grill. There was also another pizza store, Flora's, and another iconic institution on that block, Kucks delicatessen. These were, as you can probably tell, good times. We would also extend the day playing street games at night. If you have no clue what I mean by "street games," there is a wonderful video, *New York City Street Games* (NY Street Games Productions, Highbrow Entertainment, 2010), which will give you the feel and flavor of those special leisure activities, such as Johnny on the Pony, Two Feet Off, Red Light–Green Light, Hit the Stick, Running Bases, and, one of my friend's favorites, Mumphries. I hated that game, along with Johnny on the Pony, because I was very thin at the time and I would inevitably get hurt. Johnny on the Pony requires three or four boys to form a connected line, bent over at the waist, and the other team's goal is one by one to run and jump on the line of boys, hoping to break the connections (girls played some of these games but not others). In Mumphries, the goal was for one kid—who was "it"—to run through a line of other kids, who hit him and pounded on him. It never made sense to me—but could you imagine that kind of "game" being played today in an upper-middle-class neighborhood, with parents never finding out about it?

Street games bring to mind another benefit of growing up in that time and place—it gave each of us a tough exterior. You needed to know how to get through difficult situations in life. You needed to learn how to talk to people, how to negotiate with others, and how to avoid getting "beat up." Growing up in City Line taught you how to take a punch, get knocked down, get up and dust yourself off, and continue your journey. In addition, unbeknownst to me, that place was shaping my personality in a way that, later on, my students would find funny. The students in my classes think I am hilarious—and that helps them learn. When I told one of my oldest and best friend from that time and place that my students find me funny, he responded, laughing out loud, "But you were only the 29th funniest person in the group." Actually, I was surprised myself how funny my students found me to be. It was just a "nice" discovery of who I was when I became an adult.

I have already alluded to the wonders of the stoop. The stoop is where I watched the world go by. The stoop made me feel as if my family was equal to other families who were also just sitting and watching the world go by. The similar outside facades of the row houses provided a sense of equality among neighbors. On the stoop I read the *Long Island Press* (no longer published) and worried about the "Gale" warnings posed by Gale Sayers when the Bears were to play the Giants for the first time in many years. It was where I played stoopball, endlessly recreating the Yankees and Dodgers playing in the World Series. It was also where tears were shed after the Yankees lost four straight games to the Dodgers in the World Series in 1963. It was where a growing boy's eyes watched the girls of the block get older. It was where my backside sat waiting for my mother to come home after she went shopping each day with her little cart. It was the place where I thought about leaving, and then eventually did leave my block, to hang out with other friends on another block (a difficult but necessary decision). In the winter we would still hang out together—on stoops, on corners, in basements, in Nathans, and at P.S. 214 to play basketball. What I wouldn't give, just once more, to hang out with my old friends on one of our stoops or to watch *A Christmas Carol* (George Minter Productions 1951) in my friend's basement on Christmas Eve with two other best friends, eating calzones from Flora's Pizza Shop.

If you are detecting a love/hate relationship in my memories of growing up in City Line, you are absolutely correct. On the one hand, City Line was like an urban village (Gans 1962). For example, one day a woman on Forbell Street (three blocks away) yelled at me and threatened to report to my mom that I had been sitting on her car. On the other hand, the village could sometimes seem very cold. My mom was incensed when one neighbor walked past her "with her nose up in the air." Our family was somewhat "radioactive." Many people stayed away from us (including some relatives, but with the exception of one or two families on the block who had similar problems), scared that maybe they would have to get involved with my alcoholic father. In addition, the "village" ignored other obvious problems. One young man would walk up and down Liberty Avenue holding a pile of shoes in his arms. Someone, some city agency, should have intervened and helped him and his family. I am not sure how that would have happened— counseling was just something that would not have been considered in that neighborhood. Many of us only laughed at him. Another man in the neighborhood would walk up and down the streets throwing a pocket full of rocks at kids' feet. No one said anything. We children would just laugh and run away. A woman who lived in Ozone Park and who painted her house various colors over time, would mumble and yell in the street every day. Can you imagine any of those happening in Scarsdale (Westchester), NY, or Great Neck, Long Island, with no one saying or doing anything to help?

Of course, there were many instances of people helping each other. I remember when the man next door had to climb up to our second-floor apartment on a long ladder to open the door for us after I locked my mother out of the apartment (by accident) and there was a pot of boiling water on the stove. Or when the landlord came up to our apartment to kill a rat that had swum up into our toilet. In fact, a detective who lived across the street used his gun to kill a rat that was trapped down the block in a neighbor's cellar (my mom would scream at these events, being a very nervous person). There were, to be sure, elements of an urban village, but there were also disjointed, disaffected, and isolated inhabitants, and other not so pleasant facets that you will hear about from former residents in the next chapter.

NOTES

1. See Milburn and Conrad (2016) for a current review of this body of work.
2. The demographic tables in Chap. 1 give breakdowns of race and ethnicity in the area.
3. In my own research, and in opposition to some previous studies, I found the middle class to be more conformist in attitude, especially toward education. However, that is part of their cultural capital that allows them to succeed in school and later in life.
4. I also used to play "store owner"—an interesting game for a young child, which I think was symbolic of my fascination with how much "stuff" stores had on their floors, and that it all could be owned by one person.
5. Barry Saddler was injured in the Vietnam War, and, it was claimed, later trained Nicaraguan rebels in Guatemala to fight against the Sandinistas. He died from gunshot wounds after receiving death threats (New York Times, 1989).
6. Murray (2003) discusses the social and political involvement of the women of Bayside in the civil rights movement.
7. See Manheim (1952) for the sociological basis for the study of generations.
8. See Thabit (2003) for a discussion of the development of East New York as a ghetto.
9. See Bluestone and Harrison (1982) on the deindustrialization of America; and Freeman (2001) for a discussion on the rise and fall of labor power in New York City.
10. Marxists call this "false consciousness." Indeed, one could argue that the pitting of whites against blacks was a political ploy (using coded words or phrases such as emphasizing "law and order") that helped weaken labor and strengthen management (see Cowie 2012).
11. That was the same police precinct where a few years later a number of police officers were indicted and convicted on corruption charges—see the documentary The Seven-Five (All3 Media America, 2014).
12. See the demographic tables in Chap. 1 for the Presidential voting results for the area.

CHAPTER 7

Social Media: A "Reunion" of Angry (and Not So Angry) White Working-Class Men and Women

The life experiences of some of the former residents of my old neighborhood seem to have fostered an angry disposition toward the "other," while this is not the case for everyone. I would argue that this phenomenon can be explained by the different social worlds they inhabited in City Line and Ozone Park: some former residents lived hard lives, are angry and bitter, and so lash out, while others have lived more "settled" working-class lives and do not feel as angry or bitter.

After I started working on this book, I was told by a couple of old friends that I might enjoy joining social media web sites, where I would find a few other friends from the old neighborhood. After much hesitation, as I am a low-tech type, my son signed me up to social media web sites. There I met a number of old friends, and I also made some new friends who had lived in other parts of City Line and Ozone Park. After five years on social media web sites I don't have many friends or followers. My children laugh at me, since some people have hundreds if not a thousand or more friends. My friends are mostly those connected in some way to my old neighborhood. To my surprise, some of them have different perceptions of what it was like to come of age in the old neighborhood. Others have—for the most part—similar perceptions to mine, both positive and negative (most comments on social media about the old neighborhood were positive). In fact, a few of these friends, old and new, took umbrage at some of my comments that they thought were too negative in tone. To be clear, some people just did not want to hear any negative comments about that time and place, thinking that

© The Author(s) 2017
T.J. Gorman, *Growing up Working Class*,
DOI 10.1007/978-3-319-58898-8_7

social media should be devoted only to good memories. This attitude is in keeping with the adage "If you can't say anything positive, don't say anything at all." My feeling was that a truer picture of the old neighborhood might develop if both positive and negative aspects of City Line and Ozone Park were aired.

There are a couple of methodological problems with taking any social media comments as reflecting a representative sample of the residents of that time and place. Joining these social media web sites has been, mostly, a positive experience, somewhat akin to attending a school reunion. Those who have unhappy memories and experiences of growing up in City Line and Ozone Park, however, will not be well represented. For example, I have a few old friends who told me they have stayed away from social media because they don't want anything to do with the old neighborhood. Indeed, one very good friend was angry with me because she was in no mood to talk about or hear anything about those city blocks. Nevertheless, I realized that I had the opportunity to compare and contrast different memories of the same time and place. Yet, I also realized that there are ethical pitfalls in using social media comments as data. Therefore, I did not use any comments from social media sites from the point in time I realized I was going to use some those comments as data for this report (or participate in any discussion to elicit responses for the report). Then I took additional steps—to be outlined—to ensure the ethical integrity of this sociological analysis.

The other problem in relying on social media for data is the same as relying on a "call-in" radio show (or, for that matter, RateMyProfessor). That is, those who are motivated to participate may be a different population from the typical person in that population. Yet, these social media sites have become so ubiquitous that I feel justified in using it to give some flavor of how some previous residents now think about the neighborhood.

What can explain significantly varying memories of the same time and place? There are a number of possible reasons. First, it is possible that different memories represent the actual experiences people had in that neighborhood—some had better experiences than others. As stated previously, there were both "hard-living" and "settled-living" families residing in that area. Some families, obviously, had more financial resources and fewer family problems; some families owned homes while others could only rent; alcoholism and drug addiction affected some families and not others; and the children in some families did well in school while those in other families did not. Accordingly, the interaction of these and other variables could lead to people having varying degrees of satisfaction with their lives.

It might also be that the lives of children are not as busy and complicated as adult lives; thus, some people might be remembering their childhoods—50 years ago—through "rose-colored" glasses. As someone else on one of the social media sites asked, why did almost all their parents move away if City Line was such a great place to live? Our memories of "simpler times" can tend to distort reality. In *The Way We Never Were*, Coontz (1992) dispels the "simpler times" of the 1950s family that are embedded in books, television shows, and movies. Some younger inhabitants of City Line and Ozone Park also have talked about simpler times—times some my old friends now disparage. Interestingly, when the question of drugs and gangs from our era in City Line were discussed, a few people responded that they did not remember drugs and gangs as being much of a problem. At that point in the discussion, a couple of other City Liners responded "*What?*" (even some of those who usually had been singing the praises of the neighborhood). They went on to say that drug use was rampant (as I remember it also) in the late 1960s and 1970s, and gangs were present about half a mile deeper into Brooklyn and in the middle of the neighborhood, if you count organized crime gangs.[1] Obviously, the older members of my old neighborhood—those who came of age in the late 1950s and early 1960s, such as my older brother—remember a time when the drug culture had not yet reached City Line. I guess it was possible to have been part of a group of friends who abstained from drugs, but as far as I remember, one would have had to be living under a rock to have missed all the drug use and abuse at the time I came of age.

The women on social media were much more likely to complain about a lack of professional role models while growing up in City Line. Their opportunities were, in accordance with 1950s gender roles, confined to marriage, child rearing, and maybe working as a secretary in Manhattan (although there seemed to be a few teachers and nurses among them). However, most saw their lives as having unfolded according to their own choices.

Two variables may help explain the varying degrees of satisfaction of ex-City Liners with St. Sylvester School: gender and generation. Without a doubt, boys appear to have the most negative memories of their experiences at SSS. The girls who did complain voiced concerns related to the narrow focus of the curriculum, which may have limited their early education. Boys, however, spoke about the physical abuse they experienced at the hands of the nuns. A couple of girls also talked about corporal punishment being a problem, one in particular saying she hoped one of the nuns she had as a teacher burned in hell, but the consensus among both males and females was that boys took the brunt of the physical abuse. Memories of SSS also seemed to be influenced by one's age—younger men and women had more positive comments about attending, with physical abuse apparently becoming less of a factor in the Catholic school approach to education than it was for those who attended SSS in an earlier era.

It is now time to hear the words of some previous residents of City Line concerning their memories of that time and place. Although comments made on social media are in the public domain, I have taken a number of steps to protect the identities of those whose comments I have used. First, I have not employed any names. Second, the quotations have been altered to help preserve the anonymity of the speakers. In fact, I have combined the comments of some participants with those from others, keeping the dominant tone, and I have scrambled the order. Finally, I tried to make sure that the comments were from public pages. Comments that were not "public" were only summarized. In essence, no one particular comment is attributable to any one individual. Do all these precautions distort the comments being used? Only in the sense that it would be almost impossible to identify any one person's words. I kept the types of comments—negative or positive—together to give the reader a sense of the attitudes that some people from my old neighborhood now have toward that time and place, while protecting their identities. The indented paragraphs connote comments made by former (or current) residents of City Line and Ozone Park.

The first discussion clearly illustrates that many people have very different memories of growing up in City Line. The discussion started off with a comment from someone who asked:

> I see people talking about the good times but were there bad things about City Line? It seemed that back then most of the girls could be nothing but secretaries and the boys were trained in a vocational trade subject. There weren't many choices for us and just a few of us went on to college. There wasn't much in the way of culture in the area for us, also. But, it was the beginning of mothers going off to work.
>
> If anything the girls went to college, and the boys went into the Armed Services.

Then, surprisingly, another new voice started to talk about the seamy side of the area:

> I was a gang member back then—fighting and criminal activities. I don't know if many people here were into that world.

Another new voice (the topic is obviously interesting to more and more of those from the old neighborhood) reiterated the refrain espoused by others:

> My family wanted me to just have kids and to be a secretary, but I wanted more—college. The parents just wanted us to do better than they did. They tried to help us get there. But that usually did not include college.

Another person responded:

> Women worked when they got married but then didn't once they had children. But, everyone has to take responsibility for their decisions.

One more participant chimed in with:

> I didn't get any encouragement from my mother for me to go to college. I can't remember wanting to be anything except being a secretary. It's really my fault but I am fine today.

It is interesting that the discussants tended to mention only their moms when talking about their parents.

Someone else entered the discussion and tried to change the subject:

> I have only good memories when I think about the old neighborhood. Why don't we stick to those.

At that point, someone added that it was unfortunate that stores had not been open on Sundays. Someone else said that she had obviously missed the point of the question, but it might have been another attempt to change the subject.

A participant tried to sum up:

> There was good and bad about City Line.

I couldn't agree more with that statement. In a valiant attempt to change the topic once and for all, one man said:

> Kucks [an iconic deli on Liberty Avenue] WAS open on Sunday.

Even so, the topic had whetted a number of people's appetites for more. The discussion went back and forth, and a new voice added:

My family struggled. Just like some other people here, we didn't know what you needed to do for college [a lack of cultural capital]. So, I went to CUNY and I finally got a job on Wall Street—but it was an all-boys network then. But, I kept going and I am doing ok today.

Another person who was involved in gangs at the time reported:

There were gangs, drugs and lots of trouble. I got away from the neighborhood just to stay alive. I finally went to a community college. We didn't have a lot of money but here I am today and the neighborhood shaped me.

Someone else stated that he might leave the discussion because it seemed that some people didn't want to discuss anything controversial. A familiar name said:

Some don't want to stir up trouble.

This individual went on to say:

I believe we should remember that it was not all good. A lot of people used drugs and a couple of them died. Only the strong survived that time and place.

As you can see, many men and women from City Line wanted to talk about controversial matters once the discussion turned in that direction. However, it made a few others rather uncomfortable to talk about unpleasant topics that distort their "constructed" image of their childhoods and adolescence in my old neighborhood. It is true, unfortunately, that a few of these individuals did indeed discontinue their participation in discussions like the one above. Ultimately, these types of discussions would, for the most part, disappear. Honestly, they can be exhausting—even online virtual discussions. Over time, I found myself not participating in controversial topics on social media because it can jeopardize friendships, the newly acquired and those that are decades old. The few discussions that did explore controversial topics, however, pointed out something undeniable: growing up in City Line was not like growing up in Mayberry, a fictional, idyllic town portrayed in the 1960s television series *The Andy Griffith Show*. In that vein, one of my old friends said:

Fathers used to come out of bars very drunk. They staggered up and down the streets.

I do agree with those former residents who said there were benefits to growing up in that neighborhood. And from my time on social media, it looks as though a number of people from the old neighborhood have been successful. Those early years were very important for (as someone else said) who we are today. On the streets, we learned how to organize games, negotiate rules, and use humor to get out of trouble. My childhood was happy and sad at the same time, but the schooling, the era, and working-class cultural capital did not give me a broad enough view of the world and my place in it. How could it have been any other way, given the environment surrounding me? Only after a number of events (discussed previously and to come) did I begin to perceive that I could possibly have a different kind of life. Middle-class kids learn that fact earlier in life; it gives them a head start. The individual who became uncomfortable with the former discussion interjected her viewpoint firmly:

> Girls from that time and place trained to become secretaries and the boys a trade. That's just the way it was, it was not positive or negative—but, girls from our generation did start to do different things from what their mothers did.

A newbie to the discussion stated:

> College was not even talked about by my parents. They didn't talk about my future. I went to college later when I was older but it is more difficult then. I wouldn't want to return to that time and place there was a lot of prejudice and not enough people of different races and religions. It really helped me.

Females dominated the discussion of the lack of opportunities. Then, someone else said:

> I think I am going to leave this site. I want to keep the good memories I have of City Line.

One person nailed it when she said:

> There is good and bad back then and that is the same with this site. You don't always have to agree with all that is said here. We have different memories of that time and place. Some are good, some are bad. Most of the comments about that time and place on this site are positive. We all grew up the same way, how could we [have] thought any differently?

Stating what had been said previously but with a new twist, the same person went on:

> For our parents, high school was good enough, So, they thought the same for us. I attended college later in life in order to get a better job. I needed it to move up in my company.

Another added:

> My mother, believe it or not, did not like it when I won a scholarship to college. But, she was very happy when I got a job in a career that she deemed appropriate for a woman. College was not a priority—I got my college degree eventually, but I did lose out, overall because it was when I had kids.

Another participant said:

> But, we were poor and did the best we could. We had lots of children in the family.

Someone else commented:

> It's a story about two cities.

A new friend of mine immediately added:

> It's about two genders.

And another participant chimed in:

> I went to a CUNY school also, free tuition. We could have never afforded today's college tuition to go to college, and graduate school.

She continued:

> We didn't have too many things—toys and such. We got some during the holidays. But that helped improve our imaginations. I appreciated what I had. My mother would have never put up with the way kids are today.

Her point about today's kids lacking in imagination worries experts in child development (Willis 2011). Someone else, sounding very much like a sociologist, said:

Boys got to go to college back then. One of my male siblings went away to college while I went to a local CUNY college. It had free tuition and open enrollment. This is the only way for me to have gone to college but I went.

She continued with an insightful comment that sociologists who study "tracking" would be interested in:

The notion [cultural capital] that some kids go away to college surprised me. Even Adams [the local high school which had a college track] just pushed CUNY schools on us which we were told to decide from.

Someone else interjected:

Yes, nowadays the kids are college bound from middle school.

That's not true for everyone, in particular poor and working-class kids, but I understand the point. It sounds as if she has experienced some social mobility. Another person commented:

After high school I didn't go to college—it was not expected—but getting married and having kids was expected. I, too, got a job as a secretary. That's what happened. I finally went to college at middle age. I had a great childhood, life was simpler then—I have fond memories of that time and place: we played outside all day. We hung out on our friends' stoops. Kids today have it harder than we did.

But, remember that someone else said that kids today are being prepared for college starting in middle school. These varying perceptions may have something to do with a person's own current social class position, like for this participant:

My family and I went back to my old stomping grounds. They were shocked. I told them it was a much better area then.

This sort of comment confuses me, because when I visited the old neighborhood in 2011, 2013, and 2015, I found the streets clean and the structures in good shape. What had changed was the demographic make-up of those streets.

A person then asked why most people left the area if it was such a nice place to live (a very good question). One response amounted to admitting there were problems with living in City Line:

Just like previous generations who came here, for a better life.

Then, like a verbal bomb going off, a newbie to the discussion said:

> Treasure your memories because I was in the old neighborhood recently and it was very sad.

Another person agreed:

> Yes, it IS sad.

So did another discussant:

> I saw a picture of my old house. It IS sad because I love my memories of that place.

One more person said:

> The way it is now hurts badly. I will never be able to have those experiences again.

Someone else chimed in:

> I am so happy that that is where I am from. That time and place made us who we are today—strong.

Another discussant said:

> I am sad about my old neighborhood.

On another occasion, the discussion turned to the neighborhood in general. In an attempt to open some minds about the changes that took place over time, one old-time resident suggested people should read *How East New York Became a Ghetto* (Thabit 2003). A person new to the discussion ventured:

> That was then. People were forced to sell. It is improving and I am happy.

One man took a sociological approach:

> That kind of thing happened in many inner cities back then. I walk those same streets now like I did back then. But there is a lack of community now [see Putnam 2000].

One discussant's view was:

> Minorities and Puerto Ricans and people on welfare caused problems in East New York; that's why white people left. Books—huh.

In fact, Thabit's book outlines a complex web of causes of white flight, redlining, and block busting. Another discussant posited:

> Blacks and Puerto Ricans scared the whites who then left. There was a lot of racial tensions and hatred. The area had a lot of racial hatred. People moved out and then the area went downhill. That is when it turned into a ghetto.
>
> The owners of buildings in ENY used welfare tenants to line their pockets and then abandon the buildings. There is a lot of crime there now (See the demographic table in the Appendix to Chap. 1 for the current data on crime in the area).

Someone else took offense at this comment:

> No! The people there today are fantastic. There are bad people everywhere. It's not the kind of community you people are saying it is. You make it out to be a war zone today and it isn't.

Another man said:

> The neighborhood is fine today. Was Long Island any better [where many whites moved to on leaving Queens]? You all left because of the different color faces that move in. Many people moved to Long Island and it wasn't much better there.

Someone else disagreed:

> It is a ghetto now.

Some participants, especially those who still live in the neighborhood, seemed to think that City Line and Ozone Park continue to places where people are proud to live. They wondered what Long Island gave them. Equally, there were complaints about the new residents of City Line and Ozone Park from a couple of people. One said.

> Indians play their music loud into the morning hours.

Others took the opposite view:

> Its better today in the area than in past decades.

> I think it is still a nice neighborhood, everyone speaks English on some of the blocks.

Speaking English seems to be the litmus test of whether the block has really changed for the worse.

> What about all the holiday flags hanging there today?

Then, someone asked a very important question:

> If it was so good in that time and place then why did most move away?

One response was:

> Well, they liked it but wanted better.

The next response was on the tip of my own tongue:

> I don't understand that answer. So, it wasn't so good then? Why not move back?

Another person said:

> The area is not the way I remember it. I'm Italian.

Someone else interjected:

> I still live there. Change is good. Everyone on my block speaks English.

Others added:

> And there were drugs back then.

> But, people could leave their doors unlocked then.

I don't remember doing that in my house.

> There were needles everywhere.

A participant offered some insightful analysis:

It is possible that we remember with rose colored glasses.

Of course, there were a number of nasty comments about the ethnicity of those who live there today, such as:

I want Italian sauce, not curry.

Finally, someone asked what I was thinking:

Holiday flags? Oh please.

Others added:

Some countries around the world are bad you know.

There are some entertainers from Ozone Park you know, like Bernadette Peters, that's what makes me proud.

Other comments were somewhat more reasonable and understanding:

There have been crazy comments about Arab-Americans. I am a Catholic and an Arab-American. All Italians are not in the mafia and not all of people like me are terrorists.

Too many hateful comments here. People left. Good!

Many groups were discriminated [against] when they first came here such as the Irish, Italians and Germans.

Early in my time on social media (before I decided to use social media comments in this volume) I tried to use this argument, but for the most part it was unsuccessful in changing people's minds.
Other participants chimed in:

Yes, there is much hate.

I agree, people left here and they complain now.

If you are German, Italian, or Arab does not make you a fascist or terrorist. Keep that in mind.

No, we have not kept that in mind.

There are good and bad among all peoples.

Immigrants have faced prejudice and discrimination—they were called all kind of derogatory names. They were just from different cultures. The newest immigrants are just like our oldest relatives. They will try to fit in. Keep that in mind. Try to be more open. They just want a piece of the American Dream.

The discussion at this point seemed to have motivated those who were less ethnocentric to participate. It culminated with one person saying:

It's great that it is so multicultural here now.

To further protect the identities of the participants, I will summarize the next set of comments about the old neighborhood. There were a number of negative comments about the current residents, some were about their food, their personalities, and their wedding celebrations, and their "camels." Yet, there were other comments about how pleasant the new residents are. A few of the past residents thought the new residents' ethnicity and religion were the main reason for others' negative comments. As I have stressed above, they tried to remind the "haters" that the Italians, Germans, and Irish faced similar prejudices. (You may remember me saying earlier that my surname was originally O'Gorman, but my great-grandfather dropped the "O" because it wasn't a good time to be Irish in New York City.) However, someone responded that the new residents have come here to kill us, "our" ancestors did not. One man even suggested that the call to prayer that one can now hear in the old neighborhood might be an attempt by Muslims to secretly pass (terrorist) information. (Never mind that there is more right-wing extremist terror in the U.S.A., Plucinska (2015) and Eichenwald (2016)). Others did try to push back at that kind of thinking.

I posted a few passages from *A Walker in the City*, by Alfred Kazin (1951), into one social media discussion. It is about his memories of growing up in Brownsville, East New York—just down the road from City Line—and is considered a classic. Here, he is talking about what it was like to walk into the "Italian" section of his old neighborhood in the 1930s (he mentions many streets and avenues that would have been familiar to participants: Atlantic, Liberty, etc.):

> There was a new public library.... It was to the north of the Italians, just off the el on Broadway, in the 'American' district of the old frame houses.... I still had a certain suspicion of the Italians—surely they were all Fascists to a man? Every grocery window seemed to have a picture of Mussolini frowning under a feather-tipped helmet.... In a butcher shop ... the clumps of red and brown meat dripping off those sausage rings stayed with me ... did they eat such things?

It is sometimes good to refer to history, literature, and sociology when trying to understand how cities change and how the new and old residents of a neighborhood view each other.[2]

The debate on social media went back and forth, one side pleading with the other to take more of a "culturally relativistic" attitude (and not an ethnocentric one). And finally, in disgust, some said that if people don't like the new residents, there is a simple solution: just don't go back to the old neighborhood. A few former residents have never moved from the old neighborhood and feel it remains a nice area for families to raise children, with one person speaking to the fact that people still walk most places and children still play safely outside. In contrast, another former resident said that the area now resembles the Middle East—but named a non-Middle Eastern country as an example, which gave others the opportunity to say that part of the problem is that many people have a fairly narrow view of the world and have not experienced enough interactions with people from other cultures. They added with emphasis that not all Jews are cheap, not all Irish are drunks, not all Italians belong to the Mafia, and not all Muslims are terrorists.

With crime rates at record lows and the physical structures of the neighborhood in good shape, one must wonder exactly what the negative comments about the current residents are referring to. Is it the new residents' customs, food, dress, or their religious beliefs? Or is it all of the above? There is no doubt that there are two different images of the state of the old neighborhood: one as a nice place to raise a family, and another as an unsafe and unpleasant place even to visit. One other matter is without debate: there are a number of men and women who grew up in this working-class neighborhood who are now angry, bitter, and resentful of its current residents. As one former resident remarked, it is a shame that there is so much racism and hate in some of the comments. And there are other former residents who do not feel this way. I would hypothesize that those who are most angry are those who have lived "hard lives," experienced hidden injuries of class, especially those associated with a lack of the badges of ability that a college degree and/or a high-status career can confer.

I still wanted to know the answer to the important question raised by a few former residents of the old neighborhood: If City Line was such a wonderful place to live, then why did almost everyone leave? Moreover, it is quite interesting that the woman who posed that question is one of the few City Liners who still lives in the area. In those words one can also hear, obviously, a certain amount of anger and resentment. And for the first time, we were introduced to the elephant in the room when talking about Ozone Park and City Line at that time: the presence of the mob and its standing in the neighborhood. Many residents felt that the mob (and John Gotti) was a positive presence. Also, the woman who asked the question invited everyone to return to City Line if they thought it was such a grand place to live. People tend to forget that their childhood memories may not match their parents' perceptions of the neighborhood; it was our parents who decided to move away, as some ex-City Liners admitted. There was no mention either that the 1950s and 1960s were not good times for certain groups of people, including women, homosexuals, and people of color.

As you can see from the comments, some of the former residents of City Line and Ozone Park did take a balanced approach to their memories and current feelings toward the neighborhood. There were, indeed, positive and negative aspects of growing up working class in that neighborhood. I have visited City Line a few times over the last five years, and the neighborhood looked in good shape: the physical structures were sound and clean, the side streets were quiet (including my old block, 76th Street), and Liberty Avenue was bustling with shoppers. It seemed to be a fine place to live. After I stopped saving social media comments for this publication, I tried my best to lay out some basic sociological concepts on social media sites such as "ethnocentrism" and "cultural relativism": I asked whether the changes in City Line between then and now may be just noticeable "differences" and not representative of a substantive neighborhood decline.

The biggest change is the ethnic background of the inhabitants. (A number of ex-residents were shocked to learn that Queens was recently voted the number one place to visit in the country because of its diversity (NY Daily News, Rosenberg and Erikson 2014)). So, is the ethnic make-up of the area today what some of the negative comments were alluding to? Well, some people referred to the current residents as "Dot Heads" or "Towel Heads," and joked about the camels outside the sari shops. In addition, the IND "A" train that runs through City Line had been historically referred to by some ex-residents as the "Animal Express," (because it went through African-American neighborhoods) but now I have heard it referred to as the "Ali Baba Express."

Some people said they felt that negative comments about Ozone Park and City Line were not appropriate for social media. Owing to the belief that social media comments were only for positive memories, topics such as drug abuse and alcoholism were to be avoided. There were also, to be sure, some objections to the calls for postings to be only about the positive aspects of the old neighborhood. And some people did speak about the negative aspect of growing up in City Line. When some of the bad points were finally brought out in the open, one that was mentioned was the lack of professional role models, especially for girls. In this extended discussion, one can hear a great deal of "gender consciousness" and a burgeoning "class consciousness." The women here spoke about the gender role expectations of that time and place, and how these limited their future opportunities, with college not being an option for most of the women (for most of the men at that time also) and with a limited number of careers open to them.[3]

When some ex-City Liners let their hair down and opened up about their feelings, many of their comments echoed a number of the points made in this book. For instance, a few touched on what sociologists call "cultural capital," saying they were unaware that there were scholarships for college, and that you could actually go away to and live at colleges. In addition, some admitted that "with the good, comes the bad," agreeing that growing up in an urban working-class environment has some advantages: learning to be tough, self-reliance, and being able to take a punch and come back stronger. Most importantly for my research interests, comments demonstrated an incipient class consciousness among members of the working class: they saw their position in the social class structure in terms of "us" as opposed to "them" (as I discuss elsewhere: Gorman 1998a, b, 2000a, b). Finally, those who "escaped" the constraints of their class and neighborhood to go on to college and acquire successful careers pointed to a significant causal event: they left the neighborhood, with hanging out with new friends in places such as Manhattan being a common theme.

As you can see from earlier comments, many former residents' explanation for the decline of the neighborhood is that other groups "moved in": blacks, Puerto Ricans, and welfare recipients. When some people who still reside in City Line suggested that the area is still nice and filled with "good people," they were usually contradicted quickly (mainly by people who live elsewhere). A few people who still live in the area showed their anger at those who moved away to far-away places such as Florida (a very popular destination, it seems), and who have not seen the neighborhood in years but continue to disparage it, nonetheless. Sociology teaches us that tough economic times have the tendency to push people to denigrate others, especially those nearby socially and economically, a phenomenon that social psychologists call "scapegoating."

A complaint was voiced that current residents seem to keep to themselves, more than was the case in our time, but that may just be an indication that those new residents have taken more of a modern, "middle-class" orientation than our older, "working-class" approach. The common refrain that "good fences make good neighbors" resonates with many who live in today's suburbs. Robert Putnam's *Bowling Alone* (2000) sparked a debate on whether there is a trend toward an ever-increasing population becoming more and more isolated.

Keep in mind, also, that many of the comments are from individuals who have recently reached the stage in life when they look back at their life and evaluate whether they are satisfied or not with what they see (Erikson 1950). As we age, the youthful dreams we had growing up of what we could aspire to obviously narrow. It may be that some people—working-class men and women who have not shared in much of the American economic pie—find it psychologically advantageous to blame others for their current situation. This is the social psychology of social class relations in American society.

It was interesting that when photographs of City Line as it now stands were posted on social media, showing a clean and vibrant community, some ex-City Liners immediately wanted to know the date they were taken. It was as if the photographs did not provide enough evidence for their current image of the area as in decline. Correspondingly, when a few photographs of the old neighborhood painted a dreary picture, some former residents responded with comments such as "I don't remember City Line looking like that." On viewing one old photo in particular, an old friend said, "What a dump." That comment did prompt a couple of former residents to raise their eyebrows, metaphorically.

One comment is interesting in light of recent incidents involving police officers shooting young black men. A participant in a social media discussion said: "I hope that Mr. XYZ, who made those racist comments, brings a better attitude to his work when he is on the job in New York City [as a City worker]." The man who made this comment now lives in East New York and was not treated well on Social Media. Many of the comments reproduced in this chapter are about East New York more broadly, an area that has one of the highest crime rates in New York City (the 75th Precinct). It has been that way for a very long time.[4] City Line happens to be the easternmost tip of East New York and always has had a somewhat different set of demographics than the rest of the area.

To conclude, it is worth stressing that some people have an image of how the world works and almost nothing you say, or any evidence you present, is going to change their minds. Most posts on social media that presented the current state of the neighborhood in positive terms tended to be ignored. On one occasion I said that one of my best friends had compared City Line then to a ghetto. A couple of people gave me a tongue lashing, and in fact I have lost a few "friends" from the old neighborhood for questioning the special place that City Line holds in their hearts. Let me say this in respect to my years growing up there: I loved them, and I hated them, too.

NOTES

1. See Brooklyn gang books mentioned earlier for a discussion of the gangs of East New York.
2. See also Falco (2012), CNN "When Italian Immigrants were 'the Other.'"
3. The demographic tables in Chap. 1 offer a comparison of the percentage of residents who had at least some college in their background with residents of other neighborhoods in New York City at the time.
4. For sociological discussions of particular neighborhoods, see Thabit, 2003 for East New York, Rieder, 1987 for Canarsie, and Torgovnik, 1997 for Ocean Parkway.

CHAPTER 8

Conclusion: Hard and Settled Living and The Development of Angry (And Not So Angry) White Working-Class Men and Women

WORLDS OF PAIN?

In her classic book *Worlds of Pain: Life in the Working-Class Family*, Lillian Rubin (1976) vividly describes the lives of working-class adults in the United States. She tells stories of families struggling to make ends meet, working in unfulfilling jobs, and living in unhappy marriages, with few hobbies or pastimes. When I studied working-class families, I found a number of them to be like the ones she described, but I also found working-class families whose members were happy, enjoyed their work, took family vacations, and wanted their children to attend college. However, Rubin's portraits of working-class families still resonate today, and evoke some of the families from my old neighborhood.[1] While some families in City Line and Ozone Park lived "settled" lives (Howell 1973), with characteristics of some of the working-class families found in my earlier study (Gorman 1998a, b), more and more working-class families today live in "worlds of pain."

The evenings growing up on 76th Street were filled with kids playing ball, riding bikes, playing tag, waiting for the Mr. Softee ice-cream truck to come down our block, and listening to the neighbors talk, joke, and laugh about New York's sports teams, their bills, and complaints about local politicians. Many of us from my old neighborhood have fond memories of that time and place, but stress and strife were ever present. I watched my mom juggle the money, drag my drunken father out of the car in front of our apartment on a daily basis, and curse life as she knew it. I also

© The Author(s) 2017
T.J. Gorman, *Growing up Working Class*,
DOI 10.1007/978-3-319-58898-8_8

229

witnessed painful moments for other families in the neighborhood—alcoholism, low-income-related problems, and marital discord.

Rubin's portrayal of working-class couples getting married without much thought about the ramifications of such a commitment resonated with my own experience. My first wife and I got married very young (she was barely 19 and I was 20), but when college and professional careers are mostly out of the question, what alternative is there for working-class kids? How else can a working-class kid get out from under his or her parents' roof? Currently, wedding bells are more likely heard today in middle- and upper-middle-class neighborhoods (see Cherlin 2014). This social fact only points to the continued financial stresses and widening income gap that shape and intensify the "worlds of pain" for the working class. We weren't going away to college, but I never questioned my ability to acquire a decently paying job, and neither did my first wife. I had a (two-year) college degree in a specific field—graphic arts—and printing was one of the largest industries in New York City. By the same token, my ex-wife had studied stenography and typing in high school, and she acquired an entry-level job at the corporate offices of a large firm in Manhattan. Many other young women from that time and place found work as secretaries in the offices of major corporations. Also, this was almost exactly the same period of time when middle-level incomes peaked, before their historical flattening and downward trend. With this rosy outlook and generous gifts from our wedding guests, we felt as though our jobs had given us a good start to a nice, working-class life.

Some family members in the neighborhood had jobs that might have placed them in the lower middle class or, possibly, for a few, even the middle class, but they had attitudes and aspirations that were still largely working class in nature (their cultural capital). This social fact has to be front and center in any discussion of the varying outcomes of individual social mobility of the residents of City Line at that time. In fact, it seemed our lives were always on the borderline—the border between Brooklyn and Queens, the border between two gangs, the border between early and late baby boomers, and, for some members of the community, the border between the lower middle class and the working class.

Self-Confidence

This book has been my attempt to pull apart the various facets of my life to help me understand how I (and others) got to my current position in the socio-economic hierarchy. In utilizing an auto-ethnographic methodological approach, I have included as much sociological analysis as emotional content. I hope my students in all my classes come away with the ability to conduct such an analysis. One of my mentors was absolutely correct: those many facets of life are intertwined in ways that make them invisible and somewhat "natural." That is, within any social class structure, the presence or absence of certain facets is not questioned. A middle-class parent once said to me, "Of course my daughter is going to college, why wouldn't she?" Indeed, from the neighborhood in which she grew up, to the friends she has and their aspirations, to the school she attends, to the educational levels and careers of her parents, "why wouldn't she?" As my mentor said to me (or rather warned me), it is difficult to isolate these (dare I say) variables: they are in the air, the water, and the very fabric of everyday life. Yet, one aspect consistently found along this journey stands out from the rest in trying to understand what it was like growing up in City Line during the 1950s, 1960s, and 1970s: my lack of *self-confidence*.

Whether I think about my educational experiences, interactions with the opposite sex, or career choices, the self-confidence endowed to members of the middle class that is sorely lacking among members of the working class is vital to understanding what it was like to grow up working class. Middle-class kids have the self-confidence to push themselves forward in ways, and in areas, that working-class kids do not. Lareau (1989, 2003) notes this when she addresses the middle-class sense of entitlement. The belief in one's own ability to achieve—whether academically or interpersonally—is important. It is the feeling that you have the ability to be accepted at a top college, or the confidence that your crush will accept your request for a date, or the potential (plus ability) to make the school's baseball team. The self-confidence to accomplish these goals (and others) forms the basis for middle-class children's sense of entitlement. It is the determination to raise your hand first in class. It is the belief that you can take the difficult courses and programs in high school that will give you access to top colleges, and thus to lucrative employment. In fact, it is the hutzpah to take courses in areas that might not, at first, seem financially lucrative at that moment, in the arts for example, but that can lead to top jobs in theater, music, and film. It is the belief that you deserve better friends than those you have at the moment. What I am trying to do here is speak to how that sense of entitlement comes to fruition. It needs to be spelled out more directly, because it is just part of a range of "normal," everyday middle-class experiences (see Brekhaus 1998). Where does that self-confidence come from? It comes from parents who have professional, well-paying, career-oriented jobs; older siblings and peers who have attended college; and an entire neighborhood that is geared toward promoting college attendance and professional careers. It would be difficult not to have an abundance of self-confidence under those conditions.

Growing up in City Line and Ozone Park, I did not develop the self-confidence necessary to succeed in many of the important facets of a child's life. To paraphrase, with a twist, what the middle-class parent said to me about her daughter: How could I have been expected to have self-confidence with parents juggling bills and worrying about losing a decent paying, blue-collar job (in Bordens dairy), having "friends" who made fun of me about my alcoholic parent and my early failed attempts at dating, attending an elementary school that made me urinate in my pants, and lacking any connection to professional role models? Those feelings of inadequacy weigh down on a young working-class boy's attempt at building the kind of self-confidence needed to break out of the constraints of a neighborhood that did not, by any means, instill a sense of entitlement.

STRUCTURE AND AGENCY

Sociology, though, does recognize that social structure is not altogether deterministic. What factors came together to help me get to where I am today—a tenured Associate Professor at Queens College? Some of the following factors helped: an older brother who danced to the beat of a different drummer and became a Vietnam veteran with a passion for social and political issues (see Kluger 2011); a couple of key, caring teachers who advised me to reach for the stars; a mother who had a "sassy" attitude toward life; a divorce early in life; some friends who went their own way (also I believe connected to older siblings' adventurous attitudes). All together, these gave me, over time, a belief in my own abilities and the spark to try new paths. As Vance (2016) notes in *Hillbilly Elegy*, it takes a number of variables to line up for someone from the working class to move up and out from their humble beginnings. It was a long road from running an (already outdated) printing press in high school to becoming an Associate Professor in Sociology at Queens College—the very same college I was not sure I could even get through as an undergraduate student. It has been, as the Grateful Dead sang, a long, strange trip.

An early indication in my life that I could dance to a different drummer myself was the way I learned to entertain myself in my apartment when my friends wanted me to come out to play and probably "rank out" each other. Eventually, I had enough of the rank-outs, and took the bold step of breaking away from the group. Instead, I ventured around the corner to hang out with a new bunch of guys who wanted to play ball without the ritual insults. My early years growing up in City Line illustrate the intersection of social structure and agency—I was able to maneuver through constraints in a way that started to build self-confidence. Social class and social structure interacted with other active agents such as my older brother, sassy mother, a few caring teachers and counselors, and life-course events. Social structural constraints set the parameters, but active agents in my social life helped me navigate and challenge them.

Surely, differences in child-rearing techniques across social classes are important for cultivating the interests and imaginations of children. That someone in a middle-class home would have recognized my childhood interest in science goes without saying—I would have been prepared early for the Bronx High School of Science (one of the top high schools in the country for children interested in science). Middle-class parents would have also had the information necessary to make informed choices about schools and careers. However, even with these everyday realities of urban working-class life setting the stage for my future, I was still able to use the wiggle room that social structure allows in order to be an active agent. It was not easy, and the outcome would have probably been different if one or more of the mitigating factors had been absent.

Social Mobility and the Economy

My peers from the old neighborhood experienced a wide variety of life outcomes. The research methodology used for this sociological self-inquiry has not been quantitative in nature, thus it did not allow any correlations or other statistics to be calculated for those who did and did not experience upward social mobility. I have only recently been introduced, on social media, to a number of former residents from the old neighborhood. These are people who have made themselves available to discuss such matters. Others who may or may not have experienced upward mobility may not be well represented in this online forum.

How did some working-class urban residents experience social class mobility? First, we would have to distinguish between those who experienced real intergenerational social mobility from those who, because of social structural changes, experienced a changing work environment (white-collar workers in air-conditioned offices) but not true social mobility (compared to their parents who still worked in factories but earned a better living). How much social mobility would I have been able to claim for myself, for instance, if I had remained in the printing industry, estimating, planning, and scheduling print jobs, compared to my uncle who worked a linotype machine in a hot factory at the peak of the industry? That is a difficult comparison to make. Although I have worked in air-conditioned offices, sitting in front of computer screens and having the flexible schedule of a college professor, there was never any chance my wife and I could have owned two homes as he did on one income.

Today, the United States is falling behind many other nations whose people used to emigrate to it to experience greater social mobility opportunities (see Gould 2012). There are two obvious social facts that can help explain why some people from that time and place experienced upward social mobility: race and gender. Women and people of color could write additional chapters to this book about what it is like for them to grow up in an urban working-class setting. As noted previously, female friends of mine have talked about the lack of professional role models (or any role models outside of homemakers and secretaries) in City Line. Indeed, one female friend from the old neighborhood still finds it difficult even to discuss the matter with me because it makes her angry. In addition, this was a time (the late 1960s and early 1970s) when, believe it or not, there were counties in the United States that had not yet desegregated their schools (even though the Brown *v*. Board of Education ruling came down from the Supreme Court in 1954). It was also a time when African-Americans were demanding their civil rights. My auto-ethnography cannot capture all these experiences, but it can help foreground certain social worlds, with the understanding that other voices are necessary to have a deeper understanding of that time and place.

The era in which I came of age is key to explaining the kind and amount of social mobility some of us from City Line/Ozone Park experienced (See Chetty et al. 2016). The period after World War II, until about the mid-1970s, was a time when men (and sometimes women) who had completed just a high school education could find a decent-paying job that supported an entire family on just one income. Today, this is what we would call a "living wage." Now, people with the same credentials have not fared as well on the job market, and therefore neither have their children. Many parents, supported by a booming economy, strong unions, and government programs (such as the GI Bill), experienced some social mobility and benefited as a result. That is not to say that our parents did not work hard.

They did, but the opportunity to work—and be paid well for it—has to be part of the socio-economic landscape before one can show one's abilities. After World War II, the United States was the dominant economy in the world. Unions were strong, production grew, and for a while it seemed as if all boats did rise with a strong economy. In fact, right up to the time when my generational cohort entered the workforce, the economy was strong. My birth year is the midpoint of the "baby boom generation," and we entered the workforce in 1971 if we went to work after high school, 1973 if we went to work after community college, or 1975 if we went to work after attending a four-year college. Many social analysts say that the early to mid 1970's were the years when working-class wages flattened. We just got in under the wire.[2] In addition, there were more intact working-class families (for better or worse) at that time, with the effects of the women's movement of the 1960s just starting to be felt in America, especially in working-class neighborhoods like mine.[3] The later cohort of baby boomers (born in the late 1950s and early 1960s) faced a different economy when they tried to enter the workforce in the early 1980s.

A number of my old friends experienced a certain amount of upward social mobility, but very few (from what I can ascertain from social media) became lawyers, medical doctors, hedge fund managers on Wall Street, or members of Congress or other political entities. (I know of one attorney, one engineer, a couple of teachers, no medical doctors, a few small business owners, a couple of accountants, two publishing managers, one professor, one art historian, and one New York City official.) Of course, the full extent of social mobility among former residents of City Line is an empirical question and beyond the reach of this anecdotal inventory. A few women (and men), because of traditional gender roles, experienced upward social mobility through marriage to someone in a more prestigious and well-paying occupation. This imbalance within couples can lead those same people to be susceptible to downward mobility due to divorce (especially women, while men's income rises after divorce, see Peterson 1996).[4] I am convinced that our neighborhood's environment wasted a lot of individual talent and brain power.

One can only imagine what future research and auto-ethnographies will tell us about social mobility, and if the gap between the rich and everyone else will continue to widen (It will if Piketty (2014) is correct). Again, thinking back to that time and place, one has to give credence to the concept of "agency." The key question in sociology, of course, is how much of an active agent can any one person be? It is possible, given the widening gaps between the rungs of the social class ladder, that being an active agent today (and in the future) is more difficult than in the period I came of age. While some of us experienced social mobility (in education, business, and management) in that time and place, most (if not all) of us are not part of the top rung of the social class ladder that has received so much media attention lately.

As I have said repeatedly in this volume, the Catholic elementary school I attended helped offset mediocre high school and community college experiences.[5] Is the answer to the problem for everyone to attend college? No, especially if we were to have the type of vocational educational system found in countries such as Germany and Japan, where there is a tight connection between industry and schooling. We have been neglecting our vocational students and schools (with vocational schools acquiring a bad reputation, especially among the middle and upper middle class). Nevertheless, we need to make it possible for every student at least to have a viable option and the choice of attending college. College attendance has been associated with being more open to other cultures (Feldman and Newcomb 1969; Pascarella and Terenzini 1992), and that might help alleviate some of the anger, frustration, and bitterness we hear so much about today. Some research has shown, however that being tolerant of others does not necessarily translate into support for race-based solutions (Wodtke 2012; Kane 2001).

Neighborhood

Some former residents from City Line have pointed out the connection between moving away from the area and their rise in social status.[6] That a few of them consciously made the decision speaks to the ability of some individuals to rise (to some degree) above the constraints of social structure and class. As an illustration, one person admitted that she told a friend on the block that he was too smart to stay in the neighborhood. Another man, when asked if he wanted to move back to City Line, responded, "Why would I go back, I spent a long time trying to get out." One other women said "there was nothing there for me," and her friend added, "It looks so grey and dreary there."

As soon as I got my first job and got married, I had the urge to move away from Ozone Park. I wanted to move to what seemed to be a more interesting area of Queens, such as Forest Hills (with its trendy shops, nice movie theaters, book stores, and tennis club). Despite spending many years in the row housing (with railroad rooms) in City Line, we could see that other neighborhoods had unattached, single-family homes and nice backyards. One of my older friends made note of the beautiful homes in Bayside, Queens as he traveled to Queensborough Community College. It is ironic that working-class kids from Ozone Park and City Line glimpsed middle- and upper-middle-class neighborhoods while traveling to a two-year community college where they might even have been studying social inequality and social class. In this case, it might be said that the system can sow the seeds of its own destruction.

Now, some people in the old neighborhood might have been apt to talk about the "snooty" residents who live in those areas (as did the respondents in my research on education). Nevertheless, others aspired to the ways of life (culture) of these people and places. This split in attitudes toward those who were better off could help explain the variety of outcomes my old friends experienced during their lifetimes. In other words, as resistance theory has shown (Willis 1981), working-class kids get working-class jobs by having a laugh at the expense of the "man." But, those attitudes may just help reproduce social class relations. Others, however, found that the best way to "fight the power" was to adopt others' way of life—move out, move on, move up; get your degree and then work to help change the system for others who had not yet moved up the social class ladder. After my divorce, I tried to do just that—traveling through Europe, going back to school to finish my BA degree, and leaving a lower-level supervisory job in the printing industry to prepare for a professional career.

To stay put is to risk staying in place. That is, as I heard from some former residents of my old neighborhood, their moving away from the area helped them achieve certain goals later in life. The most recent research (Chetty et al. 2016) does suggest support for that notion—that the earlier (up to 13 years old) one moves away from a low-income area, the better one's chances of experiencing upward mobility. One factor identified by Hunter (1974) is the tendency for those with higher income levels (and who have children) to view their neighborhood more favorably than those with lower incomes (and who are childless). This is an empirical result directly related to my arguments in this book, adding to the explanations for residents' varied perceptions of a single neighborhood. That is to say, when a family can use its resources to take vacations and purchase all the accoutrements of a middle-class lifestyle, it can participate in the life of its community in ways that other families cannot because of limited funds. If a child grows up with a nice bicycle, decent clothes, and memories of vacations to Disneyland, is it any wonder they will tend to have positive memories of growing up in that neighborhood? (By the way, this does not mean the answer is for everyone to move to the suburbs or rural areas. They have their own problems.[7])

Other factors have been found to affect the perception of neighborhoods by others, whether they be demographics (education level, income level, etc.), social institutions (family, schools, churches, and law enforcement), or the social organization of the neighborhood (social norms, social capital, and role models). Each factor must be clearly defined for each neighborhood, and it must be shown how each factor affects a particular population within a particular neighborhood (see Sampson 2012 for the most recent research on the effects of neighborhood).

Hard and Settled Living

Some of the stories contained in this book coincide with the perceptions of others—such as Alfred Kazin (1951)—who said he "escaped" the fate of living in his neighborhood by hanging out and making friends in other neighborhoods. A family did not necessarily have to move to rise; rather, the children of City Line who started to hang out with new friends in different environments such as Greenwich Village (in Manhattan) were more likely to meet people who had different attitudes and greater aspirations for the future. My own personal story includes "moves" of that sort that made a difference in my life, the first to get away from 76th Street by hanging out on 75th Street. Admittedly, that is a small move geographically, but it removed me from the destructive friendships that were hurting my self-esteem. Another time, I moved from 76th Street and made some new friends who had started a rock band, listened to "cool" music, smoked pot, and had long hair. After adopting some of these tendencies (including the controversial hairstyle that nearly got me kicked out of high school), I returned to my old neighborhood with a different sense of self that garnered newfound respect among my old friends. Finally, at the age of 31, I moved to Stony Brook, Long Island, to pursue a PhD in sociology, far away from a career in the printing industry.

Some of the comments from former residents are also at odds with my perceptions of what it was like to grow up in City Line. It is important to remember that nostalgia provides comfort in a changing world (Lowenthal 1985). As Suttles (1968) has noted, various groups can experience the same neighborhood in different ways. That my memories would be described as more negative definitely must have its roots in the problems I experienced in the different facets of life I have explored in this book—a "hard-living" environment. That is the social reality for a large number of working-class families. For some, a "settled" working-class family was possible if one had a father who came home sober every day, minimizing the number and sound level of parental arguments; had parents who saved money for family outings and vacations; had friends who supported each other; and had a family income that allowed for a more secure—confident— existence. What the presence of these different family types in the same neighborhood suggests is an ongoing interaction between family and neighborhood. For example, many of the same neighborhoods in Brooklyn that may have been described by earlier inhabitants as dangerous, crowded, and dirty are now undergoing a process of "gentrification" by a new generation of young people who find them cool, exciting, and vibrant. How neighborhoods affect individual perceptions of an area is a major concern in urban sociology, with a vast literature (see Sampson 2012). In sum, City Line may have been a good place to grow up—for some kids, who did not experience the various hidden injuries of class felt by many of those in working-class families.

A friend of mine from the old neighborhood, Tom Crockett, an English and drama teacher and director of many plays, published in 2015 a book of 12 short stories about growing up in that time and place, which I have mentioned before. The book is funny, sad, and poignant. The stories, a combination of fact and fiction written by someone very skilled in his use of English, subtly makes many of the same points as I do in this volume. It is a set of "funny" stories that highlight the struggles of the people who lived on his block—75th Street in Ozone Park (right next to City Line). It is a celebration of the resilient culture in which we were raised, and he has made the point to me that he didn't even know we were in a (capitalist) race. The people are survivors, but their struggles are there for all to see—fear of gangs, hanging out on street corners, crowded row houses, sexual awkwardness, marital tensions, Catholic schooling and its aftereffects. I thought I would die of laughter when I read the story that our baseball coach (who always treated us nicely) had just been released from jail after serving time for (allegedly) manslaughter. It certainly was a different time and place. Crockett's book is a fine work of literature that helps the reader understand that time and place; hopefully, it may be seen as a companion piece to this one.

Angry (And Not So Angry) White Working-Class Men and Women

Looking to today, more and more of my friends from the old neighborhood seem angry at the social and economic changes that have swept the United States over the last few decades.[8] Let me add that I have also heard from many angry white females from the old neighborhood, as well as anger from both men and women in my previous research on parental attitudes toward education (Gorman 1998a, b). They seem to be angry over the lack of well-paying jobs, immigration policy, "politically correct" culture, and the welfare state. They also lashed out at those who are having a difficult time climbing the social class ladder. It seems as if it is easier to get angry at people closest to themselves in social class, rather than the CEOs of corporations whose salaries have skyrocketed while the pay for many Americans has stagnated. It is easier to blame your problems on those who you can see in your daily interactions, especially the new immigrants who now inhabit your old neighborhood. We can see some indications of these feelings (in addition to the comments on social media previously discussed) in recent national surveys suggesting that racial attitudes (specifically whites' feelings toward African-Americans) have worsened in the United States since President Obama first took office (Pasek et al. 2014). The most negative comments I came across in my previous research seemed to be coming from those who had never attended college; research has consistently shown going to college to be associated with making students more open to other groups and cultures. Obviously, we are *not* in a "post-racial" society, and we may need more people to attend college just for that reason alone.

A number of former residents from Ozone Park/City Line long for a "simpler" time when the streets were safe, children played all day on those streets, and their neighbors were just like them—Italian, Irish, and German (Many tend to think the legendary John Gotti helped provide safe streets in Ozone Park and City Line). Never mind that city streets across the United States today are about as safe as they were then (especially streets populated by newly arrived immigrants) and that parents (especially middle-class parents) today plan most of their children's activities because they fear those safe streets. Additionally, those "simpler" times did not occur for many people (women, people of color, and gays and lesbians) in many ways. The old timers were children back in that time and place when summers appeared endless and the streets of Ozone Park and City Line seemed like a playground. Yet, when their parents had a choice, they moved to bigger, less crowded, and "better" places. Their fear of the economy, however, is real and on target. The problem is that they tend to conflate their economic fears with their fear of "others"—Muslims, African-Americans, and Hispanic/Latinos.

Some of my old friends seem to be more tolerant than others, which may be because of their religious beliefs or educational level, though religion and education do not guarantee that any one particular person will change. Still, some have not changed, and if anything have become more intolerant than they were when I knew them back then—even some with a four-year college degree. One old friend has said to me that one of the problems may be that we expect our old friends to be the same people they were over 50 years ago. Indeed, some of the minor differences that were noticeable back then have grown into glaring gaps. This friend continued by asking, "How did they become so different from us?"

Sometimes, I feel sorry for those who are angry, afraid, and distrusting of the new inhabitants of the old neighborhood. They know there is a legitimate problem somewhere, but they have a difficult time clearly pinpointing the source, and instead blame newcomers. It is not easy identifying the source of our societal problems, given that there are talking heads on television, on radio, and in the newspapers spewing misinformation. Look, the old-timers say, we worked hard and experienced upward social mobility; why can't the new immigrants do it for themselves, too? Even those who are now having trouble attaining the American Dream find it difficult to identify the exact problem or set of (political/economic) problems that keeps them from it—they certainly feel stiffed and resentful (Faludi 1999).

Hidden Injuries of Class

When working-class individuals get angry at their socio-economic conditions, they can react in a variety of ways. Some will blame themselves,[9] some will blame "others" (immigrants, the poor, minorities) and vote for political candidates who promise to keep those "others" out of the country and cut back on social services, some will blame the "system" (without fully thinking through what the "system" entails) and might buy a gun to protect themselves from the government and the "others," and some will begin to understand the historical, social and economic conditions that have shaped their lives. Those who try to understand those conditions (if the pattern I observed in previous research holds true), taking a culturally relativistic approach, will tend to have had more settled lives and experienced fewer hidden injuries of class. Those individuals may be able to overcome their anger and resentment and instead make contributions toward social change (as I have tried to do, by teaching working-class students in a college setting). Of course, it is always possible that even those who try to understand current social, political and economic conditions may act in ways not conducive to helping their socio-economic situations (like Willis' (1981) "Lads").

My past research indicates that those who experience the most debilitating hidden injuries, without any social defenses against them such as a skilled blue-collar occupation, will most likely be susceptible to anger, bitterness, and resentment toward the status quo. In fact, future research on the topic could catalogue such class-related injuries and try to determine which are the most hurtful, and which are more likely to develop the angry white men and women that we have heard from in this volume and others. In addition, such research might also try to ascertain further the kinds of experiences that may inoculate working-class men and women against becoming angry (such as whether one grew up in a "settled-" or "hard-living" family, or demographic indicators such as level of education, income, occupation, and previous interactions with "others" in school and the neighborhood). This is a tall order for a researcher, but it needs to be done if we hope to have a more perfect union. The America of the 1950s is not returning, but it still has a profound effect on our beliefs and attitudes today. Past research and current events have shown that economic instability contributes to mistrust of the "others" whom the working class see as a threat economically. Yet, as this volume has suggested, there is also resentment toward other people's cultures no matter their economic ability to live in areas that the white working class previously inhabited.

Currently, Thomas Piketty's (2014) economic tome *Capital in the Twenty-First Century* is being debated in intellectual circles as to its Marxist purity. According to Piketty, the rate of return on capital will continue to increase in the near future, whereas Marx saw the rate of return on capital decreasing. His analysis, which has withstood a bevy of criticism (see Boushey, Delong and Steinbaum (eds.), suggests that income inequality will persist and worsen in the future. The economic reality for the working class today will not be returning to the kind of socio-economic world my friends and I experienced in City Line in the 1960s and early 1970s. Capitalists shut down old factories and moved them overseas or to non-union areas of the south and west of the United States. Globalization and technological innovation have made the idea of a person with a tenth-grade education supporting a family of five (as my dad had) sound ludicrous.

The job my uncle found after losing his well-paying job (with just a high school education) paid less than he had been making in printing. Granted, his new job as a print buyer for a major corporation in New York City was in a nice, clean, air-conditioned office, but he had to sell the family's summer home that they had purchased when he was a blue-collar linotype operator. And, when you talk to men and women who had a skill they had used to produce products, they tell you, sometimes on the side, that they don't respect their new jobs in clean offices "pushing papers" (see Halle 1984; Rubin 1976; Gorman 1998a, b). Today, my father would be looking, at best, at a minimum wage job.

There is a bleak outlook for the economy, health, and wellbeing of the white working class. With automation and outsourcing not slowing down, the future continues to look dismal for their life chances (with fewer unions and pensions, underfunded schools, poor diets, and little or no health insurance). Will that mean an increase in the hidden injuries of class for white, working-class young people and adults (and will those injuries be as "hidden" as in the past, with the ever-widening income and wealth gap)? If so, will we see an increase in their resentment, bitterness, and anger at their plight? Will working-class men become increasingly angry at the "system" with women now garnering the lion's share of college credentials? At the same time, however, the working class is becoming populated more by people of color. In fact, the non-white population is predicted to surpass the white population in the United States by the middle of the twenty-first century (if not sooner). Added to that is the fact that the non-white population has higher aspirations than whites. Therefore, if more and more of the working class are non-white (Jones 2016), then at whom will the working class lash out? Will they continue to lash out in a way that, ultimately, is detrimental to their best interests, as laid out in What's the Matter with Kansas (Frank 2004), or will the working class—white and non-white together, and possibly with elements of the newly struggling middle class—finally come to see where their interests truly lie, in a change in the political economy?

What Can Be Done?

What can be done? This is the part of sociology books and journal articles that are usually the weakest; we are not as good at solutions to problems as identifying and analyzing them. That is not surprising; solutions to problems are very difficult to propose. The person I have been reading lately with sensible solutions is Robert Reich, economist, former Secretary of Labor in the Clinton Administration and now the Chancellor's Professor of Public Policy at the University of California at Berkeley. Robert Reich calls for a number of changes in the US political economy in a series of books, the most recent being *Saving Capitalism* (2016). He calls for those in power to vote to raise the minimum wage, support unions, develop a tax code that does not favor those in the top 1–5 percent, make trade deals beneficial to working people, invest in training and education, provide government-funded healthcare, and rebuild the infrastructure (college graduates with a full-time job earn a median income 67% [or more depending on the study] higher than high school graduates [Lobosco 2017] and studies show that automation has hurt the working class more than the trade deals politicians demonize). We may even need to start to consider providing a basic income to everyone as a solution. These changes, however, will be difficult with the recent gridlock in the Federal Government.

Limitations

As is the case for most studies in sociology, the current work has some limitations, some of which I have addressed throughout the book. I want to remind the reader that someone who differs in gender, race, or sexual orientation might have a different experience from my own working-class story of growing up in City Line/Ozone Park (especially if one imagines how the arguments would play out in different countries). In 1998 (and as Michael Kimmel has pointed out recently), I argued that working-class white women do not seem to be as angry and bitter as the men. It could be argued that working-class white women's skills and education (women now outnumber men at every educational level, but not among the STEM subjects) are a better fit for an economy that is changing from a manufacturing to a service base.

Another limitation is my own sexuality. In City Line/Ozone Park in the early 1960s, a fairly conservative, Irish-Italian-German, Catholic, working-class community, it was assumed that most everyone was heterosexual and that heterosexuality was "normal." Those few whose sexuality was in question would hear taunts of "fag" or "lesbo." For heterosexual young males, the "conquest" of females was highly valued (at least when the guys talked among themselves). The young women had to try to protect their reputations at all costs or risk being known as a "who-a" (our neighborhood's version of "whore"). This was the macho–John Wayne–Rat Pack era, which gives the reader another context for understanding that time and place.[10]

THE STORY CONTINUES

A sociologist once said that the longest trip he ever had to make was from the Bronx to Manhattan. In reality, that is not much of a distance in miles, but he was talking about the cultural shift from his old neighborhood to his current teaching position at a university. It has been a long trip for me, too—from a vocational high school student to a full-time associate professor position teaching at Queens College (two statuses), though only a couple of miles apart. Yes, I have a love/hate relationship with my memories of growing up working class on the border of Brooklyn and Queens in the 1950s and 1960s. Yet, I still feel close to the people I knew and keep in contact with them. Whether they have experienced social mobility or not, they are tough, scrappy, and resilient. I will never forget them. Additionally, I hope I have made my equally tough, scrappy, and resilient family proud. Finally, I hope my writing, teaching, and advising at Queens College and Queensborough Community College have given my students the determination to "reach for the stars."

As for me, the story continues. I sought counseling after my mother passed away in 2009, and my therapist, after hearing my life story, said, "What took you so long to get here?" No doubt, I take after my mother; she was a very nervous person. Whether the anxiety I have experienced over the past decade or so can be attributed to nature or nurture will not be solved here. (I still do not understand why there are not more *social* psychologists.) Moreover, my mother's parents were also "nervous" types, and so were their four children. Was that affliction passed down to their children genetically, or by living in a house with nervous parents? Keep in mind that their parents had lived through the trials of the Great Depression. Likewise, one could ask whether my mother was nervous because she inherited those genes from her nervous parents, or because she was married to an alcoholic. Concomitantly, one could ask whether her three children have had problems with anxiety because they inherited it, or because they watched their father come home drunk every night and fall asleep at the kitchen table. Regardless of the answers to those questions, recent research has revealed the negative consequences of children growing up in a stressful environment. The effects of stress on a child can affect aspects of development from learning to self-esteem (and low self-esteem can foster anger, see Donnellan et al. 2005), and the impacts are found more often in low-income families. Over the years, I have tried to turn stress into the energy necessary to get things done and succeed. It certainly powers my teaching acumen, pacing back and forth in front of the classroom and up and down the aisles, sometimes leaves the students giggling, as if to say, "What is this guy on?" What they don't know is that this guy is just powered by his own energy source. Rarely do I sit at my desk while I teach. After one particularly intense classroom lesson when I could barely stand up (and was full of chalk dust from head to toe), a colleague of mine looked at me and asked if I was okay. Too much stress can eventually lead to burnout. To be sure, it has affected me to some degree outside the classroom, inhibiting a couple of projects on my agenda.

This auto-ethnography, put together a number of sociological concepts and theories, and fits into an overall critical theoretical orientation, including defiance, resistance, and the possibility of social change.[11] Above all, this project has made me a better sociologist, because I can see more clearly the many social interconnections that helped shape who I am today. Our sociological imaginations can always be improved.

Meanwhile, when some of the newcomers do "make it," many old-timers scream that "they are taking our jobs." And all indications do suggest that those who now inhabit my old neighborhood, on average, are starting to climb the social class ladder. Interestingly, many former residents of the old neighborhood used to complain that they were paying for "others" to be on welfare their entire lives. The newly arrived immigrants are "damned if they do, and damned if they don't." Some old-timers speculate on social media about how the new immigrants can afford expensive houses in their old neighborhood. I have also read some former residents' surprise to find that crime is down in those areas compared to the 1980s and 1990s.[12] In fact, recent newspaper articles have discussed the possibility of East New York (where City Line is located) becoming an "up-and-coming" neighborhood (Warerkar 2017). Mayor de Blasio has identified a segment of East New York (at the edge of City Line) for redevelopment (Flynn 2014). These promising realities just do not fit with the negative images many old-timers have of the old neighborhood and the newly arrived immigrants who now populate City Line and Ozone Park. Sure, education and religious beliefs can help these former residents untangle these problems, but their fears quite often lead them to believe certain "facts" about the poor, minorities, and immigrants. The resulting confusion leads to anger and a turn to political candidates such as Donald Trump and other populist figures. This is what can happen when you grow up working class.

Epilogue

Donald Trump was sworn in as the 45th President of the United States on January 20, 2017. All indications are that he won with a significant boost from the white working class, especially those without a four-year degree. He won an overwhelming number of votes from white men without a college degree (72 percent) and a very large number of votes from white women without a college degree (62 percent). To be fair, he also won a majority of the white male vote from men with a college degree (54 percent). Hillary Clinton won the majority of votes from white women with a college degree (51 percent).[13] What can we take away from these numbers? It seems that white working-class males—those without a college degree—are the unhappiest (you might even say, angry) with the status quo, followed by white working-class females. However, even among those with a college degree—the middle class—white men are angrier than white women. These results confirm much sociological research and the arguments made in this volume.

Some commentators have tried to show that typical Trump voter was not working class by noting that they came from households with a median income of $72,000 (Silver 2016). It is true that other demographic groups than the white working class helped Trump win the Presidency, but it does not mean that many of those households with a median income of $72,000 were not working class. For instance, if a household contained three people, each making approximately $24,000, they would be considered a household with a total income of $72,000. Furthermore, the income of voters, generally, on average is higher than the median income of the typical American household ($56,516 for 2015). Moreover, working-class men and women from my generation grew up at a time when they were paid a decent wage. That generation is now at its peak level of personal income and has experienced social mobility based on income. All in all, income is a tricky variable to use to categorize social classes. If it is employed, it tends to be combined with other variables such as educational level and occupational prestige. Educational level is the variable that is used by more and more researchers today to define social class. Those who hold four-year degrees are considered part of the middle class, and those who do not are considered part of the working class. Thus, a four-year degree is now seen (and the data supports this view) as the main road to middle-class status in the United States. This is part of the ongoing discussions about social inequality, and it looks as if the four-year degree will become even more important for middle-class status in the future. This is what I tell my students.

In addition, some pundits have tried to dissect the data on Trump supporters who are angry. Are they angry because of racist tendencies, or economic deprivation, or do they just want to poke their fingers in the eyes of liberal elites? As I have illustrated through this book, it is very difficult to pull those variables apart in real-life situations. Nevertheless, there has been a recent increase in hate crimes against Muslims in the U.S. (Williams 2017).

NOTES

1. Rubin (1976) is *the* book that propelled me into becoming a sociology major as an undergraduate student at Queens College. Because her study did not ring totally true to my own working-class background, set also the stage for my doctoral dissertation.
2. See Steglitz (2013) for a good discussion of the history of social inequality in America.
3. *The Way We Never Were* (Coontz 1992) is a magnificent look at American families during this time period.
4. However, recent research shows that men and women today tend to pair up from the same social class.
5. Today, poor and working-class students have a more difficult time affording Catholic school tuition, and they continue to populate community colleges, which will not offer them the opportunities available to middle- and upper-middle-class students in four-year colleges and universities.
6. Similarly, Alfred Kazin (1951) said that success in his neighborhood in Brooklyn (not far from City Line) was measured by one's ability to escape it.
7. See Gaines (1998), Wynne (1977), Kenny (2000), Kelly (1990) for a look at the suburban experience.
8. Kimmel, *Angry White Men* (2013), Rubin, *Families on the Faultline* (1994), and Susan Faludi, *Stiffed* (1999) all analyze this phenomenon.
9. See the recent research showing the declining health and life spans of white, working-class Americans (Case and Deaton 2015).
10. See Lareau (2003), Steedman (1986), Tea (2003), Lamont (2000), Bettie (2003), Gest (2016), and Boylorn and Orbe (2014) for working-class stories and studies from a variety of perspectives and the issue of intersectionality.

11. Also see Giddens (1984) for an explanation of the interplay of structure and agency.
12. This is not surprising, as research has shown the tendency for there to be low crime rates in areas populated by newly arrived immigrants. For example, see Rose (2013).
13. All voting figures are from CBS News (2016).

Bibliography

Adler, Patricia, and Peter Adler. 1991. *Blackboards and Blackboards*. New York: Columbia University Press.

American Yearbook Company. 1971. *Dynamo*. Jamaica: Thomas A. Edison Vocational and Technical High School.

Anyon, Jean. 1980. Social Class and the Hidden Curriculum of Work. *Journal of Education* 162: 67–92.

Appy, Christian G. 1993. *Working-Class War: American Combat Soldiers and Vietnam*. Chapel Hill: The University of North Carolina Press.

Asian American Federation Census Information Center. 2013. *Profile of New York City's Bangladeshi Americans*. Asian American Federation.

Belfoure, Charles, and Mary Ellen Hayward. 2001. *The Baltimore Rowhouse*. Princeton: Princeton Architectural Press.

Berger, Bennett M. 1990. *Authors of Their Own Lives: Intellectual Autobiographies by Twenty American Sociologists*. Berkeley: University of California Press.

Berlage, Gai. 1982. Children's Sports and the Family. *Arena Review* 6(1): 43–47.

Bettie, Julie. 2003. *Women Without Class: Girls, Race, and Identity*. Oakland: University of California Press.

Birrell, S., and D. Richter. 1994. Is a Diamond Forever? Feminist Transformation of Sport. In *Women, Sport and Culture*, ed. S. Birrell and C.L. Cole. Champaign: Human Kinetics.

Bluestone, Barry, and Bennet Harrison. 1982. *The Deindustrialization of America*. New York: Basic Books.

Bourdieu, Pierre. 1977. Cultural Reproduction and Social Reproduction. In *Power and Ideology in Education*, ed. Jerome Karabel and A.H. Halsey. New York: Oxford University Press.

© The Author(s) 2017
T.J. Gorman, *Growing up Working Class*,
DOI 10.1007/978-3-319-58898-8

Bourdieu, Pierre, and Jean Claude Passerson. 1977. *Reproduction in Education, Society, and Cuture*. London: Sage.

Boushey, Heather, J. Bradford Delong, and M. Steinbaum, eds. 2017. *After Piketty: The Agenda for Economics and Inequality*. Cambridge: Harvard University Press.

Bowles, Samuel, and Herbert Gintis. 1976. *Schooling in Capitalist America: Educational Reforms and the Contradictions of Economic Life*. New York: Basic Books.

Boylorn, Robin M., and Mark P. Orbe. 2014. *Critical Auto-Ethnography: Intersecting Cultural Identities in Everyday Life*. San Francisco: Left Coast Press.

Braun, Henry, Frank Jenkins, and Wendy Grigg. 2006. *Comparing Private Schools and Public Schools Using Hierarchal Linear Modeling*. Washington, DC: NCES.

Brekhaus, Wayne. 1998. A Sociology of the Unmarked: Redirecting Our Focus. *Sociological Theory* 16(1): 34–51.

Carr, Patrick J., and Maria J. Kefalas. 2009. *Hollowing Out the Middle*. Boston: Beacon Press.

Case, Anne, and Angus Deaton. 2015. Rising Morbidity and Mortality Among White Non-Hispanic Americans in the 21st Century. *Proceedings of the National Academy of Sciences of the United States of America* 112(49): 15078–15083.

CBS News. 2016. *How Donald Trump Won the U. S. Presidency*. Stanley Feldman and Melissa Herrman, November 9.

Cherlin, Andrew J. 2014. *Labor's Love Lost*. New York: Russell Sage Foundation.

Chetty, Raj, David Grusky, Maximilian Hell, Nathaniel Hendren, Robert Manduca, and Jimmy Narang, 2016. *The Fading American Dream: Trends in Absolute Income Mobility Since 1940*. National Bureau of Economic Research Working Paper Series.

Chetty, Raj, Nathaniel Hendrin, and Laurence F. Katz. 2016. The Effects of Exposure to Better Neighborhoods on Children: New Evidence from the Moving to Opportunity Experiments. *American Economic Review* 106(4): 855–902.

Chi-Lites. 1971. *Have You Seen Her?* Brunswick Records.

Clark, Burton R. 1960. The 'Cooling-Out' Function in Higher Education. *American Journal of Sociology* 65: 569–576.

Coakley, Jay. 1993. Sports and Socialization. *Exercise and Sport Sciences Reviews* 21: 169–200.

Coleman, James S., and Thomas Hoffer. 1987. *Public and Private High Schools*. New York: Basic Books.

Cole, Stephen. 1983. The Hierarchy of the Sciences? *American Journal of Sociology* 89(1): 111–139.

Coles, Robert, Alvin Rosenfeld, and Nicole Wise. 2001. *The Overscheduled Child*. New York: St. Martins Griffin.

Columbia Pictures. 1966. *A Man for All Seasons*. Fred Zinnemann, Director.

Coontz, Stephanie. 1992. *The Way We Never Were*. New York: Basic Books.

Cowie, Jefferson R. 2010. *Stayin' Alive: The 1970's and the Last Days of the Working Class*. New York: The New Press.

Cramer, Katherine J. 2016. *The Politics of Resentment: Rural Consciousness in Wisconsin and the Rise of Scott Walker.* Chicago: The University of Chicago Press.

Creedence Clearwater Revival. 1970. *Up Around the Bend.* Fantasy Records.

Crockett, Thomas. 2015. *Hope Beyond All Hope: New York Stories.* San Ramon: Vision Press.

Curry, T. 1993. A Little Pain Never Hurt Anyone: Athletic Career Socialization and the Normalization of Sport Injury. *Symbolic Interaction* 16(3): 273–290.

Dews, C.L. 1995. *This Fine Place So Far from Home: Voices of Academics from the Working Class.* Philadelphia: Temple University Press.

Dionne, E.J. 2015. The Hidden and Deadly Bias of Class. *The Washington Post,* November 12.

Doheny, Kathleen. 2015. Bullied Teens at Risk for Later Depression. *Everyday Health.*

Dollard, John. 1981. The Dozens: Dialectic of Insult. In *Mother Wit,* ed. Alan Dundes. Jackson: University Press of Mississippi.

Donnellan, M. Brent, Kali H. Trzesniewski, Richard W. Robins, Terry E. Moffitt, and Avshalom Caspi. 2005. Low Self-Esteem Is Related to Aggression, Anti-Social Behavior and Delinquency. *Psychological Science* 16(4): 328–335.

Donnelly, P., and K. Young. 1988. The Construction and Confirmation of Identity in Sport Subcultures. *Sociology of Sport Journal* 5(3): 223–240.

Draut, Tamara. 2016. *Sleeping Giant: How the New Working Class Will Transform America.* New York: Doubleday.

Drum, Kevin. 2011. Bullying and Social Status. *Mother Jones.*

Durkheim, Emile. 1985 (1st Published 1895). The Rules of Sociological Method. In Steven Lukes (ed.). *The Rules of Sociological Method and Selected Texts on Sociology and Its Methods.* New York: Free Press.

Dundes, Alan, ed. 1990. *Mother Wit: Readings in the Interpretation of Afro-American Folklore.* Jackson: University Press of Mississippi.

Economic Policy Institute. 2012. *U. S. Lags Behind Peer Countries in Mobility.* Washington, DC: Elise Gould.

Eichenwald, Kurt. 2016, February 4. Right-Wing Extremists are a Bigger Threat to Americans that ISIS. *Newsweek.*

Eitzen, Stanley. 2011. *Sport in Contemporary Society.* Boulder: Paradigm Publishers.

Ekstam, Helen. 2015. Residential Crowding in a "Distressed" and a "Gentrified" Neighborhood: Towards an Understanding of Crowding in a Gentrified Neighborhood. *Housing, Theory, and Society* 32(4): 429–449.

Elder, Glenn H. 1985. *Perspectives on the Life Course.* Ithaca: Cornell University Press.

———. 1986. Military Time and Turning Points in Men's Lives. *Developmental Psychology* 22(2): 233–245.

Elder, Todd. 2013. Are Catholic Primary Schools More Effective than Public Primary Schools. *Journal of Urban Economics* 80: 28–38.

Ellis, Carolyn. 1995. *Final Negotiations: A Story of Love, Loss, and Chronic Illness*. Philadelphia: Temple University Press.

———. 2004. *The Ethnographic I: A Methodological Novel About Auto-Ethnography*. Walnut Creek: Alta Mira Press.

Erikson, Erik. 1950. *Childhood and Society*. New York: W. W. Norton & Company.

Falco, Ed. 2012. When Italians Were the Other. *CNN*, July 10.

Faludi, Susan. 1999. *Stiffed*. New York: William Morrow and Co.

Feldman, Kenneth A., and Theodore M. Newcomb. 1969. *The Impact of College on Students*. Piscataway: Transactional Publishers.

Feletti, Vincent S., Robert F. Anda, Dale Nordenberg, David F. Williamson, Allsion M. Spitz, Valerie Edwards, Mary P. Koss, and James S. Marks. 1998. Relationship of Childhood Abuse and Dysfunction to Many of the Leading Causes of Death in Adults. *American Journal of Preventive Medicine*. 14 (4): 245–258.

Fine, Gary A. 1987. *With the Boys*. Chicago: University of Chicago Press.

Flynn, Gerald. 2014. Is East New York the Next Bushwick? *Gothamist*, July 22.

Foley, Douglas. 1990. *Learning Capitalist Culture*. Philadelphia: University of Penn Press.

Frank, Thomas. 2004. *What's the Matter with Kansas*. New York: Henry Holt and Co.

Freedman, Jonathan. 1975. *Crowding and Behavior: The Psychology of High-Density Living*. New York: Viking Press.

Freeman, Joshua B. 2001. *Working-Class New York: Life and Labor Since World War II*. New York: The New Press.

Freidan, Betty. 1963. *The Feminine Mystique*. New York: Dell.

Gaines, Donna. 1998. *Teenage Wasteland: Suburbia's Dead-End Kids*. Chicago: University of Chicago Press.

Gans, Herbert J. 1962. *The Urban Villagers*. New York: Free Press.

———. 1967. *The Levitowners*. New York: Random House.

George Minter Productions. 1951. *A Christmas Carol*. Brian Desmond Hurst, Director.

Gest, Justin. 2016. *The New Minority: White Working Class Politics in an Age of Immigration and Inequality*. New York: Oxford University Press.

Gleave, Josie and Issy Cole-Hamilton. 2012. A literature Review of the Effects of a Lack of Play on Children's Lives. *Play England*, January. www.playengland.org.uk.

Giddens, Anthony. 1984. *The Constitution of Society: Outline of the Theory of Structuration*. Cambridge: Polity Press.

Gitlin, Todd. 1987. *The Sixties: Years of Hope, Days of Rage*. New York: Bantam Books.

Goldhaber, Samuel Z. 1971. Tuition Rises Next Year in College. *The Harvard Crimson*, January 5.

Goldstein, Amy. 2017. *Janesville: An American Story*. New York: Simon and Schuster.

Gorman, Thomas J. 1998a. Paths to Success: The Meaning of Schooling to Working-Class and Middle-Class Parents. *Educational Foundations* 12(3): 35–54.

———. 1998b. Social Class and Parental Attitudes Education: Resistance and Conformity to Schooling in the Family. *Journal of Contemporary Ethnography* 27(1): 10–44.

———. 2000a. Cross-Class Perceptions of Social Class. *Sociological Spectrum* 20(1): 93–120. Also Included in Gagne, Patricia, and Richard Tewksbury. 2003. *The Dynamics of Inequality: Race, Class, Gender, and Sexuality in the United States*, 100–112. Upper Saddle River: Pearson.

———. 2000b. Reconsidering Worlds of Pain: Life in the Working Class(es). *Sociological Forum* 15(4): 693–717.

Gould, Elise. 2012. *U.S. Lags Behind Peer Countries in Mobility*. Washington, DC: Economic Policy Institute.

Gove, Walter R., and Michael Hughes. 1983. *Overcrowding in the Household*. New York: Academic Press.

Gruneau, Richard. 1983. *Class, Sports, and Social Development*. Amherst: University of Massachusetts Press.

Gustafson, Anna. 2014. Time After Time: Ozone Park's Cyndi Lauper Proves She Has More Than Staying Power. *The Forum*, June 19.

Guttman, Allen. 1978. *From Ritual to Record*. New York: Columbia University Press.

Hackman, Daniel A., Laura M. Betancourt, Nancy Brodsky, Hallam Hurt, and Martha J. Farah. 2012. Neighborhood Disadvantage and Adolescent Stress Reactivity. *Frontiers of Human Neuroscience* 6: 277.

Halle, David. 1984. *America's Working Man: Work, Home, and Politics Among Blue-Collar Property Owners*. Chicago: The University of Chicago Press.

Hochschild, Arlie Russell. 1989. *The Second Shift: Working Parents and the Revolution at Home*. London: Penguin (Viking).

———. 2016. *Strangers in Their Own Land: Anger and Mourning on the American Right*. New York: The New Press.

Horowitz, Irving Louis. 1969. *Sociological Self-Images: A Collective Portrait*. Beverly Hills: Sage Publications.

Howard, Mary Ellen, and Charles Belfoure. 2001. *The Baltimore Rowhouse*. New York: Princeton Architectural Press.

Howell, Joseph T. 1973. *Hard Living on Clay Street: Portraits of Blue Collar Families*. Garden City: Anchor Books.

Humphries, Stephen. 1981. *Hooligans or Rebels*. New York: Basil Blackwell.

Hunter, Albert. 1974. *Symbolic Communities*. Chicago: University of Chicago Press.

Jacobs, Jane. 1961. *The Death and Life of Great American Cities*. New York: Vintage Books.

Jemie, Onwuchekwa. 2003. *Yo' Momma: New Raps, Toasts, Dozens, Jokes & Children's Rymes from Urban Black America*. Philadelphia: Temple University Press.

Jensen, Barbara. 2012. *Reading Classes: On Culture and Classism in America*. Ithaca: Cornell University Press.

Jones, Robert P. 2016. *The End of White Christian America*. New York: Simon and Schuster.

Kane, Emily W. 2001. For Whom Does Education Enlighten: Race, Gender, Education and Belief about Social Inequality. *Gender and Society* 15 (5): 710–733.

Karp, David A., William C. Yoels, Barbara H. Vann, and Michael Ian Borer. 2016. *Sociology in Everyday Life*. Long Grove: Waveland Press.

Katznelson, Ira. 2005. *When Affirmative Action was White: An Untold Story of Racial Inequality in Twentieth Century America*. New York: W W Norton and Co.

Kazin, Alfred. 1951. *A Walker in the City*. New York: Houghton Mifflin Harcourt.

Kelly, Barbara, ed. 1990. *Long Island: The Suburban Experience*. Interlaken: Heart of the Lakes Publishing.

Kenny, Lorraine Delia. 2000. *Daughters of Suburbia: Growing Up White, Middle Class, and Female*. New Brunswick: Rutgers University Press.

Kimmel, Michael. 2013. *Angry White Men: American Masculinity at the End of an Era*. New York: Nation Books.

Kinney, David A. 1993. From Nerds to Normals: The Recovery of Identity Among Adolescents from Middle School to High School. *Sociology of Education* 66(1): 21–40.

Kluger, Jeffrey. 2011. *The Sibling Effect: What the Bonds Among Brothers and Sisters Reveal About Us*. New York: Riverhead Books.

Kohn, Melvin L. 1969. *Class and Conformity*. Homewood: The Dorey Press.

Komarovsky, Mirra. 1962. *Blue Collar Marriage*. New York: Vintage Books.

Kozol, Jonathan. 1996. *Children in America's Schools*. With Bill Moyers. Produced by Jeffrey Hayden. PBS. Documentaries.

Kruse, Kevin M. 2005. *White Flight: Atlanta and the Making of Modern Conservatism*. Princeton: Princeton University Press.

Lamont, Michele. 2000. *The Dignity of Working Men: Morality and the Boundaries of Race, Class, and Immigration*. New York: Russell Sage Foundation.

Lareau, Annette. 1989. *Home Advantage: Social Class and Parental Intervention in Elementary Education*. New York: The Falmer Press.

———. 2003. *Unequal Childhoods: Class, Race and Family Life*. Berkeley: University of California Press.

Laslett, Barbara. 1973. The Family as a Public and Private Institution: An Historical Perspective. *Journal of Marriage and the Family* 35: 480–492.

Levy, Matt. 2010. *New York Street Games.* Documentary. Highbrow Entertainment.

Lewko, John H., and Susan L. Greendorfer. 1988. Family Influences in Sport Socialization of Children and Adolescents. In *Children in Sport*, ed. Richard A. Magill, Michael J. Ash, and Frank L. Smolls. Chicago: Human Kinetics.

Liff, Bob. 1999. When City Drew the Line Double Lives the Norm in Border Neighborhood. *New York Daily News*, April 27.

Linge, Mary Kay. 2016. The Top Career and Technical Schools in New York City. *New York Post*, September 16.

Longman, Martin. 2017. Addressing the Cultural Anxiety of the White Working Class. *Washington Monthly.*

Lowenthal, David. 1985. *The Past Is a Foreign Country.* Cambridge: Cambridge University Press.

Macleod, Jay. 1987. *Ain't No Makin' It: Leveled Aspirations in a Low-Income Neighborhood.* Boulder: Westview Press.

Mannheim, Karl. 1952. The Problem of Generations. In *Essays on the Sociology of Knowledge—Collected Works*, ed. Paul Kecskemeti, vol. 5, 276–322. New York: Routledge.

Martha, Reeve and the Vandellas. 1967. *Jimmy Mack.* Motown.

McGuire, Richard T., and David L. Cook. 1983. The Influence of Others and the Decision to Participate in Youth Sports. *Journal of Sport Behavior* 6(1): 9–16.

McPherson, Barry D. 1988. The Child in Competitive Sport: The Influence of the Social Milieu. In *Children in Sports*, ed. Richard A. Magill, Michael J. Ash, and Frank L. Smolls. Chicago: Human Kinetics.

McRobbie, Angela. 1978. Working-Class Girls and the Culture of Femininity. In *Women Take Issue*, 96–108. London: Women's Studies Group.

Messner, Michael. 1990. Boyhood, Organized Sports, and the Construction of Masculinities. *Journal of Contemporary Ethnography* 18(4): 416–444.

Michener, James A. 1953. *The Bridges at Toko-ri.* New York: Random House.

Milburn, Michael A., and Sheree D. Conrad. 2016. *Raised to Rage: The Politics of Anger and the Roots of Authoritarianism.* Cambridge: MIT Press.

Miller, Kim. 1999. Adolescent Sexual Behavior in Two Ethnic Minority Samples: The Role of Family Variables. *Journal of Marriage and the Family* 61(February): 81–98.

Mills, C. Wright. 1959. *The Sociological Imagination.* New York: Grove Press.

Morris, E.W. 2011. The Hidden Injuries of Class Among Rural Teenagers. In *Reshaping Gender and Class in Rural Spaces*, ed. Barbara Panini and Belinda Leach, 221–237. Burlington: Ashgate Publishing.

Moses, Paul. 2015. *An Unlikely Union: The Love-Hate Story of New York's Irish and Italians.* New York: New York University Press.

Murray, Sylvie. 2003. *The Progressive Housewife: Community Activism in Suburban Queens, 1945–1965.* Philadelphia: University of Pennsylvania Press.

NCTE. 2014. Why Class Size Matters Today. Review.

Oakes, Jeannie. 1982. *Keeping Track: How Schools Structure Inequality* (2005 Second Edition). New Haven: Yale University Press.

Obituary. 1989. Barry Sadler, 49, Balladeer, Dies. *New York Times*, November 6.

OECD. 2010. A Family Affair: Intergenerational Social Mobility Across OECD Countries. In *Economic Policy Reforms.* Paris: OECD.

Oliver, Melvin L. 1980. Race, Class and the Family's Orientation to Mobility Through Sport. *Sociological Symposium* 30: 62–86.

Orfield, Gary, Jongyeon Ee, Erica Frankenberg, and Genevieve Siegel-Howley. 2016. Brown at 62: School Segregation by Race, Poverty and State. *The Civil Rights Project.*

Orlick, Terry, and Cal Botterill. 1977. *Every Kid Can Win*, 63. Chicago: Nelson Hall.

Pascarella, E., and P. Terenzini. 1992. *How College Affects Students.* San Francisco: Jossey Bass.

Pasek, John, Jon A. Kronsnick, Trevor Tompson, Tobias H. Stark, and B. Keith Payne. 2014. Attitiudes Towards Blacks in the Obama Era: Changing Distributions and Impacts on Job Approval and Electoral Choice, 2008–2012. *Public Opinion Quarterly* 78: 276–302.

Peterson, Richard R. 1996. A Reevaluation of the Consequences of Divorce. *American Sociological Review* 61(3): 528–536.

Pew Research Center. 2010. At Long Last, Divorce. D'Vera Cohn. *Marriage and Divorce.*

———. 2013. Roles of Moms and Dads Converge as They Balance Work and Family. *Social and Demographic Trends.* Kim Parker and Wendy Wang.

Piketty, Thomas. 2014. *Capital in the Twenty-First Century.* Cambridge, MA: Belknap Press.

Plucinska, Joanne. 2015, June 24. Study Says White Extremists have Killed More Americans in the US than Jihadists. *Time.*

Pritchett, Wendell. 2002. *Brownsville, Brooklyn: Blacks, Jews, and the Changing Face of the Ghetto.* Chicago: University of Chicago Press.

Putnam, Robert. 2000. *Bowling Alone: The Collapse and Revival of American Community.* New York: Simon and Schuster.

———. 2016. *Our Kids: The American Dream in Crisis.* New York: Simon and Schuster.

Quarantello, Richard G. 2013. *Surviving the Warzone: Growing Up East New York Brooklyn.* Philadelphia: Xlibris.

Queens College Sociology Handbook. 1982. CUNY.

Reich, Robert. 2008. Supercapitalism. The Transformation of Business, Democracy and Everyday life20081. New York, NY: Knopf 2007.... *Society and Business Review* 3 (3): 256–258.

————. 2016. *Saving Capitalism: For the Many Not the Few.* New York: Vintage.

Rieder, Jonathan. 1985. *Canarsie: The Jews and Italians of Brooklyn Against Liberalism.* Cambridge: Harvard University Press.

Rifkin, Jeremy. 2001. *The Age of Access: The New Culture of Hypercapitalism, Where All Life is a Paid-For Experience.* London: Penguin Books (TarcherPerigee).

Riley, Matilda White, ed. 1988. *Sociological Lives,* ASA Presidential Series. Beverly Hills: Sage Publications.

Rose, Joel. 2013. Does Crime Drop When Immigrants Move In? *All Things Considered. NPR.*

Rosenbaum, James E. 1976. *Making Inequality.* New York: Wiley.

————. 2004. It's Time to Tell the Kids, If You Don't Do Well in High School, You Won't Do Well in College, or On the Job. *American Federation of Teachers Report* 28: 8–10.

Rosenberg, Eli and Chris Erikson. 2014. Lonely Planet Guidebooks Calls Queens the Best Travel Destination in the United States. *New York Daily News,* December 11.

Rubin, David C. 1986. *Autobiographical Memory.* Cambridge: Cambridge University Press.

Rubin, Lilian. 1976. *Worlds of Pain: Life in the Working-Class Family.* New York: Basic Books.

————. 1994. *Families on the Faultline: America's Working Class Speaks About the Family, the Economy, Race and Ethnicity.* New York: Harper.

Ryan, Jake, and Charles Sackrey. 1984. *Strangers in Paradise: Academics from the Working Class.* Lanham: University Press of America.

Sage, George H. 1980. Parental Influence and Socialization into Sport for Male and Female Intercollegiate Athletes. *Journal of Sport and Social Issues* 4: 1–13.

Salinger, Tobias. 2014. Ozone Park Parishioners Say John Gotti Wouldn't Tolerate Virgin Mary Statue Decapitation. *New York Daily News,* January 13.

Sampson, Robert J. 2012. *Great American City: Chicago and the Enduring Neighborhood Effect.* Chicago: University of Chicago Press.

Seeley, John R., R. Alexander Sim, and E. W. Loosley. 1956. *Crestwood Heights: A Study of the Culture of Suburban Life.* New York: University of Toronto Press.

Sennett, Richard, and Jonathan Cobb. 1972. *The Hidden Injuries of Class.* New York: Vintage Books.

Seyfried, Vincent F. 1986. *The Story of Woodhaven and Ozone Park.* New York: The Leader Observer.

Sharlet, Jeff. 2016. Donald Trump: American Preacher. *New York Times Magazine,* April 17, 42–47.

Sherman, Jennifer. 2009. *Those Who Work, Those Who Don't: Poverty, Morality and Family in Rural America.* Minneapolis. University of Minnesota Press.

Silver, Nate. 2016. The Mythology of Trump's 'Working Class' Support. *FiveThirtyEight.*

Simon, Paul, and Art Garfunkel. 1966. *Homeward Bound*. Columbia Records.

Sinatra, Nancy. 1966. *These Boots Are Made for Walking*. Reprise Records.

Sony Pictures. 2014. *The Seven-Five*. Documentary by Eli Holzman, Aaron Saidman, and Sheldon Yeller.

Stephen Cole, (1983) The Hierarchy of the Sciences?. *American Journal of Sociology* 89(1):111–139

Strayhorn, Billy. 1939. Take the "A" Train. Song by Duke Ellington Band. Black Lion Label.

Steedman, Carolyn Kay. 1986. *A Good Woman: A Story of Two Lives*. New Brunswick: Rutgers University Press.

Steele, Claude. 1995. Stereotype Threat and the Intellectual Test of African Americans. *Journal of Personality and Social Psychology* 62: 26–37.

Steglitz, Joseph E. 2013. *The Price of Inequality*. New York: W. W. Norton & Company.

Stormer, John A. 1964. *None Dare Call It Treason*. Florissant: Liberty Bell Press.

Suttles, Gerald. 1968. *The Social Order of the Slum*. Chicago: University of Chicago Press.

———. 1972. *The Social Construction of Communities*. Chicago: University of Chicago Press.

Tea, Michelle, ed. 2003. *Without a Net: The Female Experience of Growing Up Working Class*. Emeryville: Seal Press.

Thabit, Walter. 2003. *How East New York Became a Ghetto*. New York: New York University Press.

The Doors. 1969. *The Soft Parade*. Electra Sound Records.

The Newest New Yorkers: Characteristics of the City's Foreign-Born Population. 2013. http://www.nyc.gov/population.

The Rolling Stones. 1965. *(I Can't Get No) Satisfaction*. Decca Records.

———. 1968. *Street Fighting Man*. Decca Records.

Thio, Alex D., and Jim D. Taylor. 2012. *Social Problems*. Sudburry: Jones and Bartlett Publishing.

Thio, Alex D., Jim D. Taylor, and Martin D. Schwartz. 2012. *Deviant Behavior*. New York: Pearson.

Tichy, Noel. 1973. An Analysis of Clique Formation and Structure in Organizations. *Administrative Science Quarterly* 18(2): 194–208.

Torgovnick, Marianna De Marco. 1997. *Crossing Ocean Parkway*. Chicago: University of Chicago Press.

Tough, Paul. 2014. Who Gets to Graduate? *New York Times Magazine*, May 18.

Trigoboff, Joseph. 2013. *Rumble in Brooklyn: A Memoir*. Create Space. Bare Knuckles Press.

Vance, J.D. 2016. *Hilbilly Elegy: A Memoir of a Family and Culture*. New York: Harper.

Walley, Christine J. 2013. *Exit 0: Family and Class in Postindustrial Chicago*. Chicago: University of Chicago Press.

Warerkar, Tanay. 2017. East New York Is New York City's Newest 'Hot' Neighborhood. *Curbed NY. Vox Media.*

Warner, Bros. 1953. *The Beast from 20,000 Fathoms.* Eugene Lourie, Director.

Watson, Geoffrey G. 1977. Games, Socialization, and Parental Values: Social Class Differences in Parental Evaluation of Little League Baseball. *International Review of the Sociology of Sports* 12: 17–48.

Weigel, Moira. 2016. *Labor of Love: The Invention of Dating.* New York: Farrar, Straus and Giroux.

Weill, Kelly. 2015. Crime Is Down, So Why Are New Yorkers Afraid? *The Daily Beast,* September 21.

Whyte, Wiilliam F. 1943. *Street Corner Society.* Chicago: University of Chicago Press.

Williams, Janice. 2017, July 17. Under Trump, Anti-Muslim Hate Crimes Increased at an Alarming Rate. *Newsweek.*

Williamson, Kevin D. 2016. *Chaos in the Family, Chaos in the Street: The White Working Class's Dysfunction.* National Review, March 28.

Willis, Paul. 1981. *Learning to Labor: How Working-Class Kids Get Working-Class Jobs.* Aldershot: Gower.

Willis, Marian. Parenting Outreach Specialist. 2011. Overcoming Overscheduling. *Parenting for High Potential.*

Wilson, William Julius. 1996. *When Work Disappears: The World of the New Urban Poor.* New York: Random House.

Wiseman, Rosalind. 2002. *Queen Bees and Wannabees: Helping Your Daughter Survive Cliques, Gossip, Boyfriends, and the New Realities of Girl World.* New York: Three Rivers Press.

Wodtke, Geoffrey T. 2012. The Impact of Intergroup Attitudes: A Multi-Racial Analysis. *Social Psychology Quarterly* 71 (1): 80–106.

Woldoff, Rachael A. 2011. *White Flight/Black Flight: The Dynamics of Racial Change in an American Neighborhood.* Ithaca: Cornell University Press.

Wynne, Edward. 1977. *Growing Up Suburban.* Austin: University of Texas Press.

INDEX

© The Author(s) 2017
T.J. Gorman, *Growing up Working Class*,
DOI 10.1007/978-3-319-58898-8

Made in United States
North Haven, CT
23 July 2022

21737994R00159